The Practice of History

G. R. ELTON, who was appointed
Regius Professor of Modern History in
1983, has taught at Cambridge since
1949, becoming Professor of English
Constitutional History in 1967. He was
born in 1921 and educated in Prague
and at Rydal School before obtaining a
London University External BA in
1943, and a PhD in 1949. He served in
the army during the war, and then held
the post of assistant in history at
Glasgow University from 1948 to 1949.
In 1954 he became a Fellow of Clare
College, Cambridge, and was made a
Fellow of the British Academy in 1967.
Professor Elton has held visiting
lectureships at the Universities of
Boulder and Pittsburg in the United
States, and also at Belfast and Oxford.

He edited the second volume of the
New Cambridge Modern History, and
among his best-known works are *The
Tudor Revolution in Government* (1953),
England Under the Tudors (1955), *Tudor
Constitution* (1960), *Policy and Police:
the enforcement of the Reformation in the
age of Thomas Cromwell* (1972), *Reform
and Renewal* (1973) and *Reform and
Reformation: England 1509–1558*
(1977). Professor Elton is the series
editor for the Fontana History of
England, and has written *Reformation
Europe* for the For____ ____ __ ___
Europe.

G. R. Elton

The Practice of History

FLAMINGO

Published by Fontana Paperbacks

First published by Sydney University Press 1967
First issued in Fontana Paperbacks 1969
Tenth impression February 1982

This Flamingo edition first published in 1984
by Fontana Paperbacks,
8 Grafton Street, London W1X 3LA

Made and printed in Great Britain by
Richard Clay (The Chaucer Press) Ltd,
Bungay, Suffolk

CONTENTS

PREFACE

There have never been more historians at work in the world than there are to-day. Among these masses of active scholars, many have presumably at some time reflected upon their craft, but only few have published their thoughts. Though in this the many may have been wise, the practical result has been that, with the exception of manuals instructing in techniques of research, most books on history have been written by philosophers analysing historical thinking, by sociologists and historiographers analysing historians, and by the occasional historian concerned to justify his activity as a social utility. This contribution seeks to avoid the last, ignores the second, and cannot pretend to emulate the first. It embodies an assumption that the study and writing of history are justified in themselves, and reflects a suspicion that a philosophic concern with such problems as the reality of historical knowledge or the nature of historical thought only hinders the practice of history. When I read discussions of how historians think, how they can claim to describe that which no longer exists, or whether historical fact has an existence independent of the thinker about facts, I marvel at the ingenuity of the writers, for usually they are men who have never apparently themselves tried to do the work, to see the manifestly surviving evidence of past fact and event, or to practise critical judgment on the materials of history rather than the minds of historians.[1] Though I have looked at a good deal that has been written around these matters, I have made no effort at an exhaustive or comprehensive investigation. What I have tried to do is to set down experience—my experience in the study, writing and teaching of history. This is a manifesto rather than a treatise, more an explanation of one working historian's faith and practice than a systematic analysis with a series of proved conclusions. I know, of course, that my experience has been limited and that my examples, for instance, will seem to have been chosen from a narrow sector of history. However, I have endeavoured to remember that there is a great deal more history than I know about, that there are methods of studying it which I have not had occasion to practise, and that there never is any single road to success.

I know that what I have to say may at times appear offensive, and I can only hope to be believed if I say that I have tried to reserve my criticisms for men whose eminence I recognize and that I have thought only of the issues involved. It would be quite improper to reduce one's personal responsibility for a manifesto by calling in the friendly support or help of others, and I shall not do so. But I must record my thanks to those who over the years have listened patiently and critically to my diatribes; and I want to express my gratitude to

---

[1] I do not mean to deny that there are some sensible books on these subjects, as e.g. W. H. Walsh, *An Introduction to the Philosophy of History* (London, 1951); P. Gardiner, *The Nature of Historical Explanation* (Oxford, 1952); W. B. Gallie, *Philosophy and the Historical Understanding* (London, 1964). Every new number of *History and Theory* is liable to contain yet another article struggling to give history a philosophic basis, and some of them are interesting. But they do not, I fear, advance the writing of history.

the Sydney University Press, and especially to Mr Michael Turnbull who not only suggested this book to me but from first to last gave me encouragement and excellent advice. Authors do not often feel well disposed towards editors; this one does.

Clare College, Cambridge   G.R.E.

December 1966

I

Purpose

1 The Present Debate

The future is dark, the present burdensome; only the past, dead and finished, bears contemplation. Those who look upon it have survived it : they are its product and its victors. No wonder, therefore, that men concern themselves with history. The desire to know what went before, the desire to understand the passage down time, these are common human attributes. Yet one must distinguish. Though creation myths and cosmogonies testify to this universal desire to give meaning to the past, not all civilizations have been equally concerned to know and write human history as it really was. Modern civilization is peculiar rather than ordinary in that it rests upon the two intellectual pillars of natural science and analytical history. Theology and philosophy can both claim to have commanded the minds of men for longer stretches of time and over larger areas than these characteristic thought systems of the twentieth century, thought systems which significantly enough, came jointly to dominance in the seventeenth. Their triumph, now universal, has itself been the outcome of an historical situation, for the political and technological advantages which gave Europe the victory in the struggle of civilizations brought to the top a complex of societies whose thinking had been influenced by the longest traditions of a real concern with the past. There is something markedly a-historical about the attitudes embedded, for instance, in the classic minds of India and China, and any history of historiography must needs concentrate on the Hellenic and Judaic roots of one major intellectual tree. No other primitive sacred writings are so grimly chronological and historical as is the Old Testament, with its express record of God at work in the fates of generations succeeding each other in time; and the Christian descendant stands alone among the religions in deriving its authority from an historical event. On the other hand, the systematic study of human affairs, past and present, began with the Greeks. Some sort of history has been studied and written everywhere, from the chronicles of Egypt and Peru to the myths of Eskimos and Polynesians, but only in the civilization which looks back to the Jews and Greeks was history ever a main concern, a teacher for the future, a basis of religion, an aid in explaining the existence and purpose of man. And even there, its present-day standing is of quite recent origin.

The study of history as a properly developed discipline is really quite young, younger by far than that of medicine or law, philosophy or theology, even of the natural sciences. *Ante Agamemnona*—before Niebuhr and Ranke—the great men did exist, but the mass of historians was neither large nor remarkable. Herodotus may have been the father of history, but for a good many centuries the child he begot was to enjoy but a restricted and intermittent life. Thucydides, Polybius, Livy, Sallust and Tacitus—great names but, for some 600 years, not a terribly impressive tally; and it is not without significance that the one historian among the ancients for whom no one has a bad word seems to be Asinius Pollio of whose writings nothing survives. Medieval chroniclers occasionally rose above their annals

to reflect and explicate,[1] and by now we have all heard
of Ibn Khaldoun. Renaissance history—Bruni, Machiavelli, Guicciardini—has received more applause than
readership, and there are those who would call Francis
Bacon an historian, on the strength of that quite
untrustworthy piece of brilliant journalism, his *Life of
Henry VII*. It was, in fact, the seventeenth century that
took the first purposeful steps towards serious historical
study. Mabillon and the Bollandists founded the science
of the criticism of sources; in England, Spelman, Selden
and Brady wrote something recognizable to modern
professionals; Wanley and Maddox investigated the past
from its true relics; a bit later, the Göttingen school
weighed in, too, and transferred the initiative to
Germany.[2] Resting on the advance made by the humanists, men like these gave history the right to regard itself
as an independent form of enquiry, seeking its own
answers to its own problems, and following its own canons
of proof and purpose. They looked for causes, for a
connecting chain in the seemingly meaningless sequence
of events, and if they could be crudely mechanical they
also taught that there is secular sense to be made of past,
present and future.

However, despite these often remarkable achievements,
the scientific, ordered, systematic study of history really
began only in the nineteenth century, because only
then did historians absorb the lessons of the antiquarians

[1] V. H. Galbraith, *Historical Research in Medieval England*
(Creighton Lecture: London, 1951).
[2] M. D. Knowles, *Great Historical Enterprises* (Edinburgh, 1963);
F. Smith Fussner, *The Historical Revolution* (London, 1962); J.
G. A. Pocock, *The Ancient Constitution and the Feudal Law*
(Cambridge, 1957); D. C. Douglas, *English Scholars 1660-1730*
(London, 1939); L. Fox, ed., *English Historical Scholarship in
the 16th and 17th Centuries* (London, 1956); H. Butterfield, *Man
on his Past* (Cambridge, 1955).

and develop to the full the techniques which enabled
them to answer the common charge that their reconstruction of the past was just a tale, amusing and instructive
enough, but without any rigour, certainty or standard of
truth. Dr Johnson, though aware that historical facts
might be known, could not trust 'the characters we
find in history, unless when they are drawn by those
who knew the persons': and Catherine Morland could
not understand her boredom with history when 'a great
deal of it must be invention . . . and invention is
what delights me in other books'. Fifty years later, history
was being written on the foundation of systematic
research. The results would still have seemed morally
uninteresting to Samuel Johnson and would still have
bored Miss Morland, but for different reasons. The
inventions and fancies, the character sketches, were
being replaced by tested certainties, and open questions by problems.

There is therefore a very real sense in which good
modern historians are superior to greater minds and
abler men who in earlier ages concerned themselves
with history. There is no arrogance in this: they are
so because they have been allowed to become better
scholars. To the literary mind, the great English historians
may be Clarendon, Gibbon and Macaulay, even though
hardly anyone reads them any longer and their readability is their main claim to fame. Surely, they are
worth reading and wrote splendid books, but they wrote
in the prehistoric age and therefore lacked the opportunities which we markedly lesser men enjoy. To the
historian, the great English historians are Maitland and
Namier, even though they never wrote long histories:
for which reason it must hastily be added that one's
admiration for them is not based on, is rather tem-

pered by, this one deficiency. It is not just knowledge or
the ability to understand motive which makes the true
historians; on those grounds, no doubt, that elderly
trinity surpasses many even of the good moderns. The
difference lies in the different attitude and purpose
brought to the study by a mind trained in history as a
scientific and intellectual approach.

It need, then, cause no surprise that with that one
civilization's general dominance in matters of standards
and beliefs the study of history should in the last 300
years have assumed the appearance of a major intellectual industry. The amount of history that is written to-day
(quite apart from the amount that, though studied, never
gets written), and the number of people engaged in
various ways in the investigation of the past, should
frighten or exhilarate, according to temperament and
the phase of the moon. Moreover, like every good
service industry, history has something for everybody.
Individual craftsmen, working for the few, exist side by
side with mass-production factories supplying the needs
of the many. All the signs are of health. The university
departments are full of students; and teachers of history,
laid end to end, might even reach from premise to
conclusion. Publishers fall over each other in the rush
for historians: even academic historians have at last
realized that they own a marketable commodity and
need not be quite so awed by the publisher's cheque-
book. The series multiply. The whole business is beginning to show the marks of a run-away boom: hectic
production leading to dilution of quality, price inflation,
and ever more insistent warnings from the apprehensive
that all good things must come to an end. Indeed, there
are signs that we may be reaching that crisis of
confidence which can precipitate a slump. At every

turn one encounters visceral investigation; the working historian's life is increasingly beset by the specialists in moral exhortation and the prophets of doom.

In some sense, this unsystematic debate is itself a sign of life, though it cannot be denied that life, as usual, involves occasional touches of disease or malformation. Nor is there a great deal that is new in all these doubts and warnings. A good many critics demand that historians should leave the shelter of their muniment rooms and libraries in order to play their part in creating a general intellectual climate; but do they know that they are only repeating the arguments of Voltaire and the eighteenth-century philosophical historians against the antiquarians whose researches they despised?[3] Those who preach the virtues of statistical, sociological or other 'scientific' methods are only reviving, after an interval so short as not quite to excuse their ignorance of the fact, the weary argument whether history is an art or science.[4] Because its materials are necessarily partial, and the products emerging from individual minds more partial still, history always has posed and always will pose the sort of problems which give rise to dispute, acrimony, and the writing of hostile reviews. Why, at the very beginning of our science stands the prototype of all these arguments: history had barely begun when Thucydides attacked the methods and purposes of Herodotus. Debates among historians are

[3] Cf. A. D. Momigliano, *Studies in Historiography* (London, 1966), 1ff. It may be unkind to remember that the claims of those philosophic historians collapsed when they were found to be sadly wanting in scholarship.

[4] Whether history is an art or a science is a dead issue. It is both. But it has always been an art; the addition of science, which is the work of the last 150 years, has turned it into something new, something appropriate to the highest abilities of the human reason

coeval with the writing of history, and like the heresies
of Christianity all the possible positions were worked
out quite early, to be repeated in resounding counter-
point through ages of controversy.

Above all, historians have always wondered just why
they do this thing—why they study history. It may be
true that a concern with the past is a widely found
human characteristic, but that does not dispose of the
question. It only puts it one stage back: why should
people be interested in the past, and especially why
should they be sufficiently interested either to devote an
intellectual existence to it or to support the lives of
those who do? The question why society should wish to
nourish historians leads to its corollary: what should
historians do to justify their existence to their society?
The simple answer that to study and write history is a
pleasant occupation, that it satisfies the practitioners and
does no harm to anyone else, is not only too obviously
narrow and selfish but may not even be true. Historical
writings can do harm; they have done so; and any
thoughtful historian must at times ask himself whether
he has a purpose beyond his own satisfaction.

The questions may be eternal; the answers tend to go
in waves of fashion, cannoning off each other in often
predictable reactions to the predominant theory of the
moment. Since historians are naturally given to sharp-
ness of tongue, the debate is likely to look savage to
the outsider: it is not only in intellectual ascendancy
that historical studies prove themselves to have supplanted
medieval theology. Nevertheless, a little bit of perspective
can fairly be demanded of men who claim to be concerned with the development of things and ideas through
time. Thus when we are told, by an historian now in
his early thirties, that in the first half of the present
century English historians had 'temporarily lost their

bearings' because the political and constitutional preoccupations proper when Britain ruled the world had
ceased to be valid while nothing else had taken their
place,[5] we should point out to him, gently, that he
has merely failed to consider the question in a proper
historical light. The many good historians whom he
thus relegates to confusion and intellectual poverty did
not, it is true, happen to hold certain beliefs that are
fashionable now. They did not necessarily suppose that
only social analysis has value in the study of history, and
they did not, on the whole, suppose that they must
justify their labours by reference to some non-intellectual
effect upon society. But this does not mean that they
were not possessed of principles and creeds as definite,
and as potentially limiting, as those proclaimed by their
critics. The first half of this century was dominated
among English historians by a conviction that the
principles of respectable historiography could be reduced
to one main precept: to study history for its own sake.
Though this austere rule could and did produce a fair
amount of narrow tedium, it also resulted in some most
remarkable monuments of the historian's craft. It is, so
far, by no means clear that those who react against it
are likely to write history anything like so well founded,
so careful in its pursuit of the truth, or so uninfluenced by
preconceived ideas and ready-made answers. Their
chances of doing so are at present hard to judge because
after quite a few years of manifestoes and occasional

[5] Keith Thomas in *Times Literary Supplement*, 7 April 1966,
275. The whole of that article, and indeed of the issue of which it
formed part (called 'New Ways in History'), is shot through with
an engaging arrogance and historically invalid assertions. But
it raises serious questions, and I shall recur to it throughout this
chapter.

learned articles they have notched up a still surprisingly small amount of identifiable achievement.

Neither the fact that the debates can become otiose, nor their zeal in so often simply echoing the points made in the past, need, however, lead one to suppose that the proper cure is silence. The debates are necessary and, even at their most jejune, not totally without worth. Like all those who practise the concrete sciences, historians are always in danger of contenting themselves with the daily grind. An age of debate is an age of stock-taking; it leads to a necessary reformulation of purpose and principle; and though the answers are never going to be really new they may yet throw new light and accumulate new insights which will assist in the real purpose, in the study and writing of history. The recent and continuing outburst of self-doubt, lavish criticism, and prescription of panaceas has been accompanied by much superficial shouting, much whoring after false gods, much petulant assertion of doubtful tastes and standards. But these defects do not rob it of its fundamental justification: it attacks a complacency which could become mindless. However, it does seem to me that the time has come to restate some of the truths of practice and experience, to rescue history from its candid friends, and to remind the historical world that there is work to be done rather than to be called for, that that work must be carried out in a cage set by certain inescapable conditions, and that bright ideas, however seemingly new, are not everything.

In this chapter I shall concern myself with three main issues. It is first of all necessary to ask once again whether history has an identity independent of other forms of study: does history exist as an intellectual pursuit, can it claim to possess its own rules and principles, or is it merely a hold-all for various other 'social sciences'?

Secondly, arising from this, its proper relation to cognate disciplines must be looked at. Lastly I shall offer my answer to the question : why should we study history?

2 *Autonomy*

The study of history comprehends everything that men have said, thought, done or suffered. That much is commonplace, but also not quite true; some reservations have to be made. In the first place, not all the past is recoverable, and the study of history is necessarily confined to that part of it of which evidence either survives or can be reconstructed in the mind. That is to say, while history may commonly be thought of as the whole of mankind's past life, it is in truth equal only to the surviving past. Historical study is not the study of the past but the study of present traces of the past; if men have said, thought, done or suffered anything of which nothing any longer exists, those things are as though they had never been. The crucial element is the present evidence, not the fact of past existence; and questions for whose answer no material exists are strictly nonquestions. True, this is a less limiting reservation than may be thought because the surviving traces of the past are not confined to material survivals; evidence can to some extent be discovered where it appeared not to exist, and the historian's techniques at times enable him to reconstruct that which is lost from that which is still around. Yet the limitation remains important, especially in practice. Lively minds of little knowledge like to charge historians with asking the wrong questions or with treating uninteresting problems. The history of princes and politics, of war and diplomacy, is often called dull and insufficient; why do we not hear more about 'ordinary people', the lives of the poor, the whole of 'society'? The charge can be true, but only if in fact the evidence for the study of such problems exists. If it does not, they have no place on the historian's table. The past is over and done with : it cannot be relived. It can be reconstructed—seen and understood again—only if it has left present matter behind.

Secondly, the definition given is in a way too wide because history is not the only form of enquiry which deals with man's past life. All the so-called social sciences—archaeology, anthropology, economics, social psychology, sociology—attend to man, and all of them can concern themselves with his past as well as his present. This is quite apart from the fact that strictly they can never consider the present : at the moment of being considered it becomes the past. These sciences are clearly autonomous; they deal in methods, questions and results which are peculiar to themselves. Is history autonomous in this sense—is it indeed a specialized form of enquiry or merely an attitude of mind employable in these other sciences? Sociologists, in particular, are capable of asserting such a claim; I once heard one of them say that the study of the past is superfluous because a true understanding of the present, arrived at by sociological analysis, enables one to extrapolate and explain the past. (He did not appear to be joking.) However, the arrogance to which sociologists are prone does not preclude the possibility that occasionally they may arrive at some not entirely obvious truth not discoverable by historical enquiry alone. We must therefore ask how history differs from other studies of man if that difference is not found in its concern with the past. The answer lies in three habits peculiar to history : its concern with events, its concern with change, and its concern with the particular.

History deals in events, not states; it investigates things that happen and not things that are. As against this, archaeology, for instance, can only uncover and describe states, conditions and circumstances symptomatic of a particular way of life; it is unable to handle the fact of life, which is movement. Archaeological states follow jerkily one upon another, without description or explanation of the movement, and it matters nothing whether the transformation is gradual (undatable), as it usually is, or catastrophic. When the archaeologist attempts to incorporate events in his analysis, he either has to confine himself to the bare fact essentially equal to the description of a state ('this site was destroyed by fire') or to resort to historical statements that do not arise from his archaeological evidence and methods, and which, if he is studying a period for which no historical account is possible, may have to be purely imaginary. Anthropology or sociology, on the other hand, may well display interest in the event—in a circumcision ceremony or a wedding, in the building of a school or the formation of an opinion—but this will not be for the sake of the event but for the sake of extracting static conclusions from moving elements. The historian may well interest himself in the state of things, the condition of society, the principles underlying a system of government or a system of thought. But if he is to understand historically and practise historical writing, he will have to think of such analyses as steps in a chain of events, as matters explanatory of a sequence of happenings. He will have to concentrate on understanding change, which is the essential content of historical analysis and description. History treats fundamentally of the transformation of things (people, institutions, ideas, and so on) from one state into another, and the event is its concern as well as ıts instrument. To suppose that causal relationships are the main content of history is an error, for they form but a particular case of the general principle that history deals in movement from state *a* to state *b*. If *a* can be said to have caused *b* the relationship happens to be causal; but it is none the less properly historical if *a* and *b* are linked by coincidence, coexistence, or mere temporal sequence, all relations very often encountered in history, however less intellectually satisfying they may be.

As for history's preoccupation with the particular, that must be seen in its proper light. It is often asserted that the special distinction of the historical method is to treat the fact or event as unique. But frequent assertion does not create truth, and this statement is not true. No historian really treats all facts as unique; he treats them as particular. He cannot—no one can—deal in the unique fact, because facts and events require reference to common experience, to conventional frameworks, to (in short) the general before they acquire meaning. The unique event is a freak and a frustration; if it is really unique—can never recur in meaning or implication—it lacks every measurable dimension and cannot be assessed. But to the historian, facts and events (and people) must be individual and particular: *like* other entities of a similar kind, but never entirely identical with them. That is to say, they are to be treated as peculiar to themselves and not as indistinguishable statistical units or elements in an equation; but they are linked and rendered comprehensible by kinship, by common possessions, by universal qualities present in differing proportions and arrangements. The historical event is like the modern physicist's atom, composed of analysable and repeatable ingredients but so composed as to be itself complex and in a measure unpredictable; and not like Newton's atom or Leibniz's monad, a basic and identical unit of matter. This is what is meant by the false assertion that the historical fact is unique, and one can see that for practical purposes the error can seem very like the truth. But the distinction is vital because reasoned analysis of the complexities of the past and avoidance of the standardizing mistakes of the social sciences are not possible unless the true definition is grasped.

We can now rephrase the earlier definition of history. It is concerned with all those human sayings, thoughts, deeds and sufferings which occurred in the past and have left present deposit; and it deals with them from the point of view of happening, change, and the particular. Since no other treatment of man's experience answers to this definition, the autonomy of history—its right to be distinguished from cognate sciences—is established.

3 Kinds

Within this comprehensive definition of history, we ought perhaps to distinguish different kinds. The writing of history and the understanding of the past take many forms, and no one, probably, who has ever thought about these matters, can avoid believing in some hierarchy among them. Thucydides, for instance, opened the story of debates among historians by questioning the possibility of any history except contemporary history. To him this was the inescapable conclusion to be drawn from the fact which has been mentioned : that history is only equal to its evidence. He thought that only personal experience and observation could guarantee knowledge and accuracy. 2500 years later, that argument is still sufficiently alive for an American historian to ask the ironical question whether the past should concern the historian at all.[6] In giving a warning against an excessive preoccupation with the contemporary, he adopted a position probably more common to-day than that of Thucydides, if only because developing techniques have given us a better control over the evidence for more distant ages and left us aware of the exceptional difficulties involved in discovering and assimilating the evidence for our own times. One also meets the opinion that special virtues adhere to this or that period of history, as it might be the European middle ages, or the nineteenth century, or some great age of Cathay. Such arguments may sometimes be valid when the purpose of study is in question; some well-worked or well-documented pieces of history may have advantages in teaching others, as some obscure or little known bits may assist the historian in marking out his claim to recognition. But no argument exists which successfully establishes a hierarchy of worth among historical periods or regions as such.

Yet though we need no longer think in those terms, we are still inclined to make distinctions supposedly based on differences of intellectual content. To some commentators, no history that does not tell a story deserves the name at all, while others object to anything but pure analysis as below the highest aspirations of the historian. Most people do not admit to such clear-cut prejudices, but the prejudices are there all the same. In truth, historians, like other people, tend to judge their world from their own experiences and practice, and it is distressing to see how narrow in their sympathies even eminent men can be. E. H. Carr, for instance, has spent a great part of his life writing the history of Russia in

[6] Charles E. Nowell, 'Has the Past a Place in History?', *Journal of Modern History*, xxiv (1952), 331ff.

the twentieth century; fundamentally, he has worked on a narrative account in very recent history. But does this entitle him to judge the state of our knowledge of fifth-century Greece from the fifty-year-old memories of a Cambridge undergraduate, or to write off a great part of medieval studies because he mistakenly thinks that the bulk of evidence surviving from the middle ages was produced by monastic chroniclers?[7] These are errors based on ignorance; another derives from his limited understanding of the historian's range of tasks. 'I have no patience,' he says, 'with the fashion . . . of pretending that Mommsen's greatness rests not on his *History of Rome* but on his corpus of inscriptions and his work on Roman constitutional law; this is to reduce history to the level of compilation.'[8] If the last sentence were true one might no doubt agree with him. But his exasperated complaint shows no sign that he grasps what Mommsen achieved when he laid the solid foundations of Latin epigraphy, or of the kind of organizing and analysing genius required in the writing of the three large volumes of the *Staatsrecht*. The sheer learning and expository skill displayed in these works exemplify historical insight and achievement of the highest order; to recognize this, which need not induce one to deprecate the sweep and grandeur of the *History of Rome*, should, in the working historian, call forth an awed admiration for greatness in his own line of work. By comparison, narrative history might almost be called easy, though Mommsen's practice of it, even if intellectually less mountainous than those other works, remains marvellously impressive in itself. But both types of writing are history.

The reason for Mr Carr's somewhat philistine judg-

[7] E. H. Carr, *What is History?* (Penguin edition, 1964), 13-14, 149.
[8] *Ibid.* 37.

ment is obvious enough : he himself has specialized in
the production of narrative history on the grand scale.
Historians naturally praise in their fellows those enterprises and distinctions which come closest to their own
mode of thought and work. It is difficult to appreciate
anything that one does not know from personal experience, easy to lapse in catholic sympathy. And this is the
more understandable because too universal a sympathy,
too ready an acceptance of all treatments of history,
would constitute an abdication of the judgment which
all historians must, as a duty, preserve. Occasional
grumpy disapproval is much to be preferred to that
general and tepid approval which pervades, for instance,
most professional reviewing of historical books in
America. The motives may be creditable (not to slay
the defenceless) or very dubious (not to call down similar
treatment upon oneself), but in any case a real duty is
neglected when no standards are set for the intellectual
and artistic treatment of serious historical problems.
Sympathy for a variety of concerns and manners of
approach does not preclude the existence of some severe
discrimination in the judgment.

However, the more obvious and more common danger
is that exemplified by Mr Carr : to write off certain
forms of historical study and to reserve approval for
those to which one happens to incline oneself. Behind
such harsh judgments lies the multifariousness of history
itself. Since the whole of history—the whole of a person,
a period, or a problem—can never be got between the
covers of one book, some means of rendering the material
manageable must be found. The commonest is to adhere
to the notoriously artificial divisions into which the study
of the past breaks up at the approach of a teaching
syllabus or an examination system. We write political
history or economic history, constitutional or administra-

tive history, history of ideas or history of science. J. H.
Hexter has called this 'tunnel history' and has castigated
it with his own brand of engaging savagery.[9] That he
has much right on his side cannot be denied. Tunnels do
circumscribe the vision. But what is one to do? To
transfer the universality of life on to paper, or even to
comprehend it in the mind, is rarely possible, and without a main line of thought nothing results except the
jumble which in fact is nearest to the common experience
of life. This would be neither art, nor understanding, nor
use. Issues and problems demand some sort of tunnel
for their clarification; the · past must be sorted into
'aspects' to become not only manageable but meaningful. There is really nothing wrong with thinking in
tunnels, provided one remembers that there is earth above
and around the tunnel, and that the shape and direction
of the tunnel are governed by the constitution of the
substance about it. 'Aspects' are just that : not separate
entities, but forms extracted from the mass with the tool
provided by the method of approach selected. All good
historical writing is universal history in the sense that
it remembers the universal while dealing with part of it.

There are, therefore, no ways of dealing with history
which are *intrinsically* superior to others. Political history
—the analysis and description of the way in which men
have conducted affairs—is not necessarily more jejune
than social history, the analysis and description of the
arrangements by which they have lived together in
ordered groups. The writer on wars and armies need
not feel inferior to the student of markets, price fluctuations and methods of production. Administrative history
concentrates on the manner in which institutions and
instruments of government are organized and work;

---

[9] *Reappraisals in History* (London, 1961), 194ff.

constitutional history, which concerns itself with the principles and conflicts embodied in the development of governmental organization, is not by that token any more distinguished. In particular, the historian of thought and ideas, secular or religious, need not think (as he is inclined to) that he is somehow more elevated or significant than he who wrestles with the intricacies of law courts or strives to understand the problems involved in the edition of charters. In these matters there are no hierarchies, and mutual respect is the only proper attitude.

This does not mean that there are no distinctions to be made, but only that the distinctions do not depend on the dominant interest or the main line chosen. The differences to which the critical mind should address itself lie solely in the manner of execution. They are not confined to the degree of art displayed, to competence in explanation or skill in description. The writing of history requires powers not universally available, but the name of historian need not always be denied to the man who cannot write well. What matters are the differences shown in the intellectual treatment of the questions asked. And here the fundamental distinction is that between the amateur and the professional. This is not always an easy distinction to make, for it is not identical with that between men who earn their living by the study of history and those who engage in it by the side of other occupations. The distinction I have in mind rests between the man who has learned his job and the man who, sometimes with touches of genius, comes to it in a happy spirit of untrained enterprise : crudely, the distinction between those who think that research means reading a lot of books and those who have grasped that research means assimilating into oneself the various and often very tiresome relics of the past. Examples of both are found inside as well as outside the academic profession.

The hallmark of the amateur is a failure of instinctive understanding. This expresses itself most clearly in a readiness to see the exceptional in the commonplace and to find the unusual ordinary. The amateur shows a tendency to find the past, or parts of it, quaint; the professional is totally incapable of this. On the other hand, the professional, truly understanding an age from the inside—living with its attitudes and prejudices—can also judge it; refusal to judge is quite as amateurish a characteristic as willingness to judge by the wrong, because anachronistic, standards. By all these criteria, Lord Acton was an amateur, and so he was, a prince of amateurs. Very wide reading and self-consciously deep thinking may have attended him; but he was for ever expressing distress or surprise at some turn in the story, was alternately censorious and uncomprehending, suspected conspiracies and deep plots everywhere. In short, he lived in history as a stranger, a visitor from Mars. The professional lives in it as a contemporary, though a contemporary equipped with immunity, hindsight and arrogant superiority—a visitor from the Inquisition. How is such professionalism created? G. M. Young once offered celebrated advice: read in a period until you hear its people speak. But this is amateurishness of a drastic kind because it is superficially professional. Who ever knew or understood people just because he heard them speak? The truth is that one must read them, study their creations and think about them until one knows what they are going to say next.

I do not mean to deny that what I have called amateur history can be very good, not only entertaining but useful and stimulating. Still less do I mean to doubt that professional history can be very bad, sterile and stultifying in the extreme. But the emotional criterion, which measures the response evoked by the historian, is a partial guide and provides no firm standard. The criterion I have offered here has about it a quality of precision. The best amateur history, however entertaining, cannot enlarge the understanding or deepen the participation because it is written from outside, through a veil woven out of strangeness and wonderment. At its best it achieves sympathy and romantic love, but it cannot penetrate to fundamental explanation; at its common bad, it is sentimental, ignorant, and an insult to the intelligence. That really fine amateur historian, G. M. Trevelyan, achieved both.

The purpose and ambition of professional history is to understand a given problem from the inside. This may well involve tedium, pettiness and pedantry, the main faults of the professional. He lacks the amateur's saving grace, for he is not doing the thing just for the love of the thing and cannot rescue himself from depression by romance and sentiment. He is struggling, sometimes grimly, with the often repulsive reality of life, and if he is a petty man or a pedant he will soon convince the reader of that. But even at his worst he cannot fail to add to learning, understanding and knowledge; he contributes truth. Thus, good or bad, he feeds the mind, while the amateur satisfies the senses. In so far as historical study is an intellectual enterprise—and that is its highest form—the professional has it every time. He is doing a job and producing results; the amateur is having fun. But there is no need to be puritanical about this. The good professional, too, has a good deal of fun in doing the job; the sad thing is to read so many professional historians who convey nothing but an agony of the spirit.

Professionalism is the product of a certain aptitude

worked upon by a specific course of training. Good historians may be born, but true historians are made. The principles and details of their training shall be touched on later; here I am concerned with the mark which that training sets upon the practitioner. In the first place, he knows his evidence. He knows the range of it, how it came into existence, what people or institutions produced it, what it can tell and what can never be got from it. In consequence he knows the 'right' questions— those capable of being answered and those that lead to further questions. His instinctive familiarity with the evidence results in a useful and necessary sense which extends his range beyond the strict confines of the evidence; even his guesses bear the stamp of truth because they fit the reality of the situation. Sir John Neale used frequently to speak of his 'hunches', and he played them very successfully. This professional hunch is based on an expert understanding of what can, what must, have happened; more than a guess, it is in the nature of an inspired forecast which often leads to the discovery of evidence supporting it. Those unaware of how the professional historian's mind works are liable to suppose that this amounts to no more than the convenient adjusting of the evidence to the preconceived idea; but though this can happen, it is rare with the properly trained professional. When the answer comes out as expected, it is because the expectation rested on profound knowledge, a knowledge which beyond the facts comprehends setting, atmosphere, possibility, probability—all those tenuous compounds in the lives of men which we call the spirit of an age. This is not to say that historians are allowed to use 'the spirit of the age' to explain things in the absence of evidence; only the amateur falls back on such vapours as the *Zeitgeist* or a national character. The professional uses his real awareness of what is 'right' in a given context in order to fight his way through to an explanation grounded on evidence. It is a tool of selection and divination, not an end to the process of reasoning and discovery. This solid kind of familiarity lies behind everything that is professional about historians; from it flows the ability to understand an age in its own terms, to judge it by the criteria appropriate to itself, to avoid the error—the 'whig' error—of looking only for what has significance in a later age, and to distinguish between the commonplace and the exceptional.

This distinction between the amateur and the professional deserves so much emphasis because it is really fundamental. Both kinds of historian require other capacities, such as ability to judge evidence, ability to construct an argument or a narrative, ability to write. The final product will owe much to these further qualities which may be found equally present or absent among amateurs and professionals alike. But the difference in the foundations will always show through. However much we may prefer to read the amusing amateur rather than the tedious professional (admitting that the adjectives may well at times be changed round), we shall trust the second when we really want to know.

It may be objected that in confining distinctions between historians to this single point I have ignored too much, and in particular that I have wilfully misunderstood the distinction between history and compilation which Mr Carr made in his comment on Mommsen. Is all work in history to be judged only by the amateur or professional status of the historian? Are there no basic differences in the kind of work attempted? Is the editing of a chronicle on a level with the writing of an imaginative narrative, the analysis of an institution equal to the unravelling of social relationships? Answers to these questions will depend on the ground upon which the enquirer takes his stand. This present enquiry turns on the intellectual worth of historical studies, and from that point of view there are no differences that do not arise from the historian's basic attitude to his materials. An honest professional job of any kind deserves equal respect; an honest amateur job merits a different and less searching appraisal. We hear to-day a good deal about the absurdities of minute research, especially in Ph.D. theses. An eminent scientist has condemned those who crawl upon the frontiers of knowledge with a magnifying glass. But what is wrong with taking a magnifying glass to the frontiers of knowledge? Surely that is precisely where it is needed. Perhaps one may want some man at times to stand up, gaze around, and look beyond; but unless they have taken an active part in the painful mapping of the advancing frontier, the visionaries are nothing but a menace. I have no patience (to quote Mr Carr) with the common attitude of contempt for the young student who labours on what may seem a narrow or petty subject and attempts to master the techniques of study which it can teach, though I would agree that the mature scholar who still seems to be at that stage of interest raises one's doubts and hackles. Except for examiners, who are paid for it, no one needs to read Ph.D. dissertations, but those who flatter themselves that they can make a valid distinction between what is important and what merely superfluous in such enterprises, elevate personal taste to the level of a critical standard. Judging thus, they have no answer to those who sniff at their own splendid and ranging edifices because they think them unsound or (this can happen) tedious. Research work of this journeyman kind deserves to be judged by the only tests it seeks to satisfy : is it honest and exhaustive, has it asked questions that are right and adequate in the context of the problem, has it found reasonable answers, does it prove the author to have learned his trade? And much the same point applies beyond the stage of the Ph.D. dissertation. Good and bad work can be done at all stages of historical enterprise; and the standard of quality to apply must be defined as intellectual honesty and intellectual penetration within the compass of the problem investigated.

The historian's ability and knowledge are as much called upon in the editing of a text as they are in writing the history of the Russian Revolution, though the result will attract different sorts of readers. There are also matters of degree and intensity to be allowed for, but none of kind. Mommsen displayed genius in his *History of Rome*; but he also displayed genius, as well as greater skill and greater knowledge, in his *Römisches Staatsrecht*. In the hand of some Professor X, neither would no doubt have been successful, though both would have been as legitimate—and as properly called history— as they were in Mommsen's hands. Naturally no one denies that historians differ in quality of mind and personal capacity. Mr A's excellence and Mr B's stupidity may mean that Mr A writes history and Mr B something else. But the point must be judged by reference to the manner in which each discharged his task, not on the grounds that Mr A's great gifts enabled him to write a history of China while Mr B confined himself to the editing of a medieval chronicle. Compilation does exist, but only rarely does it not require, embody and reflect a learned understanding of history, quite as much as it provides means for enlarging that understanding. One need not go so high as Mommsen's *Corpus Inscriptionum* : let Mr Carr try his hand at compiling trade statistics for English cloth exports in the sixteenth century and see how far he can get without a full use of a true professional equipment. And in applying that equipment to the establishing and recording of reliable figures, he would be writing *history*.

This last example makes plain that the argument is in danger of becoming absurd. Common sense forbids one accepting the view that no distinction can be made in essence between the compiling of trade statistics and the treatise on the history of trade which rests on such statistics. Yet if my premise be allowed—that judgment must depend on the question whether the work flows from adequate knowledge and is honestly executed— the deduction follows; and I certainly stand by my premise to the extent of regarding it as legitimate and important. But I agree that other premises can be found, premises which others may treat as more meaningful and fruitful, though I should hesitate to do so. In particular, Mr Carr, and others who think like him, would judge by the purpose which a piece of historical writing is meant to serve. They wish to see history justified from outside itself, and to rank its products by standards derived from that desire. It is often felt that the subject cannot claim the status, either as a science or as a useful art, which belongs to other disciplines that deal with man : it should therefore both learn from them and approximate to them. Before we can consider the purpose of studying history, we must therefore look at its relations with the mentors and rivals that have been set over against it.

4 Rivals

Autonomy is not the same thing as exclusiveness or self-sufficiency. There are things to be learned. Archaeology can assist history by recovering evidence and thus help to recreate the historical event which archaeology itself is incapable of analysing or describing; inserted into the framework of history, it can also contribute expansions of the time-scale (as in the history of ancient Egypt) or add areas of historical study by making historians ask new questions, as in the reconstruction of Roman military organization or the exploration of medieval farming habits. This asking of new questions is the chief lesson which sociologists have taught to historians who have learned to consider the 'structural' problems of society—the analysis of social hierarchies, relationship of classes, mobility among them, the importance of common assumptions and social myths. Anthropology has opened historians' eyes to the significance of social habits, the mixture of the universal and relative which goes to make up the ways in which people accustom themselves to living in groups. The obvious importance of economics and social psychology—the manner in which they enable the historian to construct wholes out of patchy evidence by teaching the general rules governing the behaviour of forces, crowds and individuals—needs no stressing. Since men's experience in the past, as at all times, was clearly influenced by what happened inside them, between them, and around them, every form of enquiry which touches on these circumstances is of use to the historian; and this may include not only the sciences of man but also the sciences of nature. Provided the instruction received is turned to historical use, provided it is used to consider and explain change in the human past, these borrowings can be nothing but fruitful.

All this is so patent that every generation produces a loud demand for more borrowing, more humility on the historian's part, more worship at the shrines of practitioners whose self-confidence springs from their claim to be scientists. They, we understand, produce certainty, where the historian is at best able to produce dialectical argument. The prophets of each generation rather touchingly believe themselves to be the first innovators, and in old age they are often found among the most bitter opponents of the next wave of prophecy. However, enthusiasm is not perhaps the best state of mind in which to contemplate questions of method and procedure. The German historicism of the nineteenth century, now so much under a cloud, took its first inspiration from two sources: the textual criticism of the philologist, and the mechanics of physical science. In consequence it was inclined to a rather mechanical view of history; it dealt too readily in plain chains of cause and effect. The attack upon it certainly came in part because the progress of historical research itself called in question many of its confident conclusions, but once again too many historians looked to other studies for instruction. Towards the end of the last century, the dominant sciences of physics and philology were replaced by biology, anthropology and sociology, with the result that history became both subtler and less certain, more relativist and more aware of the variety of circumstances that make up any given situation. Despite the conviction of some English scholars to-day that they are the first to bring the social sciences into the working habits of English historians, that trinity of mentors has remained virtually unchanged since; all that has happened is that new and often more rigorous techniques used by them have come to the attention of the historian looking for 'new methods'.

There are two chief reasons for these iterated invitations to use tools borrowed from elsewhere. One is the natural desire of young men to find new things in fields much tilled by their predecessors. Some minds

most readily formulate new questions under the influence
of some theory that has caught their attention. The
much advertised social questions—structure, habits and
ambitions—have in fact been asked by historians since
Herodotus, which is not to deny that we have refined
our techniques and occasionally enlarged our interests,
often under the stimulus of some other discipline. But
the notion that only direct borrowing from very recent
sociology or anthropology has drawn historians' attention to 'such matters as harvests and food-supply,
epidemics, and medicine, the age of marriage and the
size of families',[10] is an illusion quickly dispelled by a
little study of earlier writers. The famous antiquarians
of the seventeenth and eighteenth centuries were mainly
interested in these and similar questions, and if they
may now be despised for their preoccupation with
collecting data and their failure to produce analytical
conclusions, it is not at all clear that their present-day
successors have advanced all that much further in this
respect.

Too careful an ear cocked for the pronouncements of
non-historians is liable to produce disconcerting results.
Anthropology and sociology do not stand still; there
are probably few disciplines in which the differences
among the learned are more ineradicable and more
ferocious. The humble historian may only too readily
find himself listening to the wrong party or catch on to
views already abandoned by the *avant garde*. Thus
we are still enjoined on occasions to call in Freud when
studying people in history, at the very time when
psychologists are poised for a mass-flight from Freud.[11]

[10] Keith Thomas, *T.L.S.* 1966, 276.
[11] I cannot feel that the much-praised Freudian effort of E. H.
Erikson, *Young Man Luther: A Study in Psychoanalysis and
History* (London, 1959), contributes anything of value to an

The anthropology which influences the most modern historians is still too often at the Malinowski and Margaret Murray stage.[12] Marxist sociology, long since overtaken by more accurate and more subtle analyses, remains powerful among historians, and its influence is by no means confined to those aware of it; fragments of class-struggle theories and economic determinism are found curiously embedded in the work of scholars who at the conscious level do not believe in them but need them to satisfy their wish to be thought 'deep'. 'Lonely crowd' and 'affluent society' theories are swallowed trustingly by the alert historian who then proves less able to disgorge them again than are his sociological instructors themselves. Admittedly, the historian is not always ill-advised to be so backward; in the social sciences fashions come and go with disconcerting speed, and by sticking to his point on the wheel the historian may as quickly come to the top of the turn again as by clambering about the wheel while it revolves. Nevertheless, one is justified in asking those propagandists for more social science in history just which kind, school or doctrine they are recommending. My own experience of these debates includes several occasions on which the most fervent advocates of the use of sociology by historians were told by the priests of their golden calf that clearly they neither knew what sociology was nor had any understanding of its recent developments.

---

understanding of either Luther or his age. In so far as it has been responsible for John Osborne's play, it may even need condemnation.

12 Mr Christopher Hill accepts 'the validity of the main thesis of Dr Margaret Murray's *The Witch-Cult in Western Europe*', though he boggles 'at some of her illustrations of it' (*Society and Puritanism in Pre-Revolutionary England*, London, 1964, 187, n. 4). For this he is gently but justly criticized by Professor G. E. Aylmer (*Eng. Hist. Rev.* lxxxi, 1966, 785-6).

However, the desire to open up new lines of enquiry (even when they are not all that new) is a reputable one, and if this endeavour finds stimulus in the methods and conclusions of others it should by all means seek it there.[18] The other main reason for this constant looking over the fence is rather more dangerous in its effects, for it stems from historians' dissatisfaction with one of the essences of their calling, which is that it can never on its own terms establish scientific laws concerning the history of mankind. To use terms current among modern philosophers, history is 'idiographic', that is, it particularizes, and not 'nomothetic', that is, designed to establish general laws. An idiographic science can, it seems to me, become nomothetic only if the particulars it studies become numerous enough for statistical generalization from them to be valid, and here history is likely to be forever handicapped by the smallness of the sample. Even allowing four generations to a century, we have information about only some two hundred generations, and for the vast majority of them our information is extremely patchy. I doubt if any statistician would find this an adequate sample from which to extract the sort of general laws (the fates of civilizations, tidal movements of nations, and that sort of thing) which some historians wish to discover. Of course, the historian should generalize—that is, express larger conclusions based on his particulars. But to some types of mind that activity lacks reality unless the limited generalizations proper to the historian ('in certain circumstances men are liable to do this or that') turn into laws ('in stated conditions, the following results will predictably ensue').

18 The time may just about be upon us when literature and language are once more promoted to the task of inspiration— even if we have nowadays to call them semantics. The signs are multiplying and the prospect is attractive.

Hence the laws of economic determinism, or the biologically based determinism of Spengler and Toynbee, with their powerful attraction for those to whom the tentative and particularizing 'idiography' of history is emotionally unsatisfying. The kind of science which history can be has nothing to do with 'nomothetic orientation'—does not demand the creation of a framework of laws—for such a framework is always essentially *a priori*; but that is not to deny it scientific status in its own terms, namely the function of a descriptive and analytical science, producing a series of experimental truths.[14]

Few practising historians would probably nowadays fall victim to the search for laws; the experience of research is enough to cure such ambitions. But a good many hanker after a certainty and precision which they believe to be proper to a science and which, in their view, traditional historical methods lack. They go to sociology and the like not only for inspiration but especially for method and can speak with hope of an 'age of the historical factory' with its cooperative and organized scholarship calling upon arithmetic for aid.[15] I am less frightened by the thought of cooperative research or 'quantification' than unimpressed, so far, by its results, and I believe that these supposedly sophisticated innovators are guilty of a little naïvety. They cry for the sun of reason and learning in ways familiar down the ages, but they have mistaken the heavenly body before their eyes : in fact they are crying for the moon. There are three good reasons for this. Historical materials

[14] For a useful discussion of these and similar points see Louis O. Mink, 'The Autonomy of Historical Understanding', *History and Theory*, v. 24ff.

[15] Thomas, *T.L.S.* 1966, 276. To the best of my knowledge, Mr Thomas, a fellow of St John's College, Oxford, and the author of some excellent articles, has never worked even within sight of one of these 'factories'.

are nearly always unsuitable for the kind of studies envisaged; the comparative method conceals within itself a self-destructive error; and sociological results in history are as a rule remarkably jejune.

Sociological enquiry is distinguished by its object and its method, the object being the analysis of social relationships and the method the counting of heads in categories. History may fairly concern itself with past social relationships, and the historian may often be well advised to count heads; but it should always be recognized that, since history must analyse and relate the story of past change and must concern itself with particular people as well as categories, historical studies derived from sociological influence can never be more than a small part of the whole enterprise. In addition, they are the part least well provided for by the evidence the past has left behind. These scientific investigations of family, class, occupations, mobility and all the rest happen to excite present-day interest and began systematically little more than a century ago; since before that time interest in them was rare and unscientific, it is useless to expect to find really exhaustive materials from which now to satisfy it. Every historian encounters immense difficulties as soon as he tries to collect worth while statistics for any problem before the year 1800 or so. Too often, the figures just do not exist, and even a trained acquaintance with statistical techniques can never quite get over the problems set by samples that are not so much random as obscurely weighted both by the accident of survival and, more importantly, by the lack of concern felt for them by those who preserved them for reasons quite different from those which now motivate their study. The endeavour is not, of course, entirely hopeless, and the results of enquiry may be interesting; the trouble is that they can never be any more certain than results arrived at without these aids in method. Demographic studies, in particular, have very important uses and can sometimes rest on reasonably reliable figures; but I have never yet seen a work of this kind which did not firmly proclaim the insufficiencies of the evidence, warn against excessive reliance on its statistical tables, and then proceed to treat the explicitly doubtful conclusions as safe ground for further confident inference. Historical evidence only very rarely resolves any sizeable question for good, and it is unfortunate if particular tricks of method lead either their exponents or the reader to suppose that certainty has been at last created.

A recent and most impressive product of this sociological school of history, Lawrence Stone's *Crisis of the Aristocracy 1558-1641* (Oxford, 1965), provides some useful lessons. The vast work contains many sections in which the fashionable method plays no part, and it may be only a conventional historian's prejudice that I find these more conventional chapters the most persuasive in the book. However, the author himself clearly loves best the massive evidence of his tables on which he rests his striking major conclusions. The aristocracy, he argues, underwent a general economic decline which so reduced its social influence that on the eve of the English Civil War it had ceased to be an effective agent for hierarchic government in the members of the realm. This important generalization depends entirely on the reliability of the statistics, and very slight shifts in percentages would demolish the structure. Only one of Mr Stone's reviewers has, so far, had the necessary knowledge to reconsider both the materials from which the tables are constructed and the tables themselves, and he felt compelled to call some crucial figures in question. The acrimonious correspondence which followed showed beyond doubt that there was quite enough uncertainty about them to permit a range of inference stretching from a mild improvement in position to a rather drastic deterioration.[16] I myself have methodological doubts concerning the figures produced in the chapter on education. Not only do I find some of the 'constructed' totals, put in where the evidence fails, unconvincing, but I wonder how one takes the step from mere figures of matriculation or even graduation to an assessment of educational standards. Questions of this sort soon rattle the bones of table-making, carefully locked in private drawers.

The trouble is that such things as the wealth of the aristocracy have to be calculated from figures very hard to systematize. Before the figures can even be added up and the percentages worked out, all sorts of questions have to be solved : who comes within the categories studied, how is wealth defined (for instance, the problem of debts owed and owing), what kind of wealth can be measured, what is the real meaning of the figures in the record, how far can statistical method fill gaps in a series, what can be done about changing values of money, and a great many more. Mr Stone, of course, considers questions of this kind, but he himself very rarely claims to have arrived at certainty in his answers. Even if agreement on all these questions were possible, and there is little enough sign of this, the real meaning of the further inferences would remain troubled by the tentative uncertainty—the roughness of the estimates conceded by Mr Stone—which the nature of the evidence imposes. Yet the landed wealth of the seventeenth-century aristocracy is relatively well documented, by comparison, for instance, with the profits or losses of

[16] *T.L.S.* 1966, 285f., 347, 407. The review was anonymous. But see also G. E. Aylmer in *Past and Present*, no. 32, 113ff.

court office or the familial history of the whole group; and everything about the aristocracy is well documented by comparison with other layers of society. Historians who put all their money on this kind of study and their trust in the guiding hand of sociology come to believe in certainties they have not demonstrated; they are likely to inflict many ill-established generalizations on the history books unless they show themselves more consistently aware of the deficiencies of both materials and methods than they would appear to be. There are some questions, however interesting, that cannot be answered, and attempts to force answers to them in the teeth of the historical evidence produces at best hypo-thesis, at worst false dogma. By all means let us have more studies of this kind, but let them be a little more modest in their claims; above all, let their proponents realize that these are neither the only nor necessarily the best ways of studying the past.

In any case, investigations on the scale attempted by Mr Stone are rare, and too many of his fellow-prophets seem content with a much more dangerous practice. They in effect accept the 'models' produced by their admired preceptors and use a form of analogical argument to apply them to history. In an earlier generation, the influence of biology, and especially of the theory of evolution, on late-nineteenth and early-twentieth century historians provided a notorious example. Here historians found a doctrine in natural science which took account of their own cherished preoccupation with change, and which seemed to make undoctrinaire sense of it. Death and decay, survival and renewal, are obvious facts of human history: it seemed reasonable to see them rationalized by the theory which explained similar events in the history of species. The result was an eruption of, or perhaps only a greater authority for, conventional metaphors speaking of youth, maturity, decline, progress, survival of the fittest, and so on. The effects have sunk into conventional thinking on history and into its vocabulary; they are very hard to eradicate. The mistake may appear obvious when it leads to the biological determinism found in Oswald Spengler's *Decline of the West*, or in the sort of history which uses theories of national or racial superiority to explain sucess and failure as part of a large plan. The evolutionary theory of history has a good deal in common with that which sees the hand of God in history; after all, evolution was thought to explain the facts of natural creation in default of the existence of a creator. Such sweeping surveys, embodying the notion that what happened was bound to happen, attract by their simplicity but are among good historians readily undermined by the habits of caution and particular study to which they are trained. Less easily detected and eradicated is the biological error *in parvo*, the sort of metaphorical explanation which, for instance, treats the English Parliament at some stage as 'mature' and thinks in terms of an earlier childhood and adolescence, as though that institution—that congregation of identifiable and always adult men—had a biological history of its own, comparable to that of the individual. (When did it reach senility?)

The devotees of anthropology are particularly prone to this kind of analogical error, as when nineteenth-century Bantus and Polynesians are called in to explain things about supposedly primitive societies of the past like pre-Columbian America or German forest tribes. Study of a more strictly historical kind at once reveals such enormous differences in circumstances and situations that the value of such comparisons—even their capacity to suggest new questions and insights—becomes very problematical. In the article already quoted several

times, Mr Thomas asserts that 'Englishmen are now
disposed to see analogies between their history and
that of "underdeveloped" African countries in a way that
Victorians could never have done.' 'The gain', he adds,
'in understanding and comparative sense is incalcul-
able.'[17] But is it? Or rather, if it were properly calculated,
would it be all gain? When some writers can treat pre-
industrial England, the economically most advanced
society in the Europe of its day, as though it were like
tribal Africa or nineteenth-century India, understanding
is destroyed, not assisted. The medieval villein of England
was, unquestionably, a peasant; but this does not mean
that we can learn more or better about him by studying
other kinds of peasant still in existence than by unravelling the historical evidence (such as it is) for what
his life was really like. That perfectly useful concept,
feudalism, was not discredited till historians applied it
undiscriminatingly to any society from Aztec Mexico to
Shogun Japan in which some of its characteristics
seemed to turn up. Assuredly, analogies and comparisons
evoked by some other discipline can have their uses;
they can reactivate a mind tired of struggling with
seemingly dead or insoluble problems, and can sometimes
give meaning to details of the evidence. But unless two
things are remembered they are not so much dangerous
as pointless: the answers must still arise from a study of
the historical evidence scrutinized according to the
standards of the historical method,[18] and comparisons are

[17] *T.L.S.* 1966, 276.
[18] An interesting paper by Mr Lawrence Stone on 'Social
Mobility in England, 1500-1700' (*Past and Present*, no 33, 16ff.)
seems to me to suffer shipwreck on this condition. He starts with
a 'model' (actually quite a good one) but thereafter accommodates
his discussion to that model, deducing consequences and collecting
such material as helps the argument in footnotes which break the
rules of historical scholarship. They are eclectic, cite whole books

usually more fruitful when they draw attention to differences rather than to likeness.

Finally, one would be more impressed by the claims made for the 'new' methods if the results proved more striking and less predictable. Too often vast engines are assembled, and blows of enormous weight are struck, only to produce an answer which is either obvious, well known, or manifestly unhelpful. In his excellent study of Charles I's civil service, Professor G. E. Aylmer, intent on reducing every problem to the certainty of established figures, provides a rather fine case in point in the section which studies the allegiance, in the Civil War, of men whose only common denominator was office under the Crown.[19] The question itself is not only legitimate but important; the treatment involves no fewer than nineteen tables in twenty-three pages. The office holders in question, not so numerous perhaps as to make percentual variations appear very large, are sliced all ways, by age, social status, length of service, distribution of property, religious affiliation, and so forth. It would indeed be interesting to know whether any of these characteristics correlate with the choice made on the outbreak of war. However, the results, expressed in properly cautious language ('considerably more likely', 'a little less likely') either show nothing of significance or underline the obvious and expected, as that older men were less likely to take up arms than younger, or that men with property in the shires controlled by the king inclined a little

---

rather than specific passages in them, and make no attempt to criticize the evidence used. This was a paper intended to be read in a discussion, and as such it is brilliant; but it would be very rash to suppose that its conclusions are soundly enough based for the confidence with which they are stated.

[19] *The King's Servants* (London, 1961), 393-416.

more to his support. The climax comes with a table
which shows from a sample of twenty-three that
Catholics and High Anglicans were more likely to fight
for the king and Puritans for the Parliament. Perhaps
such 'proof' that religious convictions had something
to do with the formation of parties in the war can be
useful at a time when Church and religion are no
longer regarded as the major issues of the conflict; but
it does seem a poor reward for so much labour.

The general desire for 'new questions' seems to
suppose that the historian can get his questions in one
place and then go to another where he will find the
facts of the past waiting to be reconsidered in the light
of ideas supplied from outside his own area of activity.
It has been conceded that reading or listening to other
scholars of all sorts can sometimes give the mind a new
key, but the way in which these innovators wish to
work leads to either silence or disaster. Unless the
evidence makes the 'new' question meaningful, the in-
quirer can be only honest (that is, admit that there is
nothing to say) or dishonest (that is, construct himself
an answer by twisting, overburdening, or even inventing
the evidence). The facts known about the past are in
control. However desirable it may be that we should
have knowledge of past vital statistics and demographic
movements, it is simply the case that for the greater part
of history we shall always know very little or nothing
concerning such things. Those determined to put their
faith in 'sophisticated' mathematical methods and to
apply 'general laws' to the pitifully meagre and very
uncertain detail that historical evidence often provides
for the answering of just such interesting and important
questions, are either to be pitied because they will be
sinking in quicksand while believing themselves to be
standing on solid earth, or to be combated because

they darken counsel with their errors. Sometimes methods of counting and analysing yield valuable results, but they can do so only if there exists the sort of evidence which has already inclined historians to hold the views to which the 'sophisticated' machinery gives firm foundations. This is not at all to deny the virtue of systematic study, or even the occasional virtue of IBM machines; it is, however, to assert that these points, as all others in the historian's work, achieve virtue in the light of his evidence, his historical method, and his unprejudiced hard labour.

The sociologizing historian may well retort that to replace impressionist opinion by the certainty of figures is a true advance, and I have already agreed that not every use of these methods brings either error or the commonplace. What really matters is that, obvious or unexpected, the answers carry no conviction and are not worth the time spent on them if the alternative discipline has been allowed to be master rather than servant. The historian must not go against the first conditions of his calling : his knowledge of the past is governed by the evidence of that past, and that evidence must be criticized and interpreted by the canons of historical scholarship. New methods may improve his handling of that evidence, but they can do so only if they are controlled by the historical method, which grounds detail upon evidence and generalization upon detail.[20]

[20] Professor W. O. Aydelotte, praised (e.g. by Mr Thomas) for introducing computerizing methods into the study of nineteenth-century Parliaments, has himself been more modest and much more sensible in his assessment of the interaction between history and sociology: 'A Statistical Analysis of the Parliament of 1841 : Some Problems of Method', *Bulletin of the Institute of Historical Research*, xxvii (1954), 141ff.; 'Geschichte und Sozialwissen-schaften', *Welt als Geschichte*, xiv (1954), 212ff.; 'Quantification in

This insistence on the hard work of specifically historical research is particulary necessary because the historian who thinks that he has found better new methods in allied disciplines too often shows an inclination to accept their conclusions without critical consideration. To give an example : economists hold that a country intent on industrializing itself needs to have an accumulation of unused capital and the means to transfer it freely from the sector which accumulates to the sector trying to expand. It was therefore long axiomatic that these things happened in eighteenth-century England, and historians wrote histories of the Industrial Revolution showing them in existence and at work. The evidence, however, shows them non-existent,[21] and it has therefore become necessary to abandon whole sections of inherited lore about the Industrial Revolution, lore which was really only assumption based on the doctrine of the theorists.

One can understand why some historians fall into this trap : the historical evidence by itself may not yield any obvious generalization, and to adopt the theories of another science may provide a coherent framework within which to arrange one's thought and description. Preconceived notions are a much greater danger to historical truth than either deficiency of evidence or error in detail, and nothing entrenches them so deep as the approval of some other form of study which seems to rest on independent thought. One could make a

---

History', *Amer. Hist. Rev.* lxxi (1966), 803ff. For a thoughtful restatement of the autonomous claims of history, linked with a convincing attack on the sociologizing tenets of the *Annales* school, see. H. Heimpel, 'Geschichte und Geschichtswissenschaft', *Vierteljahrschrift für Zeitgeschichte*, v (1957) 1ff.

21 Cf. S. Pollard, 'Fixed Capital in the Industrial Revolution in Britain', *Journal of Economic History*, xxiv (1964), 299ff.

case for the proposition that the centuries of 'whig' historiography in England simply suffered from historians' uncalled-for willingness to let the lawyers dictate their scheme of argument. Similarly, the sociologist may provide a system of class structure or evolve theories of voting behaviour which are statistical abstracts from the multifariousness of real life. For his own purposes, these conclusions may be valid and fruitful, but no historian is entitled to assume their validity for his own period and problems: he is not entitled to know his conclusions before he has got there by specific study of the historical evidence.

When the externally obtained scheme becomes doctrine, as too often it does, it stultifies the study of history by reducing history to a repository of examples selected or distorted to buttress the scheme. The danger is greater when the scheme in fact claims to rest on a study of history, as in the 'whig' interpretation in which everything worked to the predestined end of a parliamentary constitution, or in Toynbee's system which enables its exponent even to classify as ages of peace eras manifestly filled with war.[22] Nowadays, the most complete case of this sort of disaster is that of Marxism, a universal doctrine of human history and behaviour based originally on some necessarily limited history and sociology and in its day a truly remarkable achievement of scientific insight and ill-controlled speculation. To-day, in those large parts of the world where it has become dogma, it seems finally to have prevented the fruitful progress of enquiry it once did so much to stimulate.[23]

A personal experience may illustrate this. Despite all the refinements it has undergone, Marxist historiography

[22] Cf. e.g. Pieter Geyl, *Debates with Historians* (The Hague, 1954), 119, n. 1.
[23] Cf. my remarks in *Historical Journal*, ix (1966) 388ff.

is committed to the view that in the sixteenth and seventeenth centuries Europe witnessed the triumph of a new dominant class, the bourgeoisie, with its own economic organization (capitalism) and ethos (Protestantism leading to secular liberalism). Specific study, on the other hand, impresses on the historian the fact that if any social group bettered its position and its share of political power in those centuries—and none did exclusively, anyway—it was the landed nobility, very conscious of its aristocratic status and ethos. After a little close acquaintance it becomes difficult to see the period characterized by any simple, socially-based transformation to which all dominant events, and in particular the Reformation, can be referred. In my introduction to the second volume of the *New Cambridge Modern History*, I said something to that effect and suggested that the essence of the Reformation should, after all, be sought in the realm of religion, in spiritual anguish and search. The argument is certainly open to dispute and should no doubt be discussed. But an eminent Marxist critic, a learned historian of the age, attacked my view not because the evidence seemed to him to point in another direction, but because he knew that in those years the bourgeoisie won their class war, with all the consequences that flowed therefrom in religion and the rest. For him no analysis not based on that piece of doctrine could be valid.[24] He simply did not see that the rejection, on reasoned grounds, of an interpretation cannot be answered by a reassertion, without argument or proof, of something that to him was true because it was decreed.

Doctrinaire Marxism is to the historian as special a case as doctrinaire Christianity once was, but special cases illumine the whole category to which they belong.

[24] L. Makkai, in *Acta Historica* (Budapest), 1963.

The historian is right to learn from all the disciplines
which concern themselves with his own chosen subject,
man through the ages. But in so learning he should walk
with great care lest he fall victim to his own humility.
He must beware of merely following fashion—the
fashion of elevating this or that study to dominance, or
the fashionable form taken at a given moment by these
other studies which, since they are directed towards the
extraction of laws, themselves suffer exceptionally from
the vagaries of fashion. He must not adopt their
methods without subordinating them to his own, and
he must not use them to do what historical evidence does
not permit him to do. Above all, he must not allow
them to dictate his ultimate conclusion or to force
upon him their so-called models.[25] Given this care, he
can and should attend to them with every intention
of learning. However, there is no need for this process to
work in one direction only. The historian has quite as
much to teach to others. He can help them to understand
the importance of multiplicity where they look for
single-purpose schemes, to grasp the interrelations which
their specialization tends to overlook, to remember that
the units in which they deal are human beings. While the
historian can profit from the social scientist's precision,
range of questions, and willingness to generalize, he can
repay the debt by giving instruction in the rigorous
analysis of evidence, sceptical thinking, and the avoidance of ill-based generalizations. Since the rashness of
the social scientist, treating his theories as facts and
intent on applying them in practice, constitutes one of
the main dangers to which modern society lies ex-

[25] Sociologists establish 'models' which they test by supposedly
empirical evidence. To an historian this seems a very dangerous
procedure: far too often the model seems to dictate the selection of
facts used to confirm it.

posed, the study of history may be said to serve a vital purpose when it combats the overconfidence of the men who see the world as categories and statistics, and who think in jargon.

5 *Purpose*

Saving the social scientist from himself (and society from the social scientist) may be a worthy reason for studying history, but not many historians are likely to regard themselves simply as specialized nursemaids and Samaritans. Some feel that they must discover that in the past which will help men to understand their present and future. The words, 'the purpose of history', have strictly two meanings: they can refer either to the purpose of the historical process, or to the purpose to be served by the historian in studying it. In practice, however, the meanings are close to each other and tend to merge. The historian who thinks that he has discerned the future towards which the past is moving conceives it his duty to instruct his readers accordingly. It becomes the purpose of his study to elucidate and demonstrate the purposes of the historical process. At the same time, it is true that even historians who do not claim to see anything significant in the way things have happened are bound to have had a purpose in mind when they entered upon their studies. No one reads or writes history in a fit of total absentmindedness, though a fair amount of history has been written by people whose minds seem in part to have been on other things.

Is there a purpose in history? Mr Carr grows very scornful at the expense of an honest man like H. A. L. Fisher, who in a famous sentence explained that he

could see none.[26] Mr Carr is surely right to denounce
the theory of the pure accident, the theory that history
is just one damn thing after another. Though in a
sense, of course, the sequence of events is just that, it
becomes history only when marshalled by the interpretative human intelligence. This is not to overlook
the importance of accidents, which do happen (though
Mr Carr would seem to suppose that they can be written
out of history), but to stress that in the understanding of
the past the accident is just another point to be explained, considered and accommodated. Accidents may
affect the course of events, but the historian, in his
analysis, must not be accident-prone. No historian, including Fisher, has in fact ever treated his subject as
though it were entirely without meaning; if he had, he
would have been unable to write. What is really at
issue is whether one may discern a larger purpose,
whether things produce effects that are continuous
and, up to a point, predictable. When Mr Carr, and
others, seek a purpose in history, they are trying to fill
the vacuum created when God was removed from history.
Even historians who hold that God reveals himself in
history would not to-day feel entitled to use him by way
of explanation, but the temperament which demands a
certain guidance from the past by way of illumination
for the future—the religious temperament—continues
to exist among historians and produce theories of the
course of history which seek this prophetic purpose.

There are in the main two ways of subordinating
history to prophecy, the circular and the linear; and
both have an ancient, respectable, and largely pre-
professional history. The first supposes that societies grow
and decay, to be replaced by others which follow much

[26] Carr, *What is History?*, 43, 100.

the same pattern. The other view supposes that the sum total of the past moves in a straight line of progress; though it will often allow that lapses, back-trackings and lateral movements may interrupt the main line of advance, it nevertheless insists that such a main line can be discovered and plotted. Linear theories are not necessarily optimistic, but their vocabulary (progress, advance) tends to inculcate a conviction that things not only move along a line but move towards an improvement.

To-day's best known cyclical theory is that developed by A. J. Toynbee, and it is not necessary at this date to demonstrate once again how little his vast edifice has to do with the facts of the past.[27] Linear theories are certainly commoner, and Mr Carr as well as Professor J. H. Plumb have recently entered eloquent pleas for a return to the allegedly discredited notion of progress, the notion that things get better in sum, however much the detail may get worse at times.[28] They both want historians to write to this purpose because they seem to regard it as the scholar's function not only to describe change but also to advocate it; the historian should be the prophet of an intelligent radicalism. Both abominate nostalgia about the past and wish to use history to teach men reliance on their powers to better themselves and their world. Mr Carr seems to think this right because he believes that this is the lesson of history; Dr

[27] E.g. Geyl, *Debates with Historians*, chs. 5-8. Toynbee may have contributed something useful to the study of history when he directed attention to areas and times little studied by the ordinary English historian. Even this is not altogether certain; as for his interpretative scheme and his treatment of evidence, they do nothing but harm to those who allow themselves to regard them with respect.

[28] Carr, *What is History?*, ch. 5; J. H. Plumb, ed., *Crisis in the Humanities* (Harmondsworth, 1964), 24ff.

Plumb adds a fear that unless historians will attend to this task of propaganda they will cease to be read and cease to play any part in their societies. Both manifestly confuse the problem of why men should be made to learn about history with the problem of the meaning of the past; or rather, to them only the particular meaning they extract from the past justifies the pursuit of history as an activity of the scholar and teacher.[29]

Let it be said at once that the underlying convictions behind the demands are in part sound. Historians cannot exist in a vacuum; they live in the society of men, influence it whether they like it or not, and should therefore be conscious of what they are about. But they should also be conscious of the dangers they run. It is all very well to regret the day when history was 'philosophy teaching by example', the day when historians thought themselves the moral preceptors of a ruling class and, aping Plutarch, used their science to instil high principles in their pupils. We cannot return to the attitude which produced a *Mirror for Magistrates* to show, by using historical instances, how those who offend against the divine order always come to a bad end;[30] and if we could return to it I doubt if many of us would. Yet such schoolmasterly ambitions are at the back of Dr Plumb's mind. When we take our more sophisticated history into the market place and the pulpit, we assume a task of some danger and must be almost pedantically careful of our integrity. Few, I daresay,

[29] Plumb, *Crisis in the Humanities*, 43 : historians' 'explanations of the past should lead to an explanation of it for their time and generation, so that, by explaining, man's control over his future may be increased'.

[30] *The Mirror for Magistrates* (best edition by Lily B. Campbell, Oxford, 1938), a collection of cautionary tales mostly in verse, first published in 1559.

would wish to deride the conviction, expressed by that
not uneminent American historian, Conyers Read, who
some years ago told the American Historical Association
that 'the social responsibilities of the historian' involved
him in the defence of 'values'.[31] But how many would
agree with him that those values must be those of
American civilization and democracy, that the historian
plays a part in 'total war'? Since no man in society,
said Read, can escape some form of social control, the
historian must 'accept and endorse such controls as
are essential for the preservation of our way of life'.
Calling, in a fiery peroration, for the suppression of
inconvenient facts, he cried that if the historian will not
offer 'assurance that mankind's present position is on the
highway and not on some dead end, then mankind will
seek for assurance in a more positive alternative, whether
it be offered from Rome or from Moscow'.

Conyers Read was expressing too frankly what others
might wish to think, though it should be recorded that
he was fully and firmly answered by a fellow-historian
from a sounder American tradition.[32] Yet he was neither
fool nor knave, and he had thought as hard about his
professional purpose as Dr Plumb, with his more radical
predilections, has done. Read's case makes plain that
the historian's function in society cannot be reduced to
that of a preacher, whether he preaches the excellence
of all that is, or the necessity of reform, or the desir-
ability of revolution. If he is to be a good preacher he
must rest his case upon a faith; but if he is to be a
good historian he must question his own faith and
admit some virtue in the beliefs of others. If he allows

[31] *Amer. Hist. Rev.* lv (1949-50), 275ff.
[32] Howard K. Beale, 'The Professional Historian: His Theory
and His Practice', *Pacific Historical Review*, xxii (1953), 227ff.;
see esp. 254f.

the task of choosing among the facts of the past to deteriorate into suppression of what will not serve the cause, he loses all right to claim weight for his opinions. An historian may be an ex-businessman, as Read was, or like Gibbon an ex-captain of grenadiers, but when he pronounces upon economics or strategy we have a duty to judge him as an historian, and only as an historian. And there the simplicities of the preacher's call at once collapse.

The trouble with all these theories about 'the meaning of history' is twofold : the great range of contemporaneous events and the shortness of historical time permit of no convincing demonstration one way or the other. It is never difficult to see purpose or direction in a sequence of historical events if one confines oneself sufficiently, especially if one limits one's gaze to the winners in any conflict. Take the seventeenth century in England : few collections of years have had more 'purpose' inflicted upon them. If one looks at the struggles of the Stuart kings with their Parliaments, one readily writes the century's history as the story of growing liberty. If one concentrates on the problems of production and distribution, one sees the age as one of expanding trade, a growth in capitalist organization, increasing dependency (decline of liberty) for certain sectors of the population. If one looks at men's minds, one comes up with an explanation based on the secularization of thought and the development of the scientific approach. There is no obvious or provable connection between these lines of 'progress', and the historian who proceeds to make one— who, for instance, argues that political liberty was a precondition of intellectual advance and economic enterprise—can no more prove his case than the historian who refuses to see any such links. Moreover, he would be ignoring other things, such as the influence of the

Reformation or the central position of land-ownership. And then there is seventeenth-century France where political liberty on the whole declined, scientific thought flourished in different conditions and in its own, quite different, fashion, and economic life followed a different line towards increasing wealth as well as increasing strain. There is the rest of seventeenth-century Europe, not to mention Moghul India, Ch'ing China, or the kingdoms of tropical Africa. How can one possibly bring these varieties of experience into a scheme depending on a single line of progress? One can do it only by seizing on some development in subsequent history and elevating that to the sole significant position. This is not the legitimate activity of selecting the meaningful; it is the idle activity of forgetting the inconvenient. As for the shortness of historical time, I have already pointed out that recorded history amounts to no more than about two hundred generations. Even if there is a larger purpose in history, it must be said that we cannot really expect so far to be able to extract it from the little bit of history we have.

Still, Mr Carr and Dr Plumb claim to be able to discern it. They deny that they have fallen victim to the cruder fallacies of progress doctrines, those that identify what is with what must be, see in the past only the triumph of the present, and thus guarantee that high degree of self-satisfaction which was characteristic of whig historiography in England. Historians who adhere to a belief in progress are always liable to lapse from description into approval, to condemn the losers as blind or wicked, and to set the judicious garland of historical necessity on the victor's head. Mr Carr and Dr Plumb try to remember the variety of the past and claim that they give it due weight in the story. They both assert that they are not determinists in the simple sense of believing that the processes of history could not have worked out differently from the way they did. In this respect, however, it is difficult to treat them as companions. Dr Plumb seems less concerned with the question whether progress is really the lesson to be learned from history than with his demand that it should be the lesson taught by historians to their own age, in order that the age may feel usefully optimistic. He trembles on the precipice which swallowed up Conyers Read. Mr Carr wishes to assert that an event like the Russian Revolution not only happened in some measure necessarily (to him, the logic of history brought it about) but in its happening testifies to the necessary improvement of mankind. That is to say, both concede a measure of determinism in their thinking, but Dr Plumb is not aware that it is there. Both are good enough, historians to avoid the more obvious traps of biased selectivity and conditioned prejudice. In Mr Carr's attitude to the Russian Revolution, and in Dr Plumb's account of social amelioration, there is not only doctrine but also much sound historical learning. Where they err is not in their history but in their propaganda, in their insistence that only their kind of interpretation will do.

Progress in history is in great part a matter of value judgment, a personal matter, and though every competent historian can discover a measure of necessity in events, none can prove that they are truly determined.[33] If our authors see progress and necessity in history, they are justified in saying so and in trying to persuade others to agree with them. They are not justified in supposing that no one can honestly see things in any other way than in the light of their simplifying handtorch, and I

[33] Cf. Isaiah Berlin, *Historical Inevitability* (London, 1954).

object to their claim that history *must* be understood and proclaimed in their single fashion. For myself, I believe that they are wrong to concentrate so exclusively on the progressive and deterministic elements in the story. All talk about progress, if it does not simply mean change, rests on the assumption that the historian can tell what is better and what worse; but one man's better is usually another man's worse. I agree with Mr Carr and Dr Plumb that twentieth-century technology has greatly improved material life. I agree that in England, at least, social attitudes have in many ways grown better, that the nation is less given to violence and cruelty than once it was. I should, however, hesitate before supposing this to be a universal experience; and though, like Dr Plumb, I am temperamentally hostile to the school of thought which sentimentalizes the past and worships a chocolate-box substitute for the reality, I cannot forget that material progress has often been linked with deterioration, even material deterioration, in the quality of life,[84] and that the decline in active cruelty has been accompanied by a decline in active indignation against despotism and arbitrary rule. I do not pretend here to make an assessment or strike a balance, a thing each man must do for himself though the historian can assist him by illuminating the past; I only wish to point out that progress and necessity are doctrines which cannot be derived from, can only be superimposed upon, the study of history. And above all, I do not see why there should be only historians like Mr Carr and Dr Plumb, *laudatores temporis futuri*, why they should claim authority for their manifestly highly selective history, and

[84] Mr Carr (*What is History?*, 143ff.) comes very close to identifying technical progress with the expansion of true reason. One does not have to be a sentimentalist to regard this as a crude and misleading point of view.

why other points of view should be not so much controverted as despised and condemned.

Does this then mean that there is no very positive purpose in studying history, that it really is only a matter of the student's private satisfaction? Are there no standards by which one may call historians good or bad, adequate or inadequate, right or wrong? I think there are, but they cannot be discovered if the purpose of history is approached from outside the discipline itself. The sort of arguments put forward by Mr Carr and Dr Plumb do not arise from their concern with history but from their personal involvement in the present and future of their own society.[35] This is comprehensible and can be creditable, but it in no way helps to explain the purpose of studying history, and it begs the question of what history means. Mr Carr and Dr Plumb are, at heart, 'whigs', looking into the past for reassurance; they begin with the assumption of a social purpose stated (that the historian must offer to society a demonstration of its power to advance itself) and they then eliminate any use of history which does not contribute to this purpose. For this reason they do fall into the deterministic error of choosing from the variety of history the line of events and detail which leads to their own present position, their preconceived end; everything else, if they do not ignore it, they explain away. The right approach would surely start from the other end. We must first explain in what manner the past can truly be studied—that is, we must accept the despised tenet that the past must be studied for its own sake—and then enquire whether this study has any contribution to make to the present.

[35] I do not, of course, mean to deny that at other times they are also very much concerned with history.

In short, we are once again faced with the autonomy of history : the study of history is legitimate in itself, and any use of it for another purpose is secondary. That secondary use will be laudable or deplorable in proportion as the autonomous purpose has been served well or ill. If I have rather more respect for the progress doctrines of Dr Plumb or Mr Carr than I have for the historical racialism of Rosenberg or the historical inevitabilities of Marxism, it is because I think their history better; if I have my reservations about their preferred interpretations, and especially about their prescriptions to other historians, it is because in my view they still ignore far too much about the past. The task of history is to understand the past, and if the past is to be understood it must be given full respect in its own right. And unless it is properly understood, any use of it in the present must be suspect and can be dangerous. One cannot use a corrupt means to a worthy end. And the creation of the sound instrument involves not only obvious things like doing the serious work of study, avoiding anachronism both in interpretation and judgment, devoting attention to the defeated as well as to the victors; it involves, above all, the deliberate abandonment of the present. The historian studying the past is concerned with the later event only in so far as it throws light on the part of the past that he is studying. It is the cardinal error to reverse this process and study the past for the light it throws on the present.

However, it does not in the least follow from this that the study of history, treated as autonomous and justified within itself, has no contribution to make beyond its frontiers. In the first place, let it be remembered that this pursuit of history in its own right is not only morally just but also agreeable. A good many people simply want to know about the past, for emotional or intellectual satisfaction, and the professional historian fulfils a useful 'social' function when he helps them to know better. He is also, of course, satisfying his own desire for knowledge, and he also is, after all, a part of society. This might be supposed to reduce the historian to a mere entertainer, but in fact it gives him a cultural role : he contributes to the complex of non-practical activities which make up the culture of a society. When he stimulates and satisfies the imagination he does not differ essentially from the poet or artist, which is not to say that he should be picturesque. There is an emotional satisfaction of a high order to be gained from extending the comprehending intelligence to include the past.

Next, it would certainly be untrue to suppose that history can teach no practical lessons. It enlarges the area of individual experience by teaching about human behaviour, about man in relationship to other men, about the interaction of circumstances and conditions in their effect upon individual and social fortunes. Its lessons are not straightforward didactic precepts, either instructions for action (the search for parallels to a given situation) or universal norms (history teaches that every thing progresses, history teaches the triumph—or futility —of moral principles); there is far too much variety about the past, far too much confused singularity about the event, to produce such simple results. Nevertheless, a sound acquaintance with the prehistory of a situation or problem does illumine them and does assist in making present decisions; and though history cannot prophesy, it can often make reasonable predictions. Historical knowledge gives solidity to the understanding of the present and may suggest guiding lines for the future.

Yet these emotional and practical uses of history are not its main contribution to the purpose of man. The study of history is an intellectual pursuit, an activity of the reasoning mind, and, as one should expect, its main service lies in its essence. Like all sciences, history, to be worthy of itself and beyond itself, must concentrate on one thing: the search for truth. Its real value as a social activity lies in the training it provides, the standards it sets, in this singularly human concern. Reason distinguishes man from the rest of creation, and the study of history justifies itself in so far as it assists reason to work and improve itself. Like all rational activities, the study of history, regarded as an autonomous enterprise, contributes to the improvement of man, and it does so by seeking the truth within the confines of its particular province, which happens to be the rational reconstruction of the past. In this larger purpose it has no sort of monopoly, for this it shares with every form of intellectual investigation, but it happens to have certain advantages in that it attracts a wide variety of intelligences, can do its work without too much demand on technical specialization in the learner, and can rest its capacity to train on its capacity to entertain.

In these advantages, which it possesses over both the natural and the social sciences, lie its temptations and perils: absence of technical specialization can lead to lack of rigour, entertainment to meretricious superficiality, variety of appeal to bias and propaganda. But the dangers do not deny the advantages; the possibility of corruption does not cast out the possibility of excellence. Integrity, resting on professional training and professional attitudes, is the safeguard. All historical work which satisfies the conditions of professional competence and integrity fulfils the historian's very important social duty; none that falls short of that standard can be trusted to fulfil any social duty safely, however conscious it may be of its obligations or however earnestly it may preach progress, the goodness of man, or the inevitability of revolutions. The quality of an historian's work must, as I have said, be judged purely by intellectual standards; the same is true of his contribution to society, though moral consequences may well flow from adherence to these principles of the reasoning capacity. It is not the problems they study or the lessons they teach that distinguish the historical sheep from the goats, but only the manner of their study, the precision of their minds, and the degree to which they approximate to the ultimate standards of intellectual honesty and intellectual penetration. *Omnia veritas.*

II

Research

The study of history, then, amounts to a search for the truth. But whether in fact such a thing as historical truth can exist has been a much debated problem; in particular, some philosophers, who show no sign of ever having tried to write history, like to arrive at the conclusion that, since historical knowledge cannot, strictly speaking, exist, there is no way of establishing truth in history.[1] These denials follow, as a rule, one of two lines of argument. They either maintain that the past, being dead and irrecoverable, cannot be known about in any meaningful sense; or that the impact of the historian upon his material renders all the history supposedly known a matter of private choice and interpretation, so that in the end there is nothing but subjective opinion, the very opposite to truth. Both these superficially cogent arguments betray an essential lack of acquaintance with the principles and practice of historical research, and it matters nothing that such relativist, even nihilist, views can sometimes be held by men generally regarded as historians. These opinions also show some ignorance of the matter studied by the historical discipline and forget that inability to know all

[1] For a sensible analysis, by a philosopher, of philosophical objections to the possibility of historical knowledge, see Arthur C. Danto, *Analytical Philosophy of History* (Cambridge, 1965), chs. 3-6.

the truth is not the same thing as total inability to know the truth.

1 *The Possibility of Historical Truth*

The problem of whether the past can be known at all—since it is not now here in the presence of the observer and cannot be brought back for study—arises from the attempt to make history seem a science, comparable in purpose and method to the natural sciences. The natural sciences have, it would seem, virtually abandoned the concepts of truth and falsehood; phenomena once regarded as objectively true are now seen to be only a statistical abstraction from random variables, and the accusing finger of the uncertainty principle further insists that, since observation alters a phenomenon, nothing is capable of being studied except after it is changed from the state in which it was meant to have been investigated. Practising scientists have therefore permitted the philosopher to remove the word true from their vocabulary and to substitute some such phrase as more probable, more accurately descriptive, more aesthetically or intellectually satisfying. This has not stopped scientists from continuing their efforts to investigate and understand nature, and in so far as it has reduced their positivist pride in the possession of the only strictly based truth the new philosophy may be thought of as gain. But historians have always been inclined to doubt the value, even the possibility, of their studies; they require not the new humility preached in the wake of Heisenberg, but some return to the assurance of the nineteenth century that the work they are doing deals with reality.

As a matter of fact, in a very real sense the study of

history is concerned with a subject matter more objective and more independent than that of the natural sciences. The common argument that, unlike the scientist, the historian cannot verify his reconstruction by repeating the experiment at will can be turned round to give him greater assurance of objectivity. Let it be granted that verifiability is the basis of the method employed by the natural sciences, and that in any acceptable sense it is clearly impossible for the historian. He can reconstruct in the mind, but he cannot re-enact. However, the fundamental reason for this disability ensures that his subject matter is to a remarkable extent quite independent of him. All scientific experiments are essentially constructs, and this applies to both the physical and the biological sciences. The scientist poses his problem, designs his experiment, and—if successful—can repeat problem, experiment and solution as often as he likes, just because he has himself determined the form in which the experiment is cast. Of course, he obtains his problem by asking questions of nature—of something outside himself—but his method enables him to treat nature wilfully and to compose for himself the argument which he wishes to resolve. Scientific experiments—dissection in taxonomic studies, for example, or the treatment of cells for purposes of study in biochemistry, or even the dropping of a stone from the tower of Pisa—are artificial; these things would not have happened but for a deliberate act of will on the part of the experimenter; the matter studied may be taken from nature, but before it is studied it is transformed for the purposes of the investigation. It is not going too far to assert that nearly all scientific study deals with specially prepared artificial derivatives from what naturally occurs.

The historian's case is very different. True, he may select his problems to suit himself. He may ask the questions he likes or believes capable of being answered; he may, and probably will, include himself in the equation when he explains, interprets, even perhaps distorts. But he cannot invent his experiment: the subject of his investigation is outside his control. When the problem of truth is under consideration, his essential difference from the natural scientist works in his favour. He cannot escape the first condition of his enterprise, which is that the matter he investigates has a dead reality independent of the enquiry. At some time, these things actually once happened, and it is now impossible to arrange them for the purposes of experiment. It may well be true that, for one reason or another, exactly what happened, or when and how and why, cannot now be known; no historian would suppose that his knowledge can be either total or finite. But this does not alter the fact that it is knowledge of a reality, of what did occur, not of something that the student or observer has put together for study. Just because historical matter is in the past, is gone, irrecoverable and unrepeatable, its objective reality is guaranteed: it is beyond being altered for any purpose whatsoever. Let it be noted that what is in question here is the subject matter of history, the events of the past, not the evidence they have left behind or the product of the historian's labours. However biased, prejudiced, incomplete and inadequate that product may be, it embodies an account of events that happened quite independent of the existence of him who now looks at them. Anyone who approves the tedious opinion that history is bunk does so because he prefers to ignore the reality of the past: but it is commandingly there, and the historian is not a free or purely wilful agent.

It follows from this that the historian's study is capable of concerning itself with a truth which is more

absolute than mere truthfulness. Verifiability is the
enemy of objective truth because it consists of the operation of the observer and experimenter upon the subject
matter studied. The historian cannot verify; he can only
discover and attempt to explain. In the work of discovery
he has the assurance that he is looking for something
that once had existence and is therefore, in theory,
discoverable. We may not know precisely why William
the Conqueror decided to invade England; we do know
that he did invade and had a reason for doing so. We
may argue over his invasion and its motive; we cannot
argue them away. Nine hundred years ago they had
existence; and just because they are irrecoverable in
the flesh now, they are indestructible in the past reality.
Thus while history will rarely be able to say : this is the
truth and no other answer is possible; it will always be
able to say : this once existed or took place, and there is
therefore a truth to be discovered if only we can find it.

Whether the truth of these past realities is in fact
discoverable is a question that shall be discussed later.
So far, I have been concerned only to deny the charge
that because the past cannot be re-enacted therefore
there is, by definition, no such thing as historical truth.
This leaves the second argument against the possibility
of its existence, the argument that the past has neither
meaning nor purpose, being merely a random accumulation of things and events, until subjectively ordered, by
selection and arrangement, in the historian's mind.

What is here in question is not the truth, once again,
of the historian's reconstruction, but his alleged inability
ever to know a truth about the past because all he knows
has had to pass through a cognitive process in his mind
which inevitably involves selection, interpretation and
perversion. An older, rather naïve, trust in the absolute-
ness of 'historical facts' has now been replaced by a

general supposition that the facts of history are only
historian's constructs, elevated among many other possible constructs to a special place of honour and importance. Mr Carr, in particular, who usefully reviews
opinions on this issue, has made a very pretty distinction
between facts as such and facts of history.[2] Though they
are relevant, it would be only cruel to consider the really
weak parts of his argument, especially his ignorance of
the many things that can be discovered in ancient or
medieval history. It is also unnecessary to do more than
draw attention to the fundamental error he commits
when he confuses the actuality of an event with the
accident of the evidence surviving for it. But there
is one passage in his discussion which summarizes his
view of what makes a fact of history, and since this view,
or something like its relativism, commands quite wide
implicit approval it is worth a little analysis.

Mr Carr holds that there is a 'process by which a mere
fact about the past is transformed into a fact of history'.[3]
He quotes the case of a man who was killed by a rioting
mob in 1850 and says that this event, once no fact of
history at all, is on the way to becoming one because it
has been mentioned in one book. It will achieve full
status when it gets into one or two more historical
accounts. The difference between facts about the past
and facts of history hangs upon 'the element of interpretation' which the historian adds to the former in order
to create the latter, though general acceptance of the
interpretation offered is required before the fact's new
status is secure.

This is really an extraordinary way of looking at
history; worse, it is an extraordinarily arrogant attitude
both to the past and to the place of the historian in

[2] *What is History?*, 1off. [3] *Ibid.* 12.

studying it. A man was kicked to death in 1850 : that is a fact, an event, which took place and which nothing now can either make or unmake. It is quite immaterial whether the fact is known to an historian or used by him in analysing a problem. If the event were unknowable—if no evidence of it had survived at all—it would certainly be neither fact about the past nor historical fact—it would have ceased to exist and that piece of potential history would never have materialized—but it would still, of course, have occurred, independent of any historian. However, the event can be known, and that is all that is required to make it a 'fact of history'. Interpretation, or general acceptance of a thesis, has nothing whatsoever to do with its independent existence. The point matters so much because Mr Carr, and others who like him think that history is what historians write, not what happened, come dangerously close to suggesting either that it does not much matter what one says because (interpretation being everything) there are always several reasonably convincing interpretations of any given set of events, or that history is altogether unknowable, being merely what happens to be said by a given historian at a given moment.

Mr Carr links his invention of special 'facts of history' with the by now conventional attack on Acton's programme for the old *Cambridge Modern History*. Certainly Acton was too sanguine when he supposed that 'ultimate history'—universally accepted and finally proven accounts of anything—would soon be possible. Though over a large range of historical problems this ambition will indeed never be achieved, the notion behind it was nevertheless true, for ultimate history is what actually happened, even though we shall never be able to rediscover it in full or with total assurance. Acton inferred from his positivist view of history that bias can be eliminated by strict attention to the facts and their meaning, so that in his cooperative history he hoped it would be hard to tell where a bishop left off and an agnostic took over. This demand has also received much ridicule, and Mr Carr duly laughs at it. Yet any reading of the old *C.M.H.* quickly shows that the ambition was fulfilled only too frequently, with a great increase in dullness and loss of life, but also a great increase in precision compared with what had been written before. That historians are prejudiced, blind and wilful, like any men, is true enough, and one may also agree that history written by men not afraid to allow themselves to appear in their discourse is both livelier history and probably better history. But that men cannot ever eliminate themselves from the search for truth is nonsense, and pernicious nonsense at that, because it once again favours the purely relativist concept of history, the opinion that it is all simply in the historian's mind and becomes whatever he likes to make of it.

Mr Carr's own work, and his reaction to criticism of it, prove conclusively that he does not in fact hold so whimsical a view of his profession. Yet his curious distinction between facts of the past and facts of history betrays two common failings: a lack of humility in the face of the past, and a confusion between the event and the meaning it acquires in the reconstruction attempted by the historian. The historian need not be too humble towards his fellows (though in an age of mass-reviewing and of jockeying for academic positions that is the humility he is likely to practise), but if he asserts a sovereignty over his facts he is a traitor to his calling. To say it once again : those things we discover, analyse, talk about, did actually once happen. They happened

to real people, people quite as alive as we are and quite
as entitled to respect for their humanity. They may not
have known exactly what was happening, and historical
interpretation and judgment are (as we shall see later)
thoroughly legitimate activities : the historian is entitled
to think about his discoveries and to find a significance
in them which may well have been invisible at the time.
But his doing so does not affect the independent reality
of the event; the historian is not entitled to suppose that
he alone, by choosing this fact and ignoring that, creates
history. On the contrary, no investigator is more firmly
bound by his material, less able to invent or construct
the object of his study. This problem of the relationship
between the genuine truth of the historical event and the
discovery of that truth from the evidence left behind
is the subject of this chapter.

2 Facts and Method

In denying the extreme relativism of which Mr Carr is
only a recent and by no means an extreme exponent, I
may well be taken to believe that facts about the past
are simple, discrete, knowable entities which need only
be collected in order that a structure called history may
emerge. However, this naïve theory concerning the facts
of history, possibly once widely current, has suffered
sufficient bludgeoning to require no discussion here. But
while no one will nowadays hold it in its naked simplicity,
the time has come to point out that it has a little more
validity than is usually supposed. In so far as it was
ever believed, it was after all a theory of their enterprise
developed by historians themselves, and some of those
historians at least knew what they were doing. Its
downfall has been largely the work of philosophers of

history, psychologists and social scientists who certainly penetrated the weaknesses of the unreflective historian and showed him how unsatisfactory his often unconscious presuppositions were, but who did not as a rule try to write history. When, like R. G. Collingwood, they did, it is not possible to analyse their history in the terms of their philosophy: it is just ordinary sound history.

The effect of these anti-positivist criticisms has been to make it at present virtually axiomatic that historians never work with the materials of the past raw: some cooking process is supposed to have invariably intervened before the historian becomes even conscious of his facts. If that were so—if there were no way of knowing the knowable in its true state—historical truth would indeed become an elusive, possibly a non-existent, thing; one could at best then hope to find an historian learned, wise and sensitive enough to have cooked his materials in such a way that their natural flavour appears in the dish. That would still make the knowledge of history a matter of pure faith which, if it is to deserve the name of an intellectual discipline and to fulfil its social function of promoting the search for intellectual truth, it ought not to be. The theory differs from that already discussed in being more total and less arrogant. Where Mr Carr's relativism makes the historian the creator of history, this more subtle version of a similar relativism supposes more inexorably that the necessary intellectual processes involved in the study of history themselves interpose a barrier between the historian and the true reality of the past. But though more subtle, this second view is no more correct. The doubts comprised in it resolve themselves into two—the necessary existence of an observer and the necessary selection of evidence.

Is the historian ruled by some version of Heisenberg's uncertainty principle? Is it true that he cannot make

contact with the historical fact without, by that very
action, distorting it? The answer to this must be that,
though in theory there is no need for this to happen, it
is in practice a difficulty one should be aware of. The
independent and real existence of historical events implies
that, in theory at least, they can be observed absolutely,
and for a very large number of somewhat basic facts this
holds good. No matter how many observers may concern
themselves with such questions as the day on which
Britain declared war on Germany in 1914, who the
eldest surviving child of Henry VIII was, or where
Napoleon confronted the allied armies on a given day
in 1813, they will all come up with the same answer.
There is, in short, a very large body of agreed historical
knowledge on which no dispute is possible, and though
this body of knowledge may not by itself provide a
very sophisticated interpretation of the past it is entirely
indispensable to any study of it. One sometimes encounters among those who think about history a predilection for arranging facts in hierarchies. Mere dates or
names—lists of kings and popes—are supposed to be
more lowly than tables of trade statistics or the arguments
used to defend a political philosophy. This is a game
not worth the playing, for the peasants of this hierarchical
society are as vital to it as its princes. Without the
simple details of accurate chronology, genealogy and
historical geography, history would have no existence.
And of these simple facts an enormous number are
precisely known.

However, while all the facts of history are theoretically
in this knowable category, not all are so known, and
as soon as more complex or private facts and events are
involved the problem of the observer does arise. Different
historians will differently regard the precise course of
the battle of Hastings or the precise meaning of Hobbes's

view of human psychology, not because they differently interpret agreed facts but because they see differences in the facts. The reason is plain enough : historical facts are knowable only by the evidence they leave behind, and in many cases that evidence is not clear-cut. To repeat, this is not a question of interpreting fact but of establishing it, and the differences resulting are likely to be differences in the degree and depth of knowledge, no more. Thus, for instance, anyone trying to establish, as Sir James Ramsay did, the totals of royal income and expenditure in the era of the Lancastrian kings, will resort to the receipt and issue rolls of the Exchequer. If, as Ramsay did, he takes them at their face value, he will total them up and suppose that he has the right answer. It takes a deeper knowledge of the material to understand that these totals are meaningless because the records contain quantities of repeated or fictitious entries. Thus the observer's understanding of his evidence will alter his historical knowledge, and increasing knowledge may also lead to a revision of supposedly established facts because facts do not occur in isolation. Most frequently, perhaps, the need for such revisions arises in connection with an ascription of originality. Wolsey, according to A. F. Pollard, created new machinery for the administration of the crown lands. However, since Pollard's day it has become clear that the machinery existed before Wolsey came to power and that he was responsible only for giving to existing arrangements the authority of an act of Parliament. This one change in the structure reverberates through any study of Wolsey's work which may end up by seeming quite differently inspired than it did when, in this one matter as well as in others, he appeared to be an administrative inventor. The historian's main 'uncertainty' lies in his ignorance; increasing knowledge genuinely produces increasing agreed certainty. This in itself proves that possibility of exact knowledge for which I am arguing and shows that differences of opinion may spring from differences in which the observer's personal intervention plays no part. Correct knowledge is not inherently impossible : it exists and constantly augments. In so far as variety of opinion reflects the move from ignorance to knowledge—and a great deal of historical debate amounts to just that—it firmly underlines the existence of real truth, not the prevalence of individual and arbitrary attitudes.

A more serious problem arises as soon as the historian proceeds from the establishment of a fact to the asking of complex questions. This is the notorious problem of the selection of evidence. The process of historical enquiry and reconstruction must work by means of selection. The mass of extant history cannot be rendered or even recorded without a deliberate choice by the historian, preserving this and discarding that. This is true of even the simplest forms of history. A medieval city chronicler will record outstanding events, such as deaths or floods or celebrations. Hundreds of men will have died that year within his knowledge, but he will commemorate a mere dozen. In so doing he applies a principle of selection : he answers the historically valid, if not very high-powered, question—who of importance died this year? Yet no two people may agree on the answer to this question. I may well wish to include my uncle and see no point in your second cousin, even if he did hold office as town scavenger. The very discovery of evidence depends on a selection of facts upon some principle of choice implicit in the question one asks, and there are therefore two variables involved at once : the question asked, and the arbitrarily determined choice. It is for this reason that some would deny the possibility of objective history at all and would claim that there is no history, only historians. In actual practice, however, the problem is not quite so devastating as it may appear in theory. We are often told that by the very act of asking a question the historian artificially limits his choice of material—that he finds in the evidence that for which he looks. Out of this limited range come further questions, themselves predetermined by the first question asked. The evidence is allegedly never in a position to play freely upon the enquiring mind, to suggest questions which are forced upon the historian, not forced by him upon the material. This sounds a convincing indictment, and there possibly are historians who proceed in this unsatisfactory way.[4] One can speak only from personal experience, and I must say that things do not happen quite like this.

The proper—and, as I believe, the common—way is different. The historian must certainly make one initial choice, of main area of study or line of approach. But after that (if he is worth considering at all) he becomes the servant of his evidence of which he will, or should, ask no specific questions until he has absorbed what it says. At least, his questions remain general, varied, flexible : he opens his mind to the evidence both passively (listening) and actively (asking). The mind will indeed soon react with questions, but these are the questions suggested by the evidence, and though different men may find different questions arising from the same evidence the differences are only to a very limited extent dictated by themselves. The part they themselves will play

---

[4] If the term historian were allowed to include the great system-makers, such as A. J. Toynbee, the indictment would obviously apply. But selection of evidence on that scale, to prove a fore-ordained case, removes the practitioner from the ranks of historians. Of course, his proper title may be more honorific : some people like prophets, especially of doom.

in these differences lies in different responses to the suggestions put out by the evidence. After this initial stage, the questions arising will be pursued specifically, and at this point the master-servant relationship is reversed. Now the historian specifically seeks evidence to answer his questions, and if his selection is ill-considered or too narrow he may introduce distortion. The interaction of the material and the questions asked of it is very intricate and sophisticated, but it is not true that in the proper pursuit of his study the historian's need to select destroys the independent existence of history. If that happens we are confronted by a bad historian writing bad history; but once again, the difficulty is not really inherent and can be overcome. There is no need to suppose that the bad or ill-trained historian is more typical than the good. This is not in the least to deny that the study of history depends on the asking of questions, or that the mass of historical facts acquires meaning only through being treated by the historian. It is to assert that the obvious dangers involved in this process can be provided for.

The two uncertainties of the historian—lack of knowledge, and the need to select—have their cure in the proper practice of scholarship and research. The methods of the trained professional historian are designed to protect him against his human difficulties, and they very often do achieve their purpose. Naturally, they do not render him immune to error, nor do they automatically eliminate bias and inadequacy, or the simple problems of time and space which hinder full or fully accurate knowledge. History is an unending search for truth, with the only certainty at each man's end that there will be more to be said and that, before long, others will say it. The historian's method does not give him the powers of a god, but it reduces the effects of human frailty and creates a formidable foundation of certainty beneath the errors and disputes which will never cease. Anyone doubting this might care to take any sizeable historical problem—the decline of the Roman Empire, or the rise of industrial England—and study its discussion in the serious literature of the last fifty years. He will encounter a great deal of disagreement, much proven error, and probably a fair amount of plain nonsense; but if he is at all alert he will be astonished by the way in which the body of agreed knowledge has augmented and by the manner in which variations of interpretation come to be first increased and then reduced by this advance. Historians are so fond of parading their disagreements—and the study does, indeed, progress as often as not by the reopening of seemingly settled questions—that the cumulative building up of assured knowledge of both fact and interpretation is easily overlooked. Yet it is indeed impressive, the product of systematic, controlled, imaginatively conducted research.

Two fairly common attitudes to historical research and method have done something to give the dog a bad name. On the one hand, there are the 'methodologists' who make a laborious and tedious science out of the historian's techniques, teaching it (as in some American graduate courses) almost as an independent discipline. On the other, we have the remaining inspired amateurs (this is an English failing) to whom the study of evidence presents no problems that cannot be solved by the common sense available to any reasonably intelligent man. Neither attitude has much to recommend it. The first turns a necessary tool into a nightmare mystery and is liable to produce egg-bound history or no history at all; the second promotes the exercise of prejudice and dilettantism, and is liable to produce pointless ephemera. There is further the difficulty that different fields of study, or different periods of history, seem to require methods of their own; but to think so represents the not uncommon confusion between method and technique. In fact, every historian needs to master some techniques, that is to say, he needs to know some technical tools which help him understand his material. Certainly the medievalist's palaeography, diplomatic, knowledge of Latin, understanding of lost administrative and legal processes are skills more obviously technical than those required of the historian of the nineteenth or twentieth centuries; they are, moreover, techniques requiring to be formally taught and capable of being so taught, which is not quite so true of the basic techniques used in investigating modern diplomatic history, though the problems, for instance, of modern economics require some highly technical learning. The best known training schools for historians, as the École des Chartes in Paris, the various national schools at Rome, or the London Institute of Historical Research, have consequently been dominated by medievalists who have reduced their techniques to a teachable science, and historians of more recent times have, understandably but mistakenly, reacted like Renaissance humanists confronted by the subtle and tedious irrelevancies of the schoolmen. Yet all these techniques—whether palaeography or statistics, medieval law or modern technology—are only particular aspects, conditioned by the surviving evidence, of the historical method which itself is the same for all historians.

Historical method is no more than a recognized and tested way of extracting from what the past has left the true facts and events of that past, and so far as possible their true meaning and interrelation, the whole governed by the first principle of historical understanding, namely that the past must be studied in its own right, for its own sake, and on its own terms. It is a way

of turning the evidence to account, and though there
is nothing mysterious about it, it is nevertheless rigorous
and not to be confused with the so-called common-
sense approach of the intelligent but untutored enthusiast.
Its fundamental principles are only two, and they may
be expressed as questions, thus : exactly what evidence is
there, and exactly what does it mean? Knowledge of all
the sources, and competent criticism of them—these
are the basic requirements of a reliable historiography.
This essay can attempt no specific description of historical
technique; that is a large subject of its own, covered in
some useful textbooks.[5] This demonstration that history
can be 'scientifically' studied must not be burdened with
systematic instructions to intending practitioners; it must
concentrate on analysing the working principles of the
method, in order to show that it does indeed overcome
the difficulties interposed between the historian's search
and the truth of history.

3 The Sources

To know all the evidence. Ideally the student should
never consider less than the total of the historical material
which may conceivably be relevant to his enquiry.
Though in many circumstances this will be an impossible
counsel of perfection, it remains the only proper ambition.
One of the demands embodied in it can, in any case,

---

[5] E.g., on a descending scale of size : J. G. Droysen, *Grundriss
der Historik* (first published, Leipzig, 1868, often reprinted);
C. V. Langlois and C. Seignobos, *Introduction to the Study of
History* (English translation, London, 1898); C. G. Crump, *History
and Historical Research* (London, 1928); M. Bloch, *The Historian's
Craft* (English translation, Manchester, 1954); G. Kitson Clark,
Guide for Research Students Working on Historical Subjects
(Cambridge, 1958).

always be observed : the historian must know the range and types of sources available to him, and he must have done his utmost to learn what has been written in and around the topic with which he is concerned. In other words, he must learn to compose a full bibliography of his subject and keep it up to date. Knowing what other historians have written is vital to a proper job, even though in the present context of explaining the connection between the historian and historical truth it has little importance. But knowing one's fellow-workers at first hand is not only a sensible precaution to prevent needless duplication or the repetition of exploded error; it also assists in covering the range of the sources, suggests questions, and opens lines of fruitful discussion. That it can in addition provide the relief of disputation, anger and abuse is a further but accidental gain to writer and reader alike.

However, what matters are the sources, that is to say the physical survivals from the events to be studied. And here the first demand of sound historical scholarship must be stressed : it must rest on a broad-fronted attack upon all the relevant material. Historical research does not consist, as beginners in particular often suppose, in the pursuit of some particular evidence which will answer a particular question; it consists of an exhaustive, and exhausting, review of everything that may conceivably be germane to a given investigation. Properly observed, this principle provides a manifest and efficient safeguard against the dangers of personal selection of evidence. Where there is a manageable amount of material, either because the question is very restricted (for instance the administration of a particular estate over a limited number of years) or because little enough has survived (as in most of the problems with which ancient history deals), the prescription can be followed to the letter. Not

that even here it is always easy. To take our examples :
studying one estate may involve studying a great many
others if the special case is to make sense, and the
ancient historian, spared an abundance of written evidence, may *inter alia* have to assimilate the work of
the archaeologists, possibly on the ground. Nor need we
forget the very different obstacles raised by the survival
of too little evidence. Still, anybody working in any
aspect of European history before, say, A.D. 1100 should
find it possible to see everything that bears on his
problem; and though materials rapidly increase in bulk
thereafter the task can still, as a rule, be discharged.
But it cannot be discharged once the historian enters
the nineteenth century. Indeed, from about 1450 on-
wards there are many large issues of historical investigation for which the rule that all the evidence be searched
becomes so full of difficulty that the daily sufferings of
the historian of recent times are, at least in some
measure, also familiar to his colleague working on the
earlier periods.

No doubt, the austere answer would be that when all
the evidence cannot be seen that piece of history cannot
be written. This might have the possible advantage
of freeing the world from a good deal of so-called contemporary history, but it is clearly not an acceptable
solution to say that the writing of history must wait for
neglect, accident, water, fire and rats to do their work of
rendering the labour possible by reducing the evidence
to piecemeal obscurity. Historians must be able to produce
sound and trustworthy history even in circumstances
which do not permit them to see everything; there
should be rules of scholarship applicable in such very
common cases to ensure that even a partial view of the
evidence avoids the uncertainties of personal selection.

It is one of the shortcomings of more recent history

that its practitioners, overwhelmed by the task of mere study, have done almost nothing so far to work out proper rules of this kind. The most obvious solution of the dilemma consists of relying on the preliminary work of others. This can mean taking other historians' writings on trust, an expedient so desperate as hardly to deserve the name; but it may occasionally be necessary if anything is to be done at all. In practice, of course, all historians gain information from the work of others: but some check on the methods of even the best established and reputed of scholars—some sample-testing of their use of evidence—is always advisable. More satisfactory are short-cuts to the material, where these exist. Thus for considerable stretches of English history the enquirer is provided with lists and calendars of documents which he could never in a life-time work through himself. Naturally, much depends on the manner in which the work is carried out, and the accumulated experience of scholars quite quickly establishes degrees of reliability or completeness in these predigested forms of the evidence. Again, however, some genuine rules apply: the criteria are by no means purely subjective.

Such ground-clearing operations are the better the more closely they adhere to the state of the material as they found it and the less they permit an editor to intrude. Thus the least dangerous of them are those that take a given body of records and without rearranging it present it in abstracts, as is done, for instance, in the *Calendar of Patent Rolls* or the *Calendar of State Papers Domestic*. Here the historian gets an accurate list of the material which can be used as an index to the originals, so that the overwhelming mass is reduced to manageability. Less satisfactory, and full of dangers to be remembered, are calendars which comprise materials chosen by the editor on some non-archival principle.

The famous *Calendar of Letters and Papers of Henry VIII*, for instance, collected in chronological order all the material for the reign which its compilers could find or accommodate. In other words, the calendar was intended not as a guide to the sources but as a replacement of them, a point underlined by the very full abstracts used; and indeed, a good deal of the history of the period has been written in reliance on these printed abstracts only. Since the work was done competently and, on the whole, with integrity (there are exceptions to both qualifications), the calendar proved not only usable and useful but also produced some valuable history, as in A. F. Pollard's massive work which rested entirely on its existence and dispensed with manuscripts altogether. But the manner of its composition was responsible for two traps characteristic of the method and quite independent of any bias in the compiler. Since it did not simply describe one existing archive, it gave a quite misleading impression of completeness; and since its makers rearranged their materials in a pattern chosen by themselves (in this case chronological) they destroyed the original arrangement and deprived the historian of much important knowledge. The provenance of documents—the way in which they came to be produced and deposited—is one of their most telling aspects, and this is something that, disastrously, cannot be established from that calendar.[6] These are serious deficiencies in the production of competent men; if in addition the compiler was inadequate—if he neither understood the way in which the material had been created, nor the importance of presenting it

---

[6] In this instance the originals do not assist because some devil prompted the Public Record Office to rebind their share of the material—the greater part of what was used—in the order of the calendar.

in a neutral manner, nor possibly even the real meaning of his records—he could, as W. A. Shaw did in his *Calendars of Treasury Books and Papers*, frustrate his enterprise and obscure the evidence he meant to render accessible. When materials become too many to be read in full, short-cuts not only may but must be used, but always with a full appreciation of their shortcomings and not forgetting that there is a difference between the whole and its parts. In practice this means two things. The historian should, so far as possible, use these productions as guides to the originals: he should with their help limit his area of search, not confine it to the printed aid. And he should treat them as he would treat all his evidence, by subjecting them to critical study: he must know how they came into being.

In any case, for large areas of history no such aids exist, and here the choice would seem to lie between the impossible (reading everything) and the undesirable (giving up work). At the perfectionist level the dilemma is inescapable, but at the perfectionist level action always ceases. We are seeking that possible which remembers and approaches the ideal. The problems of the historian faced with too much material are no more insoluble than those of the historian frustrated at every turn by the absence of evidence; neither can ever be made truly happy, but both can continue to strive.

The problem of abundance can, up to a point, be managed by controlled selection, that is to say by choosing on principles which have nothing to do with the real question asked or the ultimate product. To begin by selecting in answer to specific questions introduces the arbitrary, the personal and uncertain, and the first selection should therefore rest on different grounds determined by the material itself. It should arise from a total survey of the material and be systematic with reference to it, not to the historian's purpose. Thus an historian landed in this 'recent history' predicament should acquaint himself in general with the categories of evidence available in his field of study and then concentrate on the fundamental. If, for instance, he wishes to study the manner in which English government after about 1840 came to concern itself with public health, he will soon learn that important evidence is found in parliamentary papers, newspapers, memoirs, biographies, and the resources of municipal archives. But he is likely also to realize that the first basis of his research lies in the records of certain government departments, and he might therefore make a systematic study of these. Even so, severe limitations, for instance of the time covered, may become necessary. Once he has really worked through this class of documents, he can apply the method of selection by answer to specific questions to the rest of the ground with the degree of safety and objectivity produced by the exhaustive study of a body of 'master' records. Control of choice—reliability in the choice—depends on a high standard of professional learning which alone overcomes the perils of the amateur's pick-and-choose method; and it can be achieved only by a really thorough study of a body of material chosen not because it all contributes to the solving of a particular problem but because it has the organic unity arising from a particular archive-producing process.

None of this may sound very satisfactory, and there need be no doubt that the quality of the historian will always determine the quality of his research. Nevertheless, the procedure outlined reduces this personal element and offers valuable safeguards because it depends on two things: a real training in the craft practised, and a real concern with history (the past as

such) rather than with the formulation of theories about
it. No procedure can guarantee invariable soundness,
but some are more likely to produce it than others.
And when the obstacle to success lies in the imposed
necessity of severe selection, the safeguard lies in the
separation of selection from conclusion, in delimiting
the area of enquiry in the first place by criteria different
from those which determine the ultimate selection of
the material used to solve the problem posed.[7] The rule
has an inhibiting consequence which to some will seem
to render it stultifying: it strongly urges that, for the
present at least, work in insufficiently explored regions,
overwhelmingly equipped with material, should confine
itself to the study of very restricted topics. Certainly it
would seem sensible to make clearings in the forest before
laying out the garden. However, this goes counter to one
dubious and one legitimate desire. The dubious predilection is for the study of large tracts in outline because
this seems more important, more impressive, better
worth while, more likely to lead to fame than any
detailed investigation of limited bits of the past; in the
laity, in particular, though not only there, one meets a
strong enough inclination to call no one historian who
does not sweep and survey. Unfortunately people will not
believe that bird's-eye views are strictly for the birds.
Some who should know better sometimes give support
to such anti-scholarly views, as did Hugh Trevor-Roper

---

[7] It has always been plain to anyone engaged in training
historians that the trade is learned better in manageable areas.
This supports the view that it would be nice if historians of
recent times could bear to be trained as medievalists, acquiring the
competence to handle tools where the techniques are better
developed and the paths more clearly blazed. Thereafter they
could take their training to new pastures. But few men, thoroughly
soaked in the waters of one historical pond, feel inclined to swim
in another.

who in his inaugural lecture as Regius professor at Oxford, appeared to identify precise research with a narrow mind and a pettifogging dullness.[8] The more legitimate objection to avoiding the big book is that without attempts to see aspects of recent history as some sort of a whole, without some effort to fit together a story and a synthesis, the problems which need answers and whose solution could advance real understanding of the whole do not become apparent. This is perfectly true and justifies the writing of 'premature' general studies, provided it is remembered that their chief purpose should be to define the work of further investigation which waits to be done.

Nevertheless—and without overlooking the dangers of the narrow mind and the petty concern, about which more shall be said in the next chapter—in regions of superabundant material the real work of discovering historical truth must for quite a while concentrate upon particular studies of restricted problems. Ultimately, the man who has proved his trustworthiness and professional skill in this kind of labour not only has a right to be heard on what he cares to say on a larger topic or by way of creative synthesis : he will have deserved confidence. It is one of the principles of historical research, proved by experience but unprovable in any other way, that a genuine training and mastery obtained by systematic work on a restricted body of material will show themselves in producing instinctive rightness when bodies of material too enormous to be fully worked through are tackled in a more superficial or selective way. Those

[8] H. R. Trevor-Roper, *History Professional and Lay* (Oxford, 1957), esp. 12-13. Ph.D. theses—Mr Trevor-Roper's special target—may reflect a narrow and pettifogging mind; grand sweeps may demonstrate shallow and superficial glibness. Neither deficiency is ineluctably wedded to a particular method of working.

likely to be put off by the mountains rising before them can take comfort in the fact that one mountain is much like another; real acquaintance with a part of the range enables the explorer to tell much more about the rest without walking all over it than at first he would have supposed possible.

4 Evidence and Criticism

There is no perfect substitute for total acquaintance with the relevant material, even as there is no perfect way of overcoming severe losses of evidence. Thus there is no absolutely satisfactory way of studying history, which to some may put the subject out of court, but to others, unwilling to see an end to their metier, may seem its chief attraction. In any case, it is not enough to have seen everything; a mere accumulation of pebbles does not make a building, or even a highway. It is certainly even more important that everything seen should have been looked at in the proper light. If the independent reality of history is ever to be apprehended, the real meaning of the surviving material must be elicited from the surface appearance. Once the first stage of discovering the evidence has been got through, the methods of historical research boil down to the orderly and controlled assessment of it. Here again, common sense is not quite enough.

A good deal has been written on the criticism of sources, and some have tried to reduce it to scientific accuracy. There is good reason why historians should convince themselves and others that their way with sources enables them to establish, or at least come very near to establishing, the kind of truth which, I have argued, lies behind the history we find in books.

The laity—and this is liable to include professional academics in other disciplines—take a good deal of persuading that the historian can really tell what happened and why. Marc Bloch was driven to such exasperation by uninformed scepticism that the largest part of his unfinished *The Historian's Craft* turned into a practical description of the use of evidence quite as puzzling to the uninitiate as silence on the subject would have been. Not so long ago, the B.B.C. televised a play called 'Lloyd George knew my Father' which had much fun at the expense of historians sadly misled by the deliberate destruction, invention and perversion of evidence provided, for historical use, by the actors in some imaginary scandal. Neither author nor audience appeared to know that this is a commonplace problem to the historian for which he has time and again found solutions. The whole training of the historian is designed to help him dispose of deliberate manufactures. He may not be, and the professional historian too often is not, brought up to understand imaginatively and sympathetically, but he is certainly taught to be critical and sceptical, sometimes too much so. True, mistakes are frequent enough, and evidence can be misinterpreted. I often wonder what the illustrious dead make of all the things historians discover about them; if the Elysian fields ring with Homeric laughter, a continued interest in historical writing may well be the cause. But this is, at once, to display that excessive scepticism which lies at the heart of every sound historian and must be guarded against. That the truth can be extracted from the evidence by the application of proper principles of criticism should not be doubted, any more than that the enterprise will not always succeed.

Criticizing the evidence means two things : establishing its genuineness, and assessing its proper significance. The first is largely a technical problem. Forgeries have been successful in their time, but sooner or later they have got found out, from the Donation of Constantine to the Protocols of the Elders of Zion.[9] As a matter of fact, big forgeries of this kind are rare; producing them is much too laborious a business and only to be undertaken for some very cherished purpose. Altogether the deliberate manufacture of historical evidence is extremely uncommon; few people seem to think it worth their while to invent a documented history for themselves, or perhaps they find distortions and pretence in their otherwise genuine memoirs adequate. Why have we no false testaments of Napoleon or forged policy statements of Ghengis Khan? A distinction must be made : a spurious document is one written by someone other than the pretended author or at some time other than that pretended in it. False statements produced at the alleged time and by the alleged author are lies and require a different treatment.

It may in general be said that no one ever forged evidence to deceive historians; the intention, nearly always, is to deceive contemporaries, and most commonly a court of law. Financial statements and title deeds are the main preoccupation of the forger, and medieval charters the best example. According to V. H. Galbraith, 'forgery was the medieval monk's peccadillo', and his motive as a rule was to supply evidence of rights which he, or his house, regarded as perfectly well established but which unfortunately were not founded upon genuine

[9] Although it was not until Lorenzo Valla's famous attack in the early fifteenth century that the spurious Donation was generally exposed for the fraud it was, the facts were apparently well known to papal officers by the late tenth century (W. Ullmann, *A History of Political Thought: the Middle Ages*, Harmondsworth, 1965, 98n.).

deeds. The impulse to rectify the unfortunate deficiencies of the muniment room in the interests of true possession was generous and understandable, and if it has given medievalists many a happy hour distinguishing false from genuine it has had long-term beneficial effects. Nowadays, the techniques involved in this sorting are sufficiently established (ability to do this work does not prove possession of the higher intelligence), but it should be remembered that even thirteenth-century judges could apply such scientific tests as the search for discrepancies between alleged dates and the design of the seal, or for errors in royal styles mistakenly antedated by the forger. The historian needs only to establish the correct form and context of the genuine document in order to be able to detect the false, and this is rarely a problem once he leaves off using printed editions (though good editors will do the job for him) and looks at originals.

A good example of what should not happen was provided by R. B. Merriman in his edition of Thomas Cromwell's letters. In that collection, nos. 163 and 180 appear to be blackmailing notes from Cromwell to priors of monasteries allegedly saved from suppression by the minister; they have consequently loomed large in the usual denunciations of him.[10] There is nothing in the edition to raise doubts. But one glance at the originals shows that they were written and signed in a hand quite different from that of Cromwell or any of his clerks; that is to say, they were bits of private enterprise on someone's part who hoped to cash in on the minister's position and reputation, and since they were found among Cromwell's papers we may suppose that the trick was discovered and the minister informed. Read

[10] R. B. Merriman, *The Life and Letters of Thomas Cromwell* (Oxford, 1902). Even Dom David Knowles was taken in (*Religious Orders in England*, iii. 337).

rightly, these letters therefore tell in his favour, not against him. As forgeries they present no problem at all, and that would generally seem true of such documents. Admittedly, successful forgeries by definition escape detection, but it is neither apparent nor likely that this happens at all frequently. The evidence suggests that successful deception is very difficult, that it is practised for immediate and usually financial purposes and not in order to influence historical accounts, and that the techniques for establishing genuineness are sufficiently refined to cope with it. This is not to say that the historian should not be on the alert for forgery; there is probably no record-using historian living who has not at times wondered about the genuineness of some document before him. The rules are simple: if it can be proved genuine by internal and external evidence, use it; if such evidence shows it clearly to be forged, use it with that knowledge in mind (that is, it now means something different); if there is doubt about it, discard it. The true forger is not a serious enemy to the truth-seeking historian.

Genuine evidence, however, poses every sort of problem, and it is now necessary to agree with the well-established opinion that while the facts of history may exist in their own right they come to use and notice through the mind of the historian who selects, interprets and employs them. What guarantee can there be that one historian's opinion or interpretation is better than another's? What are the principles of scholarship upon which safe knowledge can stand?

There is a single question which the researcher must ask himself in assessing his evidence: how and why did this come into existence? From the historian's point of view, all evidence divides into two kinds: that produced specifically for his attention, and that produced for

some other purpose. What survives from the past was
put together either by someone who wished it to survive,
or by someone who had a purpose to serve in which the
prospect of the historian's interest played no part. The
first comprises in the main evidence of a literary and
often secondary kind: chronicles, memoirs, notes of
self-justification, letters intended for publication. To
the second category belong pretty well all documents and
records, most but not all letters and state papers, official
memoranda whether published or not, reports of com-
missions and of lawsuits—the products of policy, business,
and the ordinary events of life—but also the material
relics of past societies, such as buildings or artefacts.
These lists are not exhaustive; the categories are, and
the historian should always first become clear with
which of the two he is dealing. His task differs according
as he faces an attempt to influence and persuade his like
or an attempt to influence men long dead—or sometimes, to influence nobody. Material in the first category,
being designed to affect the writing of history, can be
judged with relative ease. The purpose which produced
it was rational and therefore identifiable; the interests
of the producer can usually be ascertained without
trouble. Whether actor or himself historian, he is likely
to have a case to make: his case once determined, one
can judge both his own production and the material
which he provides accordingly.

Things are rather more complicated with evidence
of the second kind—far and away the most important
and common. At first sight it might seem that a financial
account, the record of a court case, or a house cannot
bring trouble to the historian; as long as he can read or
recognize them, they will, since they were never meant
to deceive him, tell him the truth. But the point is, on
the one hand, that to see them is not necessarily to

understand them, and on the other that they may well have been intended to deceive someone else. A proper understanding of a given document involves separating the specific from common form and grasping the process by which it came into existence. It is here that professional learning comes into its own; only full ranging knowledge of what occurs in the papers of a given period or problem will prevent misapprehensions.

A few examples will show this best. In the Tudor Star Chamber, complainants invariably charged the opposing party with a violent or riotous act; but since this was requisite if the court was to have jurisdiction, it may be no more than a matter of form. On the other hand, it may record a real event; only the experienced student, weighing up the various documents in the case, will be able to arrive at a reasonably safe opinion whether the assault and disturbances had really taken place. Thomas Cromwell almost invariably signed himself as his correspondent's 'loving friend'; it would be extraordinarily rash to base any deductions as to relationship or personal feelings on that phrase, though something may quite possibly be inferred from its absence. That eminent historian, A. F. Pollard, encountering in fifteenth-century royal grants the phrase 'datum de mandatu parliamenti', concluded that Parliament had authorized the gift; but the words were common form and referred to the dating of the grant which, by a statute of 1444, was appointed to be the date of the delivery of the authorizing warrant into the king's Chancery. In the accounting system of the English Exchequer, 'arrears' represented unpaid items of revenue supposedly due to the king but often irrecoverable; they were carried over from year to year and swelled totals, if these were given at all; failure to recognize this would sadly pervert any calculation of the crown's revenue.

Every field of history yields examples of this kind, and only training—acquired knowledge—can save the historian from obvious howlers and bad misjudgments. On the other hand, such training saves him with ease. The understanding of all evidence depends on a proper apprenticeship in its use. The student would do well to suppose that he does not grasp the true meaning of his material until he has thoroughly acquainted himself with the organization that produced it, the purpose for which it was produced, and the difference between common form and the exceptional.

This phase of the job needs instruction and should receive it. The question of false intent needs intelligence and should receive that. Obviously a great deal of historical evidence now extant was at the time of its production intended to create a given effect. Diplomatic correspondence is a good case in point: communications to foreign governments can prove very revealing when placed side by side with instructions to one's own representative. Few would take expressly propagandist literature at its face value. But the matter can be less obvious, as in the letters of honourable men presenting some view of themselves to others, in the *ex parte* statements of litigants, or in legislation serving given interests but justified on grounds of general utility. Here the historian, trained to a critical scepticism, is on the whole unlikely to surrender to the bias of his sources; at least, the professional is not. Instead he faces, curiously enough, two difficulties working the other way. One is this very scepticism. It is all too easy to see deep deviousness in everything and to doubt the apparent meaning of every piece of evidence. However wise it may be to question motive at all times, and however capable of deliberate perversion all men may be, it remains a fact of experience that simplicity, straightforwardness and transparency also exist. The historian cannot therefore proceed on any single line of judgment; his mind must be forever open to the two possibilities that the evidence means what it says and that it does not mean what it says. To achieve as secure a judgment as possible, the historian here requires his most rare and almost most dangerous gift: an all-embracing sympathy which enables him, chameleon-like, to stand with each man in turn to look upon the situation. The gift is dangerous because it may in the end bring him to a total inability to judge or even to make up his mind; it need not do so but it often does.

In practice, too many historians here allow bias to intervene. They finish up by believing those they are inclined to and doubting the rest. Take, for example, the various conspiracies against the government of Elizabeth I. Among the traditional Protestant historians, it was taken for granted that Catholics, and Jesuits in particular, justified all means by reference to the end and thus were evidently always engaged in deep deviousness and double thinking. Of course they would plot. Therefore the word of the government's police was always to be accepted when it indicated that treasonable conspiracies had been uncovered. More recent Catholic historians have inverted the principle of judgment: it is now sometimes taken for granted that Elizabethan statesmen were 'Machiavellian', so that of course Sir Francis Walsingham's 'discoveries' were all in fact carefully engineered and the alleged conspiracies were organized, for its own purposes, by the Queen's government. In consequence both sides have displayed a remarkable respect for the other's supposed powers of deception and convoluted plotting, as well as more obviously a naïve trust in the honesty of their own champions. They make the enemy appear devilish clever, while their own side come close to being holy fools. A less committed attitude would treat them both as humans of the more familiar kind; it would quickly discover that neither side was invariably 'Machiavellian' or invariably incapable of deceit. Genuine plots, with all the purposes ascribed to them by the government, existed all right, but the Queen's agents fostered them further in order to discover and exploit all their ramifications. Both sides behaved as a reasoned reflection would expect them to behave: one, despairing of overthrowing a Protestant queen in any other way, sought to organize subversive violence, while the other, convinced that such dangers existed, magnified them and even encouraged the more inept plotters in order to squash them the more successfully. This case demonstrates well how all-round sympathy and understanding (a form of impartiality) can unravel the problems of the evidence; but though obvious it is also typical.

Excessive scepticism must therefore be guarded against as much as a childlike trust, especially as both reactions (two sides to the one coin of insufficient thought) are liable to be called forth by the historian's private, and sometimes unconscious, attitudes. A more serious and probably insurmountable difficulty lies in the fact that all assessment of evidence must be the work of the intellect, of the reasoning faculty. The historian cannot but work on the assumption that whatever happened is capable of a rational explanation and that evidence is the product of an act discoverable by reason. And yet we all know that this is not quite true, that we act, react and even reflect from motives which have little to do with reason and under influences—such as ill-health, a quarrel with people not involved in the transaction, whim and lack of thought—that can but rarely appear in the results of action, that is, in the evidence. Though at times these untouchables in history may become known to us, as a rule they do not; and we remain ignorant of them at the very times when, being most accidental, they would be most influential. Some historians, and above all biographers, therefore believe that a knowledge of psychology (especially of morbid psychology) is indispensable, with the result that one too often encounters some pretty awful bits of Freudian or post-Freudian commonplaces in the analysis. I do not discount the value of a real knowledge of the springs of human action, provided it is used with an almost excessive caution and with an overriding respect for what is actually there in the evidence. However, such methods are themselves fundamentally rational because they apply reason even if they deal with the non-rational; at best they reduce the area of uncertainty created by men's unwillingness always to act rationally, and at worst they greatly enlarge it. Yet on balance this matters little in most cases: over a series of actions or events, the irrational, so to speak, levels out, and a reasoned analysis can discover the truth. The difficulty does not, in fact, arise so much in the most obvious instances. It may be true that Napoleon's behaviour during the Waterloo campaign was influenced by deteriorating health and an increasing inability to judge reality, but in part these elements can be assessed and in part they vanish in the fact that the campaign was also based on perfectly rational, if erroneous, decisions.

The historian's predilection for the rational explanation causes most trouble when the evidence is thin or non-existent. Thus one would often like to know the forces or groups behind a piece of legislation, and it is natural to assume that interests benefited by a law were also instrumental in demanding it. Yet where the evidence exists, it often shows that men do not by any means always recognize their own interests: the facts of the past as well as experience in life occasionally demonstrate that the simple equation of interested party and instigator can break down. Rather than base his argument on the identification of reasonable conjecture with ascertained fact, the historian ought to be aware of the difficulty and admit ignorance. Not everything can be known, and the historian, since he deals with men, must concede the limits of rationality. However, reason also exists and men do act upon it, consciously, much of the time; again, as in the case of proper scepticism, the answer lies in maintaining a balance controlled by a rigorous study of the evidence, in considering the probable and possible as well as the obvious, and in avoiding oversimplification one way or another.

All this, no doubt, might help to confirm the belief that, no matter what has been said here, historical knowledge is strictly speaking not possible. It may be available in an ideal and theoretic fashion since that which is to be known is real; but it can never be available in practice because the interposition of the historian's personality and his inability to re-enact the event introduce too many variables. It must therefore be reasserted that these uncertainties by no means cover the ground: a great deal of history, simple and basic as well as more complex, is knowable and known beyond the doubt of anyone qualified to judge. In another very large sector, the proper techniques of the trained professional establish further secure knowledge, and constant work of research is all the time adding to that established knowledge. The rest of the field contains some things that may never be known and a great many more of which knowledge will never be so certain that disputes will cease. For the reasons already stated, this is particularly true of motive, of the reasons behind action, thought and speech. But even in this region we are not simply at the mercy of individual historians and their idiosyncrasies; here, too, rules apply, though these rules depend more extensively on the historian's abilities than do those which govern the detection of forgery or the understanding of individual pieces of evidence.

5 *Imagination*

The ultimate problem of historical evidence, as has often been recognized, is that none of it occurs in isolation. The interaction and interdependence of things are so manifest that some would doubt whether 'fact' is a term of meaning in history. Once again, this may be a perfectly justified tenet for the philosopher; the working historian, enquiring what the law was in a given dispute, how much a man was paid by way of salary, which of two particular despatches embodied the real policy of a government, which specific road was used by some army on a stated day (and all these are legitimate and important questions in the reconstruction of history) must answer the philosopher's doubt in the manner of Dr Johnson's reply to Berkeley. Yet at the same time, the working historian is even more aware than the philosopher that every question he asks involves him in a congeries of facts and specific details, that even if the final answer is a single figure or place or name, he has got there by means of a great many other figures and places and names as well as other parts of the evidence. However controlled his selection, it is still selection; however full his evidence, it is never complete; however impartial his assessment, it is still *his* assessment. Is there then no ultimate standard, independent of the historian, which applies as soon as the matter becomes more complicated?

The frank answer to this is that no absolute standard can, or perhaps should, exist, but once again it must be added that the trained and experienced mind comes so close to one that on the, as it were, Newtonian level of the universe historical truth is ascertainable. The discovery of truth requires not only the equipment already discussed—acquaintance with the available evidence and scholarly assessment of it—but also imaginative reconstruction and interpretation. Evidence is the surviving deposit of an historical event; in order to rediscover the event, the historian must read not only with the analytical eye of the investigator but also with the comprehensive eye of the story-teller. The truth is the product of this double process: understanding what the evidence really says, and understanding how it fits together. But if the product is really to be the truth, controls, once again, are necessary, and here there are two: the asking of right questions, and the application of informed standards of probability.

Right questions means fruitful questions, questions capable of producing answers. They must therefore be geared to what is contained in the matter to be enquired from: the evidence need not by any means supply answers to all the questions the historian would like to ask. Secondly, they must be penetrating; they must really exhaust the possibilities of the evidence. It is no use asking what the views of the peasantry were on the truth of religion as purveyed by the thirteenth-century Church if all we have to go by are statements from the governing sort. However much one may want to know, it is no use asking what people's living standards were at a given time in a given place, if there are absolutely no figures from which an answer could be constructed. Of course, questions that at some time seem unanswerable may become answerable in the hands of the historian who realizes that the evidence can after all be made to yield relevant replies; though this happens often enough and is one of the chief instruments of historical progress, it still leaves much of the past permanently dark. One might, for example, like to know figures for cloth production in England between 1300 and 1500. The only evidence in existence gives an account of such cloth exports as paid duty; beyond that lies an area of obscurity in which cloth smuggled without paying duty (probably a negligible amount) and cloth consumed in the country of production (certainly a large amount) remain forever unassessable. But right questions which seek in the evidence new answers based on real foundations will control the amount of genuine truth that can be added to knowledge. The purpose of a proper research training must therefore include the recognition of the right questions, which means a penetrative analytical approach to the material with a mind alert to every possibility as well as the ready discarding of any questions which turn out to be wrong either because they yield no answer or because they result in no fresh knowledge. The framing of new right questions is the most difficult task the historian can face, and it is therefore reassuring to know that it is a task not often imposed on him. New right questions are occasionally asked by some men of outstanding ability, or by someone who has receptively listened to the practitioners of some other discipline concerned with men; thereafter it takes as a rule more than a generation of historians to apply the new question to the many varieties of human history and societies.[11]

[11] In the last few years, 'demographic' questions—vital statistics

But even when the right questions have been asked and the resulting answers subjected to the rigid controls of technical scholarship, there remains one last aid in the search for truth. The answers must be probable; they must agree with what is known to be possible in human experience. This is not to suggest as vague a criterion as may at first sight appear. No one supposes that the historian is entitled to assume for true something that seems to him possible in human terms, and in practice historians tend to be better aware of the danger of arguing by analogy than are sociologists and anthropologists. The point is that the historian comes to this stage of his work at the end of a process which has taken him through the much more independent standards of judgment produced by a rigorous study of the evidence; it is only in the end, when he considers the answers so obtained, that he is entitled to apply the last test: could this have been? And if it clearly could not, he is entitled—indeed, obliged—to reconsider his evidence imaginatively, for he knows that it does not tell him all unless his imagination recreates the circumstances and interdependencies within which the evidence has arisen. The problem most commonly occurs when a sequence of events needs to be explained in which there are gaps. For instance, we know beyond doubt that in the course of the sixteenth century the English Privy Council changed its composition, working habits, and real place in government. We can say with certainty that its

---

of all kinds—have become immensely popular, and rightly so because they analyse some fundamental issues in history. But fashions always get out of hand, and historians working in periods where the evidence to answer such questions simply does not exist should accept their fate with an equanimity born of the recognition that there are other questions capable of being answered.

numbers were at some point reduced by the exclusion of
certain men, hitherto members but thereafter described
as councillors at large, not privy councillors. We do not
know when this happened; no order exists making the
change. Two ways of explaining the sequence are therefore possible. The historian may say that the change was
carried out on some particular occasion of which we are
ignorant. Or he may say that the reorganized body
developed gradually, or by stages, from the other. The
latter has usually been the alternative chosen, for historians faced with uncertainty, trained to adhere to the
known facts and unwilling to stick their necks out,
commonly prefer the supposedly safe vagueness of a
gradual transition. But apply the criterion of probability,
and what happens? Is it possible to envisage a situation
in which one part of a group of men is gradually turned
from privy councillors into councillors at large, a title
hitherto unknown? Could such a change happen without someone telling them that from now on they would
be known by this new title, with its reduced functions?
And if someone told them, must he not have done so
at some particular point in time? In short, is not the
second, and usual, explanation simply an evasion of the
answer, a vague attempt to cover up ignorance, rendered
unconvincing by an imaginative reconstruction of how
things must have happened? Known experience and a
little thought prove that they could not have happened
according to the formula usually used.

Imagination, controlled by learning and scholarship,
learning and scholarship rendered meaningful by imagination—those are the tools of enquiry possessed by the
historian. He knows that what he is studying is real;
he knows that he can never recover all of it and that
within his area of recovery the certain, the probable
and the speculative will coexist. In short, he knows

that the process of historical research and reconstruction will never end, but he is also conscious that this does not render his work unreal or illegitimate. But it is incumbent upon him to reduce the uncertainties to a minimum, whether they are introduced by the deficiencies of the evidence, by the intrusion of the enquiring mind, or—most inescapable of all—by the incomplete relationship between the process of history and the evidence it leaves behind. Therefore he must train himself to his trade and become a man of learning and hardheaded attention to his materials. He must subdue his imagination to the controls which scholarship provides. But he must not destroy it; on the contrary, he must nurture it carefully. The means by which he does this, and the purposes to which he puts it, indispensable enough in the task of research, are also the basis of success in his next task, the writing of history.

III

Writing

If historians thought that their labours involved nothing but research, they would lead easier lives. Honest and thorough research can be exhausting and tedious. But honest and thorough writing will certainly be those things, and the agony of forcing thought into order and pattern should not be despised. The writing of history is no easier than the writing of anything; compared with, say, the writing up of scientific research or even the working out of literary analysis or philosophic argument, it presents difficulties of a peculiarily drastic kind. It may even be thought that the common doubts about the possibility of historical knowledge, which have engaged our attention, sometimes represent unconscious but more justified doubts about the possibility of conveying that knowledge. The more the historian knows, the more he despairs of his ability to tell it, for the sheer complexity of the historical process stands inexorably in the way. At times it seems as though, contrary to reasonable expectations, real understanding and the impossibility of conveying it grew together in steady harmony. Every simple statement immediately seems too simple; every piece of description and explanation calls forth informed doubt in the writer; every clear expression of opinion seems to him to demand qualification, even denial, as he contemplates the variety of experience which he is trying to reduce to order on paper. It does not require the inevitable presence of critics in the wings to teach the honest historian the inadequacy of his own work, and any really learned man among them will be better able than even his dearest enemies to diminish and contradict what he has said.

Small wonder, then, that historians are commonly charged with hedging their bets, with qualifying all they say, with obscuring their subject in a welter of back-trackings and reservations. Life—and therefore history—are like that: they defy the sun-lit clarity and clear-cut road through the wilderness which good writing requires. Indeed, in a very real sense history cannot be correctly written. The processes to be analysed and described occur on a broad front, simultaneously and interconnectedly; writing is a linear development quite unlike the matter to be written about. The human mind is perfectly capable of holding a variety of interacting events, personalities and influences in a well-ordered amalgam; for physical and technical reasons, the pen is vastly less well able to convey this true comprehension to another mind. People talk of straightforward narrative history and seem to think that complexity is introduced by the writer. But what can be straightforward about a narrative which has to hold an infinity of threads in a single skein? What can be simple about a process which demands constant selection and rejection, a permanent multiplicity of choices, an inescapable awareness of the matter left out, the arguments on the other side, and the insufficiency of the activity engaged in? There is a theory that a ready ability to write comes only to the historian equipped with full knowledge. One could wish it were so, but in fact only ignorance makes the writing of history easy. In history, as elsewhere, fools rush in, and the angels may perhaps be forgiven if rather than tread in those treacherous paths they tread upon the fools instead.

Of course, there are ways of escaping the dilemma. One of the more popular is not to write at all, or at least to write very little. Some quite solid reputations have been built in this way. A man known, privately, to be learned can be thought impressively austere and formidable because he cannot bring himself to commit his learning to paper, except perhaps in the occasional small article or the more frequent attack upon others rash enough to write. Except for the reservation that no one who has not offered himself for slaughter has any right to savage others, there need be nothing disreputable in this. Writing is difficult, and to some it can, through no real fault of their own, become impossible. Nevertheless, unless the historian writes he will bury his learning and render his labours sterile : history, to exist, must be written as well as studied. A more respectable way out of the difficulty is to confine one's writing to the manageable, to choose topics which reduce the inherent problem of historical reconstruction to a minimum. Hence the learned monograph, tackling a carefully circumscribed issue usually by way of analysis and description rather than narrative. The account of an institution, the tracing of an idea, the dissection of an economic process, all lend themselves more easily to being presented on paper than does the progress of events in a complex setting of social, economic, political, intellectual or personal circumstances. But more easily does not equal easy; the fundamental difficulties of historical writing remain, as well as the conditions which that writing must fulfil.

Nevertheless, historical writing we must have, or— whether we must or not—shall have. What does it involve? What distinguishes good from bad, adequate from distressing, useful from useless? All historians differ, and the man who does not suppose that he can do at least as well as any other is rare. Any analysis, by a practising historian, of the purposes and qualities of historical writing is bound to be personal and bound to sound self-centred; any advice may well be regarded as arrogant. Yet on the point that there are differences of quality to be found among practitioners the opinions of both historians and non-historians are clear; and while I am aware of the impression which an attempt to define and prescribe must make I cannot feel justified in evading it. In any case, there is a second side to this. The higher the horse mounted by my principles, the happier the critic who can compare them with my practice.

1 Controls

The first question is whether the writing of history, however difficult, is in fact possible. I have tried to show that the historian can discover something fairly described as the truth; it remains to prove that his exposition of the past can claim more than an aesthetic quality and is more than an intellectual game. Is it true that though research may be governed by rules which severely limit the accidental, personal and selective in the search for truth, writing firmly reintroduces them? Up to a point, these doubts were answered in the demonstration that the trained historian works in ways which minimize his intrusion into the story. In the process of learning, he already constructs, and in so far as the first is governed by the integrity imposed by the evidence the second flows from that evidence rather than from the historian's mind. However, it is he who uses the evidence : he chooses, arranges, interprets. As a researcher, he has his defences; we must see whether as a writer he can escape the relativism of personality.

An anonymous reviewer, in the *Times Literary Supplement* of March 24th, 1966, replying to criticism of his article, maintained that historians can write history only by selecting from such facts of the past as past observers have thought it desirable to select for preservation. This double process of screening was inevitable and compelled attention to the historian, not the history he writes : 'this is how all historians work'. Quite possibly he is an historian himself, and it may be that the kind of history he writes is indeed produced in this way, though I find it hard to credit. The historian does not just 'select' facts; he employs them in controlled reconstruction of that past of whose reality he knows them to be evidence. Nor does the critic seem to be well acquainted with the manner in which evidence comes into existence, for that which is deliberately preserved by observers is a drop in the bucket compared with that which is left behind by action and without thought of selection for preservation purposes. Anyone who has ever had occasion to labour among the records of even one law court in even a short period of time will know how inadequate the notion of 'preservation by observers' really is. Nevertheless, limited and somewhat naïve though his view may be, it quite rightly stresses the historian's activity in processing what he uses. Whether he is trying to tell a story or to give an account of past problems, the historian must arrange his comprehension of the past in some intelligent and intelligible pattern of his own, and while this does not permit him to exclude evidence for improper reasons (that it will not fit in or makes his point of view untenable, for instance) he must still make distinctions among the details supplied by his evidence. Some is to be used and some to be discarded as irrelevant, and of the first some elements are treated as more meaningful or useful in explanation than the rest. This is certainly an activity which cannot be reduced to the rigour of the scientific experiment and which accounts in part for the continued and frequent disputes among historians.

But to suppose from this that the historian is in sole control is as false as was the argument, already dealt with, that the historian controls the very existence of his material, and it is false for the same reason. The proper rules of evidence and reason, the instructed processes of historical research, severely limit the historian not only in the interpretation of the remnants of the past but also in his choice of them on grounds of relevancy. The choice is made by seeking answers to questions. The historian wishes to say how the American colonies came to revolt against the mother country, or to account for the spread of cattle-farming across the Argentinian grass lands. He wishes to discern the influence of Aristotle on Christian thinkers in the middle ages or to elucidate the causes of Marlborough's victories over the French. All these are questions one may very properly ask of the evidence—and ask of evidence which can also, as a rule, yield answers to other equally legitimate questions. As the searchlight of the question moves about, it will bring into relief different aspects of one given mountain of evidence. To that extent the selecting mind exercises some control. But if the mind asks questions to which the evidence can supply no answer—if the searchlight points straight upward into the empty sky of pure conjecture—the mind remains a blank. The evidence controls the writer of history and his questions quite as much as he controls it, and its control comes first in time. That is to say, there can be no meaningful (answerable) questions without evidence, but the evidence will still be there, ready to answer questions, though no historian may have been bright enough to ask them. Of course, the whole process is one of interaction and interchange. Reading his material stimulates the historian into questions penetrating enough to give new meaning to the material and lead to further questions pressed upon the historian by the material. The writing and reconstruction of history amount to a dialogue between the historian and his materials. He supplies the intelligence and the organizing ability, but he can interpret and organize only within the limits set by his evidence. And those are the limits created by a true and independent past.

Unfortunately, one common opinion, as expressed in the anonymous letter mentioned before, puts all the weight upon the activating mind and overlooks the acti-vated and activating material. It would seem to derive either from lack of self-awareness in an historian, or from lack of historical experience in a commentator. The notion of the historian formulating his questions and then applying them to whatever he can find, in such a way that the answer is really determined by the question, is unreal.[1] The only questions that the historian can possibly ask before he has started seriously reading his sources are either so large and general ('I wonder what did happen when the American colonies revolted') as to leave the answer quite open, or so particular to the process of research ('I wonder what evidence there is concerning this or that') as to submit him at once to the

[1] I do not deny that some things that pass for historical writing may have been done in this way, but I am concerned with history, not with propaganda or fiction.

discipline of his training. When the work has started the questions will, of course, continue to come, but they will continually arise out of the work, not be sovereignly imposed upon it. One can speak only from experience; this is not only mine alone but of those also with whose work I have had first-hand acquaintance. The theories, for instance, concerning Tudor government which I have proposed and which have met with a good deal of argument and criticism, came to my mind not (as some of my critics would have it) because mine was a naturally authoritarian mind looking for virtue in rulers, but because the evidence called them forth. When I started on that evidence, my mind was as well stocked with received notions as a solid course of reading other people's writings could make it; it was the real evidence of the past which destroyed those notions and replaced them with fresh thinking. I may have misinterpreted the evidence, but I did not adjust it to my questions and preconceptions.

Thus, whatever may be argued in the abstract, and remembering that on top of his reconstruction the historian will express opinions which are a great deal more personal than the intellectual solution of problems, the selection and control employed by the historian are themselves guided and controlled to a very high degree by the materials to which he applies his treatment. It is, however, important to note that in one respect the materials are a great deal less concrete than has so far been alleged. That the evidence of the past can change shape and meaning under the historian's questing eye has already been admitted, and all that was said in the preceding chapter was designed to show how proper observance of the rules will limit the extravagances of such changes. What is less easily reduced to approximate certainty is the evidence that is not there. Especially for ages of which little has survived, the student depends not only on extant material but also on that which is missing but must have existed—the gaps in the text, the lost books known to have been written, the additional documents unquestionably produced by a known administrative process but no longer there. Historical writing involves both learning and imagination, both knowing what exists and understanding the complexity of the missing materials within which it exists. Evidence invariably grows in the process of interpretation beyond the mere surface appearance which it might continue to present to the layman. But it can grow only within the rigorous terms set by the rules of evidence and probability, not laws of nature but guiding lines rendered strict enough by training and insight to reduce the variable, once again, within pretty narrow limits.

The exercise of this kind of imagination can run all the way from the incontrovertible demonstration to the highly problematic guess. Certainly, the fact that historians conjecture and imagine beyond what they hold in the hand, and that they are right to do so, will keep argument and controversy alive; but argument and controversy are themselves controlled by the historian's principles of learning. (Sometimes they are controlled by malice and envy, but we are concerned with the real thing only.) The whole process of interpretation and analysis, already described, involves exercises of personal thought which reduce the scientific accuracy, even the agreed substance, of the historian's work. Those who would put all the emphasis on these variant factors would seem to me to place their bets on the wrong horse. A mind trained in the double technicalities of historical research—precise learning and imaginative understanding—will eliminate so much of the merely haphazard that the accuracy rather than the uncertainty of his work will strike the eye first. Some historical writing is simply and obviously right, some is a good deal more likely to be correct than not, some is pretty doubtful, some even good work may be wild. But the very practice of historical writing, and the occurrence of historical controversy, demonstrate that historians think themselves capable of reproducing the truth, whether they have worked out the grounds of this belief or not; and whether they are right or wrong—good historians or indifferent—they really have this conviction because they have been through the mill of learned investigation and reconstruction.

There is no final end to the study of history; the true and complete past can never be described because not enough of it survives and because what survives must be interpreted by human minds. All problems except the simplest, and sometimes so simple a point as a date or place, continue to be open to argument and doubt. Yet the freedom of exploration which this guarantees is firmly circumscribed by the reality of the past, independent of any observer, and by the tested practices which take the observer, with all his personal quirks and human imperfection, towards that reality. The historian's freedom is responsible, and in his case as in others responsibility confines rather than liberates. The study of historians can be very interesting, and a knowledge of the writer usually has something to contribute to an understanding of his work; but the study of history remains valid in itself, and a writer's contribution to knowledge stands apart from the mind he has brought to his labours.

2 Patterns and Bias

When it comes to transferring understanding to paper, the historian faces new difficulties which, in the eyes of some, may deprive him of any right to claim authority. The practical difficulties of writing—of rendering in convincing words what may be perfectly plain to the mind—are perhaps especially large in so complex an intellectual game as the writing of history. However, as has already been said, these can be overcome by art and skill, based on thought. Two more inherent obstacles resist removal. One is created by the need to make sense of things; the other by the fact that the mind which makes sense of things is not a photographic plate, blank until exposed to the light cast by the evidence.

Since historical reconstruction is a rational process, only justified and indeed possible if it involves the human reason, what we call history is the mess we call life reduced to some order, pattern and possibly purpose. This is not to say that the historian needs necessarily to see a 'larger' purpose at work in the fates of generations—God, or inevitability, or even personified History itself. I have already ruled out this prophet's ambition as irrelevant to a man's capacity as historian. The point is rather that whatever piece of the past the historian reconstructs must, to be present to the mind, achieve a shape of beginning and end, of cause and effect, of meaning and intent. If, as he ought to be, the historian is in addition an artist, a man wishing to create (in words) a thing of interest and beauty, the constructive element in the process can become overpowering; and if political motives supervene it becomes really dangerous. Take a very well known case, the seventeenth-

century revolutions in England. The almost universal
notion that that age was one in which everything in
society underwent revolutionary experiences seems supported by the evidence of events—civil war, a king killed,
revolutionary governments, dispossessions. The aesthetic
pattern also demands, and gets, the arrangement of
a true drama, a conflict between opposing truths and
rights fought out at a high level of passion and tragic
beauty. On top of that, the outcome produced the
politically weighty interpretation of a struggle for liberty
and rights, very properly won. Thus everything combined to create a very durable pattern for that century
which no historian has yet tried to recast, though many
have taken important parts away or quite refurbished
others. The axiom that this was a 'century of revolutions'
is no longer tested, it seems so obvious; and in turn it
produces new 'revolutions', as for instance ingenious if
implausible links between social rebellion and intellectual
reorientation.[2] Yet an attempt to free the mind from the
pressures of a conventional pattern, to absorb the results
of research, and to think about the whole age afresh,
suggests that the pattern is at the very least too simple,
possibly quite wrong, and that the appearance of
revolutionary changes has been allowed, for one reason
and another, to hide the curious absence of really
meaningful change in society, politics, or the distribution
of wealth.[3]

[2] The most extreme manifestation of this is Christopher Hill's
Intellectual Origins of the Puritan Revolution (Oxford, 1965)
which argues that Puritanism and an interest in the new natural
science are facets of the same state of mind. The evidence will not
support this view which really springs from the deep conviction with
which a certain historical pattern is believed in (cf. *Past and
Present*, no. 31, 104ff.; 32, 110ff.; *History and Theory*, v. 61ff.)

[3] Taking into account our new knowledge of the surrounding
centuries, and deliberately applying a possibly too sceptical

Pattern-making cannot be avoided; interpretation forms the historian's proper and necessary task. To make it possible to understand an historical event or phenomenon means to show how its pieces fitted together. Meaningful interconnection in the particular, illuminating generalization beyond the individual case—these are the marks that distinguish the inspired and inspiring historian from the hack. Anyone who reads a work of history, whether he be a professional colleague or not, should derive from it some mental elevation, the elevation which comes from seeing reason at work in ordering the seemingly chaotic. But in this activity, of course, the historian must intrude or even impose himself; what he is, will come out very strongly. Impersonal history is dead, whether the impersonality applies to the writer or to his matter. Certainly, this has its dangers. The most insidious consists of that preference for the rational which has already been discussed. Discovering the pattern in history, making sense of it, depends on the application of reason, and it is always possible that no such rational thinking took place in the actual fashioning of the event described. This is a danger that cannot be escaped. One can allow for the irrational, emotional, even insane elements in history, but even in allowing for them and fitting them into the explanation one uses reason and consequently may distort or misrepresent. However, this is not only inevitable but also insignificant : as I said earlier, reason does in measure work in men's lives, and on balance actions and motives are much more commonly explained correctly on the assumption that some form of thinking has taken place, rather than

---

attitude, I have argued a case for treating the century as markedly less than revolutionary, in *Annali della Fondazione Italiana per la Storia Amministrativa*, ii. 759ff.

that they welled up out of some unconscious which defies analysis.

Then there is the danger of overdoing the pattern-making. Since the historian is fully entitled to construct the probable from his well-founded knowledge, using both his understanding of the humanly possible and his living comprehension of the age studied (and distinguishing honestly between knowledge and conjecture), he will commonly be tempted to make sense everywhere. But a good many things in life, and therefore in history, are truly extraneous to other things, do not in fact belong with them or play upon them. Isolated events, lost thoughts, false starts, eremitical existences do occur. The insufficiency of the evidence bars too universal a view. Temperaments differ : some historians like to see 'profound significance' (usually of a morally based kind) at every turn; others take a delight in discovering only the commonplace or petty or accidental. The wise historian will be aware of his quirks and will temper both his imagination and his cunning with the caution born of active research. Above all, he will remember that sometimes he simply does not know or cannot explain or cannot fit in. He does not have to love the imperfections of his labours, but he had better resign himself to living with them.

There is a particular case of this general problem which deserves mention even though it has been discussed often enough before. Perhaps the historian's most difficult handicap—much worse than any mere prejudice—lies in his inevitable hindsight. It is true enough that only knowledge of what came after makes him into an historian at all, but (as is so often the case with the little gifts of the gods) that with which he can least dispense also most subtly corrupts him. Since we know how things worked out, we are twice tempted to suppose that they were bound to work out in this way, and to consider the known outcome to be in some way 'right'. The first frees the historian of his basic duty to explain : if what happened was inevitable no thought is required in understanding it. The second makes him into a tedious defender of accomplished fact and leads him to consider the past only in the light of the present, the notorious weakness already denounced. These are genuine errors to beware of. The historian must not simply assume rightness in a cause which triumphed and error in one that was defeated. He may still express views, even moral judgments, but not on the mere grounds of survival and disappearance, of victory and defeat. His right posture will be inside the event, though as a being exceptionally gifted, for purposes of explanation, with know-ledge of what came next. And in seeing things in shape and order, he must avoid like the plague any conviction that the course of events was necessary or determined. Whether all things seem to him to work inevitably to a new heaven or tread a path of doom, the ready determinist is a bore who uses criteria of explanation that he cannot derive from the materials or techniques of history. It is not these that enable him to make the equation 'what is was bound to be', but his faith which encourages him to ignore the multifarious and particular. That certain events were clearly and perhaps predictably the consequence of others is a conclusion at which the historian may at best arrive at the end of his studies and with an appreciation that their turn could not have been predicted at the time with any certainty. Hindsight is a help, an enlargement of the understanding, not a substitute for argument and empathy.

This business of shaping the pattern and the explana-tion is beset, it seems, by serious philosophical problems involving the very question whether historical explanation (deducing consequences from disparate facts) is possible at all. This need not concern us, except to note that what troubles the logician and the philosopher seems least to worry those even amongst them who have had some experience of what working among the relics of the past means. From the point of view of understanding the past, the many learned discussions concerning the sense in which historians explain it are quite remarkably barren and irrelevant. When it comes to explanation, it is a more serious matter that the historian may evade the task by using some of the short-hand terms with which convention has equipped him. A strange conviction dictates that a pattern becomes the more intellectually respectable the more it is expressed in abstract language. The concept of cause being under a cloud (because it used to be employed too crudely) historians have for a time been hunting for a substitute. Wherever one turns in history to-day, one runs head-on into factors. There no longer are any causes of the Reformation; instead there are factors that made it possible. This is to go from the tolerably dubious to the quite abominable. A cause is something real : people do things in order to produce results. A factor—outside mathematics and trading stations and Scottish estates— is a meaningless piece of tired jargon. Events are not the product of simple causes but of complex situations in which a variety of people and circumstances participates, but this does not mean that they are produced by factors. A word to be forgotten.[4]

---

[4] Sometimes 'factor' is used—because it sounds more scientific?— even in place of poor old 'fact': 'A major factor retarding the deterioration of Anglo-American relations was the dispute that called James Monroe to Madrid' (Bradford Perkins, *The First Rapprochement*, Princeton, 1955, 177). For some wise words on this nonsense see J. H. Hexter, *Reappraisals in History*, 195ff.

This fault is probably only verbal. More serious trouble arises for the historian for whom events take place in a setting of the purely impersonal. Ever since economics started impinging on historians we have heard of forces; since statistics were added to their equipment, we have met trends. That both these concepts are ugly and often dull may be no good reason for avoiding them; but what of their meaning? Do the 'forces' so readily resorted to by some historians have any reality? The pressures of the market, the influence of inflation, even the mental climate of an age, are not without independent and significant existence. Trends, too, do exist: that is to say, it is possible to extract from a sequence of facts a general movement or a general condition which suggests direction, upwards, downwards or see-saw It would be quite improper to condemn every use of these or similar words, every reference to abstractions from human activity. The trouble arises when they are used improperly, when forces are made to act without agents, and trends—statistical definitions of a movement in events—are themselves made to act. Abstractions describe; they must not be personified into activators. That there was a trend to this or that is something the historian may say, though as a rule he will do well to find a better choice of words. That a trend ever decided or did anything is, given the real meaning of the word, palpable nonsense, and people cannot therefore ever be said to have done, said or suffered anything because of a trend.

All this accumulation of factors, forces and trends—others will be able to add their own dislikes to the list—reflects a form of mental indolence. In briefly summing things up to himself, the historian may employ such terms because it saves time to do so, because it may define main lines of the pattern for him, and because he is (or should be) carefully aware of the inadequacies of such language. In explaining things to others, he has little right to use them because then they only represent one of two things : his inability to think clearly, or his ignorance. To use these evasions by way of explanation is to explain nothing and to reveal one's failure to understand. It is a more subtle form of that sort of mysticism which uses unfilled concepts like national characteristics or the spirit of the age as though they held a meaning precise enough to explain phenomena. There is a perfectly simple cure for these besetting sins of vaporous abstraction. History does not exist without people, and whatever is described happens through and to people. Therefore let us talk about people, by all means imposing categories on them and abstracting generalizations from them, but not about large miasmic clouds like forces or busy little gnomes like trends.

There remains the question of bias in the historian, an ancient topic of debate and a somewhat tired one. To me, the understandable reaction against claims to 'ultimate history', free of all personal preconceptions, has gone too far. No one now supposes that what the historian is in himself does not affect his writing, but (as we have seen) most people who express themselves on this point seem a little too ready to see the historian and forget the history. This attitude ranges from the sort of view held by the anonymous reviewer already cited to the growing habit, especially strong in American universities, of studying problems through the contrasting opinions of selected writers rather than from the evidence. Historiography has its uses, as an auxiliary science as well as a parlour game, but when it takes the place of history it arrogates to itself a position it is unfitted to fill.[5] That

[5] See below, p. 192.

every generation rewrites history from its own point of view, and that every historian worth reading has a mind filled with attitudes of his own, are common-places, largely true, which need not be laboured any further. Yet in all this preoccupation with the historian, people do seem to fail to notice how the supposed products of bias and preoccupation come to be the common property of all, including those most deter-mined to reveal the bias and preconceptions that went to the making of them.

When Sir Lewis Namier, a man rather good at making enemies, exploded his bomb in 1929, he claimed to be doing nothing but look at the evidence.[6] He showed that the conventional categories in which eighteenth-century political history had been discussed did not rest upon the facts of the past. Because he could be said to be a tory delighting in combating whig views, resistance could evade the issue, and it took some fifteen years for his 'revolution' to penetrate into the general accounts. This triumph of conservatism incidentally shows that not every generation always re-writes history in terms suitable to itself. Then, after 1945, Namier's views became embalmed in a general adulation from which few dissented, until now, after his death, the protests and revisions come thick and fast. As is usual, the protests seem often to assail irrelevancies or views he did not hold, but what matters is that even those who most object to the Namierite explanation of English politics talk entirely in terms first established by

[6] *The Structure of Politics at the Accession of George III*, a collection of essays demonstrating the real purposes and relation-ships in eighteenth-century politics and attacking the notion of organized party which had hitherto underlain all discussions of that time. Namier did not make acceptance easier by failing to provide an alternative coherent structure for the one which he removed.

him.[7] No one now would dream of interpreting the
England of the unreformed Parliament in the way
universal before Namier wrote. Even those who still
want to use the terms whig and tory, or who would
give a higher place than Namier did to the political ideas
and convictions held by eighteenth-century politicians,
have completely absorbed his essential demonstration
of the parliamentary scene. It may be that Namier's own
personality—his own attitude to politics or his anti-
liberal bias—helped him to break out of a conventional
framework, but what made his revision so solid that it
has now become, even to opponents, the new conventional framework was his firm foundation of scholarship. He was studying history—trying to find out—not
promoting a personal point of view, or merely (as
some do) wishing to create a stir by being different.

Namier's case shows the real place of bias, of the
historian's personality, in the business of writing history.
It enables him to look afresh at the facts of the past. If
it goes further, it commonly defeats its purpose. This is
as true of unconscious bias as of conscious. The historian
who deliberately sets out to prove a case agreeable to
his own prejudices is no real problem as an historian,
though like any propagandist he can be dangerous on
a wider stage. Notoriously, the nationalist convictions
of most nineteenth-century German historians helped
to indoctrinate generations with misleading and sometimes pernicious beliefs about the past, and unlike most
notorious things this one contains some truth. The

[7] This is especially true of the more serious writers, e.g. H.
Butterfield in *George III and the Historians* (London, 1957). For a
fine example of silly criticism, allegedly employing the tools of
political science but in fact displaying only obscurantism and
self-advertisement, see Harvey C. Mansfield, 'Sir Lewis Namier
Re-Considered', *Journal of British Studies*, ii. 28ff.

falsely glamorous view of the Stuart monarchy, and the obscurely apologetic air concerning the Reformation, which one still finds among a good many people who read history of a sort, owe less to the true revisions of an older bias made by historians than to the falsehoods purveyed by Cardinal Gasquet and Hilaire Belloc. The real study and understanding of history have been virtually unaffected by such things. As long as discussion continues, and especially as long as the issues discussed are alive, the obvious or hidden preferences of the historian will intervene but are quickly discovered and allowed for; what remains are the positive products of scholarship, originally often directed in its search by some bias, products which endure only if thanks to scholarship they have risen above the mere expression of prejudice. This is not to deny that prejudiced views are sometimes difficult to combat (the influence of so-called left wing attitudes in English economic history is a fair example); misleading interpretations can have a long life. Constant vigilance is needed, both towards others and, what is much more difficult, towards oneself. But the corrective exists, in the proper training of the professional historian.

Historians' personalities and private views are a fact of life, like the weather; and like the weather they are not really worth worrying about as much as in practice they are worried over. They cannot be eliminated, nor should they be. The historian who thinks that he has removed himself from his work is almost certainly mistaken; what in fact he is likely to have proved is the possession of a colourless personality which renders his work not sovereignly impartial but merely dull. But though dullness is no virtue, neither is self-conscious flamboyance. The historian need not try either to eliminate or to intrude himself; let him stick to the writing of history and forget the importance of his psyche. It will be there all right and will no doubt be served by his labours, but really it matters less to the result than critics lament or friends acclaim, and it matters a great deal less than does his intellect.

3 *Style*

History, then, can be written; historians pursue a humanly possible task. Indeed, for purposes of discussion, history does not exist until it has been reconstructed and written down by the historian. It lives by the word, and the historian's first concern must be to respect and regard words. Styles and methods of expression differ and there is room for many of them in the capacious mansions of historical writing. However, there is room only for those that fulfil the conditions set by the fact that no one writes except to be read. It is in this sense that history is an art. No matter how scientific the process of research may be, that of presentation requires skills of exposition, explanation and persuasion which all turn upon the right use of words. I am far from supposing that a single manner is appropriate to all forms of historical writing, or even to any single form of it, and I know of no worse prescription than that which advises the beginner to form his style upon some eminent model. What the writer is, both as a man and as an historian, will appear in the style of his writing. This is not to say that one cannot learn from others, both from their excellences and their mistakes, but one cannot copy the style of a Macaulay, a Gibbon, or a Maitland except to write pastiche, which in history is not worth the effort. However, no matter what writing comes naturally to the historian, it must be readable and may be judged by that standard.

Readability is not the same thing as meretriciousness. Some widely read historians, criticized by the less successful, come to believe that they are blamed for lack of scholarship when the hidden charge is that they attract readers. At one time there was something in this complaint, and in some parts of the world there still is. In the earlier part of this century, a good many scholars seem to have thought that the more readable their colleagues were the less they merited consideration. Difficult things, 'real problems', could not be dealt with in lucid or attractive language but required obscure technical terms and a style which reflected the agonizing processes of thought that had gone into their analysis. Any historian who expressed himself well and showed some respect for the remarkable possibilities of the English language was automatically assumed to have achieved ease of expression by sliding over the difficulties of the matter. Perhaps he was not even aware of them; perhaps he had deliberately sacrificed depth and accuracy to his ambition to become a publisher's dream; it was hard to say which failing deserved the more severe censure. The work of so popular an historian as G. M. Trevelyan gave some substance to this embittered attitude: he, and some others, too often achieved literary distinction by an easy saunter around any problem of intellectual gravity and by superficial methods of explanation which left the serious and involved student gasping. Only Maitland was free from this censure, and what made him exceptional was his manifest willingness to tackle the most recondite and technical problems without any concession to the reader's supposed inability to grasp them, yet in language so splendidly lucid that he invariably did grasp them.

In those years, it seems to have been the fashion to think that only a particularly austere and even repulsive style of writing could entitle the historian to the name of scholar, and some men appeared to reserve a special vocabulary and syntax for the occasions on which they wished to claim that distinction. That eminent medievalist, James Tait, who taught at the University of Manchester for nearly forty years, is reported by those who heard him to have been a singularly lucid and brilliant lecturer. No trace of this comes through in his writing which is obscure and painful; his one major work, a study of *The Medieval English Borough*, is quite as tiresome to read as (to judge from the length of time it took to appear) it was to produce. That very competent scholar, A. F. Pollard, wrote biographies which all could read and many read with pleasure; but when he turned his hand to a learned article, fluency turned to a stammer and proper precision to pernickety obscurity. Scholars took pride in writing only for other scholars. This should not have absolved them from the demands of art, but since those others could not escape reading what was offered, the manner of presentation was at best thought a point of little importance. The attitude extended, however, beyond the needs of scholars. A. W. Ward, who dominated the *Cambridge Modern History* after Acton's death and edited the *Cambridge History of British Foreign Policy* in the 1920's, was one of the most influential men in the profession. Allegedly an interesting talker, he wrote without colour and drained the colour from others, too. On one occasion he explained the difficulties he had with a contributor's

chapter by saying that 'it's a bit lively'.[8] There, from
the mouth of one who at Manchester had taught not
only history but also English language and literature,
spoke the voice of the profession. The learned dullness of
those histories stands as a monument to a mistaken
puritanism. This gild attitude to scholarship promoted
real delight in involution, in being comprehensible only
to what were sometimes called one's peers. The stumbling
solemnity that often hung about that attitude reflected a
measure of uncertainty about the activity engaged in :
mumbo-jumbo, private language, the barriers of techni-
cality are not so much intended to keep the mob out
as to pretend that there is something of value inside
the zareba. Intellectual enterprise which prefers to hide
behind obscurity and mere clumsiness cannot be very
sure of itself or its own ultimate worth.[9] Even justified
contempt for the intellectual softness of many popular
writers does not excuse this attitude. The historian must
not always write just for a small circle of his fellows;
the way to combat bad popular history is to write good
popular history, not to retreat from the world.

In England this rather tiresome pose has been in
retreat for the past twenty years. It is not dead, any
more than helpless bad writing is dead, nor has the
determination to write so as to be read always led to
happy results. One or two historians have publicly
replied to valid scholarly criticism of their works by citing
their sales charts. Others, less innocent, may be less
candid but are too often willing to adjust to the market.
Yet neither the desire to shock nor the desire to pander to

[8] Cf. S. C. Roberts, *Adventures with Authors* (Cambridge,
1966), 112-113.

[9] In this respect sociologists have now taken over from the
historians. They are welcome to that part of the inheritance, at any
rate.

modest understanding are very good fairies to attend at the production of historical research. However, the general level of historical writing has clearly risen. Not only has the expansion of higher education called forth an increasing number of well-presented historical accounts; not only is there something of a boom in history for the intelligent layman, a fair amount of it being 'real' history; but it is, at least, my impression that those expressions of scholarship which can never have a wide audience are to-day less hedged about by poor, obscure or lifeless writing than once they were. In such respects, America has still to follow suit. There one still encounters the old double standard; men who express themselves very prettily in conversation or, occasionally, on the platform, pull out some special dictionary of polysyllabic jargon when they come to write, in the conviction that the fraternity will not otherwise recognize them as scholars. The rank growth and the high repute of the social sciences seem to overwhelm too many American historians with a desire to sound learned. Of course, generalizations of this order carry with them any number of exceptions, but on the whole it looks as though English historians are now better able to fulfil the claims of history as an art, without losing their scholarly rigour and the right to scholarly regard, than are those of America, or for that matter those of Germany. At least, one no longer hears a man decried just because he writes well.

But signs of improvement do not equal the millennium, nor is deliberate art used to disguise an inferior product the same thing as good writing. Unless the substance is good, the appearance, painted even an inch thick, will not please. However, we cannot spare time here for skilful writing pretending to be good history. We are concerned only with history sufficiently good to have the compliment of good writing paid to it. And it has to be admitted that much of what appears as the result of genuine labours and real thought is still hidden in dull and bad writing. What makes writing dull and bad? Rising high above all other faults is lack of life which results from an unwillingness to think and a readiness to repeat other people's thoughts parrot-fashion. There is not much to be done about this by anyone except the writer himself: he alone can distil the necessary elixir from his own brain and bones. But there are two main technical pitfalls on which it is worth offering advice: the use of jargon in place of real words, and incompetence in the use of real words themselves.

One must distinguish between jargon and technical terms. No one can, and no one should, discuss medieval law without such words as dower or novel disseisin, the Reformation without referring to justification by faith alone or the spiritual presence in the eucharist, the growth of industrial economies without admitting profit margins and interest rates to his discourse. History necessarily comprehends many studies and disciplines that are highly technical in themselves and must therefore have a technical vocabulary. But history is not itself a technical study in this sense, which is why those bewitched by the spurious precision and the law-discovering unrealities of the so-called social sciences dislike and despise it. It should explain itself in terms accessible to all men, not to experts only, and if it is obliged to use technical terms, because in the circumstances they are the right ones, it must both understand and explain them. What is not permitted to the historian is the use of technical terms borrowed for no specific reason, used to suggest a non-existent profundity or a spurious scientific framework, and manifestly not expanded in terms of plain language. This rule unhappily eliminates those usefully vague metaphors taken from biology—the institutions that 'evolve', the bodies of opinion that 'mature'.[10] It particularly inhibits recent developments in social history where phrases like class struggle, social mobility, demographic curve and the like are bandied about without being given the real content that historical method and understanding require.[11] It even invalidates such seemingly harmless evasions of the historian's task to explain as the use of words like 'inevitable' or 'predetermined', for words like these, at home in logic and theology, have no accurate meaning in a study which at best can say that y was the result of x, never that only y could have been the result of x.

The rule which distinguishes technical terms from jargon is simple enough in theory though a good deal more difficult to apply in practice. Technical terms become jargon when they are used out of the context in which they are technical, or when they are used as substitutes for an explanation. The test by which jargon can most commonly be detected is this: take a piece of writing full of seemingly weighty phrases and try to transcribe it into English. If it then appears as a genuine argument, all is well. If the transcript produces tautology or nonsense, you have been exposed to jargon.

Strictures of this sort are unacceptable unless they are backed by examples, but here to give examples is manifestly to add to one's list of enemies. Still, the risk

[10] A. F. Pollard called one of his books *The Evolution of Parliament*; from one species into another, by a process of natural selection preserving or losing genetically determined characteristics? And what else, if not that? Biological metaphors are the devil: what are we to think of the writer who allowed 'a small misstatement [to] breed a big misconception' (G. R. Elton in *Eng. Hist. Rev.* lxvi, 1951, 508, n.1)?

[11] I.e., even the rules of good writing dispose of Marxist history, a marvellous repository of jargon.

must be run. I will take a book which, I believe, contains some valuable insights and analysis, but which I also believe is marred by the faith in jargon that destroys style : C. H. and K. George's *The Protestant Mind of the English Reformation* (Princeton, 1961). On p. 4 we read :

> Theology constituted the fundamental intellectuality of the seventeenth-century *Weltanschauung*.

Weltanschauung means an intellectual view of life; therefore this sentence says that in the seventeenth century theology formed the intellectual foundation of the fundamental intellectual attitudes of the time. Tautology. On p. 248 :

> There is, in fact, a curious vein of social atavism in the clerical commentary on the mores of the aristocracy.

This (to judge from the context) is intended to say that the authors are surprised to find preachers nostalgically praising chivalric virtues, later called, naturally enough in this pompous language, 'prowess at arms and *gloire*'. The surprise, in fact, rests on preconceived notions which the evidence shows to be false; the jargon could serve to disguise the poverty of the thought and the lack of historical discernment. On p. 396 they say :

> In this disproportion between institution and belief— the somewhat schizoid quality of the English Church —there undoubtedly exists a tension-producing capacity which is fully exemplified in the presbyterian agitation.

Translated, this reads (if I have got it right) : 'because the Church of England claimed general authority as an institution but permitted variety of belief, an extreme attack on it as an institution, namely presbyterianism, could be promoted from within it'. Here we have both tautology and the trite, made to appear portentously significant by misapplied technical terms, schizoid and tension-producing. The authors are not ascribing the phenomenon they discuss to the vagaries of group or individual psychology but to aspects of organization. Those terms, though deplorably ugly, have their place in psychology; there is no occasion for them here.

These examples, intentionally taken from a work of real merit, may suffice to explain the issue. *Weltanschauung*, atavism, schizoid are all quite proper and possibly useful terms in their technical meaning. This does not entitle the historian to use them out of their technical context or by way of avoiding thought. If he does, he will produce obscurity masquerading as profundity, emptiness pretending to be significance.

But technical terms are not the only ones to get misused; far too often one finds careful and competent historians paying too little heed to the manner in which they employ the ordinary language. The conventional rules of style are no less weighty for being familiar : say exactly what you mean, no more and no less; prefer the concrete to the abstract, the active to the passive mood, directness to circumlocution; attend to the rules of grammar and syntax. Everybody will have his pet hates; mine include pendant participles ('being given to dubious behaviour, the divine wrath struck down Sodom and Gomorrha . . .') and the confusion of 'who' and 'whom'. Again, the rule ought to be simple : make sure that you have said exactly what you meant to say, observing the accepted usages and canons of the English language. However, everybody who has to read a lot of history knows how readily even respectable writers fall

into clumsiness and muddle, sometimes to the point
of real obscurity. The cause may be only tiredness or
an inadequate training, or it may be an incurably bad
ear, but the results are distressing. A recent article
quoted, apparently with approval, a short passage from
a doctoral dissertation which will illustrate the point.
Dissertations do not need to be masterpieces of writing;
indeed, dullness is probably unavoidable in a work
which is required to spell out everything and comes
from a beginner in the craft. On the other hand, the
beginner should also from the first be trained to write
reasonably well and clearly; no more than any other
kind of historian should he be allowed to commit
solecisms or employ bad grammar to produce ambiguity.
  The passage in question reads :

> Collective references or designations of political align-
> ments were usually made with regard to the respective
> sides of the House, to administration and opposition,
> and, less frequently, to the majority and the minority.
> Little use was made of the terms whig and tory. On
> infrequent occasions a member might assert he was
> expounding whig doctrines : never did any claim to
> be a tory, but the term was sometimes used as a
> method of reproach.

This perpetrates more minor howlers than one would
suppose possible in a few lines. It avoids the clarity
of directness with determined success, is grammatically
obscure, and misuses words. The first sentence has to be
read more than once to discover its meaning, which
turns out to be that certain expressions were commonly
used to describe the two sides of the House of Commons.
'On infrequent occasions' is a flabby circumlocution, and
the omission of 'that' after 'assert' throws out the rhythm

of the sentence. 'Never did any claim' is an unsuccessful attempt at brightening the writing which adds ambiguity : one stumbles over 'any' for an appreciable moment before one is sure that the word belongs to 'member' and not to 'claim'. Finally, a term cannot become a method. The passage could be rewritten as follows :

> When men wished to give collective names or descriptions of political alignment to the two sides of the House, they usually spoke of administration and opposition, more rarely of the majority and the minority. They almost never used the words whig and tory. Very occasionally a member might assert that he was expounding whig doctrines; none ever claimed to be a tory, though the term was sometimes used by way of reproach.

This is a plain statement of fact, interesting in the context of the question posed; it needs no 'fine' writing, but that does not mean that the writing can be forgiven for being slipshod, tired and unrevised.

How, then, can one avoid these far from uncommon faults? Not all history can be written vividly and with the drive of verbal passion; the subject matter may not permit it. Nevertheless, all historical writing should approach the ideal in two respects : no one should ever write a sentence which he has not personally thought through, and one should always remember that what is said did actually happen. The historian who says things not just because others have said them before him but because he has re-thought each point or issue afresh will not, in most cases, come up with a new answer; but it will be *his* answer, assimilated in *his* mind, expressed in *his* words, and it will thereby renew its freshness. And the historian who remembers that his material has a true life, a past life of its own, that the things he discusses happened to and through live people, should have gone a long way towards giving vitality to his writing. He who thinks all the time and is thoroughly aware cannot go to sleep; by the same token, he will not inflict sleep on others.[12]

4 Audience

The writer of history wishes others to read the history he writes. Does this mean that in writing he should keep his audience constantly in mind? This would certainly seem to be the usual advice. Books should differ with the people to whom they are addressed. One writes in one way for schoolboys, in another for one's colleagues, in yet a third for those 'general readers' whose avid desire for agreeable history it is the ambition of authors and publishers to satisfy. On the face of it, this sounds like a counsel of sense; yet I believe it to be both wrong-headed and rather pernicious. It leads to a subtle arrogance in the writer and to that gild-spirit which at times bids fair to drive the life from the work of the profession. What right has anyone to say, 'this is too much for little minds; this I must reserve for others as able, as gifted, as profound as myself'? And is it any wonder that a man convinced that he is dealing in mysteries too deep for the generality will in the end just tend that feeble flame in the inner sanctuary, forget the world, and live in the sinful pride of the initiate?

[12] Another example: 'This organizational growth, territorially fragmented if denominationally uniform' (G. R. Elton, *Reformation Europe*, London, 1963, 57)—horribly ugly and burdened with a bogus metaphor ('growth') and a false 'if'.

Whether it is worse for the historian to retreat into the exclusiveness of the sect or to proclaim his sectarian arrogance by a vast condescension in writing for the multitude may be a moot point; speaking for myself, I can respect austerity, but I know nothing worse than the sort of book which on every page announces that of course these matters are very difficult for the reader and (if not ostentatiously omitted) had better be explained in simple (and inaccurate) language, by means of so-called modern parallels, by references to the supposed commonplace concerns of the reader, by images and metaphors and slang (usually slang just out of date) supposedly current in the world in which history has to make its way against a main preoccupation with mundane things.[18] I can feel regretful respect for the historian who decides that the world has nothing to do with him and that he will wear his hairshirt exclusively in the pages of the *English Historical Review*; but I feel much less happy about one who, mounting the pulpit, addresses his inferiors in terms suitable for them. No audience, in any case, will respond favourably to being treated as unintelligent; why should it? It is, obviously, the task of the practitioner to explain the difficult things, not to push them considerately out of sight, and there must always be a suspicion that any historian who supposes that he has things to tell which only the expert can understand has not yet himself succeeded in understanding them.

There is really no need for these coy and displeasing

---

[18] A common fault is coyness, often expressed in long words: 'Elizabeth showed herself her father's daughter by abandoning affairs of state in favour of a round of amusements mixed with dalliance' (G. R. Elton, *England under the Tudors*, London, 1955, 324). The cliché is not redeemed by being accurate enough in point of fact.

attitudes. One can, in such matters, speak only from personal experience, and I must say that in writing and lecturing I endeavour to give no thought to the supposedly differing needs and standards of readers or listeners. Of course, I want to explain myself to them, but my concern has been to expound what I believe to be the truth, or at least what I believe to be the real problems, in the language appropriate to the subject, not perhaps to the audience. Regard your audience as intelligent though possibly uninstructed, and they will indeed prove intelligent and (one hopes) depart better instructed. No problem of historical study that I have come across, in my own work or that of others, has seemed to me incapable of being explained with full clarity to any person of reasonable intelligence, and no person of insufficient intelligence will anyhow be in the way of reading or hearing historical analysis and description. If the historian has really explained things to himself, he can explain them to others; and nothing whatsoever justifies him in supposing that the others need a different treatment, a different language, a lower intensity of thought than himself. In all writing, three dignities must be observed: the dignity of the historian who must play neither the high priest nor the clown, the dignity of the audience who must actively and intelligently cooperate, and above all the dignity of the matter treated. This is no call for pomposity; there has to be respect for the rights of all involved without superior condescension, deliberate simplification, or ostentatious pity. Of course, the type of audience addressed may determine the length and detail of the explanation; it may affect the amount of technical language used. But there can be no reason for it to determine the amount of technical matter or the degree to which the problems receive explanation.

However, historical writings manifestly differ in some quite fundamental ways—in length, in subject matter, in structure and purpose, and in the line of approach. What, then, should decide these differences if not the audience addressed? The answer is simple enough : the questions to be asked and answered. What and how the historian writes depends not on the capacity of those for whom he writes but solely on what he is trying to do about history. Whatever he is there trying to do, he must attempt with a full equipment, a full understanding, a total involvement, and a best use of language, all these qualities being deployed simply to one purpose—to answer his question. Only in this way can he serve the true purpose of history, its contribution to the intellectual improvement of mankind. If instead he decides to entertain, to preach or make propaganda, to persuade people that all is progress or all is disaster, to attract an audience by playing down to them, to follow in fact any purpose other than the sovereign demand of historical study, he not only betrays his calling and his integrity, but he will be found out. When it comes to these matters of high principle it is always well to have some mundane sanctions in hand; and the sort of historian who prides himself simply on selling a lot of his books, or on pleasing an audience, should sometimes listen to what he likes to think are the voices of envy proceeding from less successful colleagues. There is absolutely nothing wrong with selling a lot of books or delighting an audience : solitude guarantees no virtue, nor is there vice in the pleasure of communicating with many. But it is fatal to elevate these considerations above all others. The reactions of one's fellows offer a reasonably true barometer by which to measure one's own sense of standards; and if their criticism were to grow not only contemptuous but justifiably so, the larger multitude, too, will not be long in discovering the truth. Those who barter their soul are especially to be pitied if in the process they lose the world as well.

Thus, the real differences evident in historical writing derive from the differences inherent in what one wants to say. And here, at last, there are hierarchies, or at least there is a line drawn between the higher and the lower. All pursuit of historical truth is, as I have said, respectable, but some forms are less respectable than others. To elucidate this statement it is necessary to classify historical writings by their manner, content and purpose.

5 Categories

Historical works belong to one of three categories: description, analysis, and narrative. Though the first two are in practice rarely divorced, and both are often involved in the third, one may for purposes of classification treat them separately. Description attempts to display a manifestation of the past without giving it the dimension of a change in time; for example, an account of a defunct government department or of a medieval village which simply explains the details of their composition and constitution. Analysis is still fundamentally static but sets the situation or thing described in a wider context of adjoining situations and things, studies interrelations, and attempts to establish causal connections and motives. To take an example: in 1536, the English government created a new office, the Court of Augmentations, to administer new revenues coming to the crown. A descriptive account would explain the structure of the Court, set out its officers and their duties, list its income and expenditure, describe its dissolution. Analysis would add such matters as the place of the Court in the general scheme of government, the reasons for a new court, problems of patronage and influence in the appointment of officers, success or failure in terms of administrative purpose and efficiency, the reasons for its abolition. Narrative tells the story, and it is not material how long the time span may be. Thus both a history of the Court of Augmentations which goes chronologically through the fortunes of the seventeen years of its existence, and a narrative of the sixteenth century in which the Court is mentioned as part of a story of government activity, would rightly be classed as narrative history.

The distinction here is one of purpose and manner, not of quality. Description and analysis are likely to arrange the available material by topics, running repeatedly over the same period of time; narrative uses time as the main backbone of its structure and may have to refer repeatedly to the same point or issue as they reappear in the course of the story. Differences in quality exist but do not provide a useful analytical tool; within the range of historical writing, the good and better, the poor and worse, legitimately share the same categories. However, a real qualitative distinction can be made within these three types, or at any rate in the first and last, for it can be maintained that in analysis there are only varieties of competence. Description and narrative, on the other hand, have two guises, one of them higher than the other. Their lower forms are antiquarianism and chronicle; their higher the meaningful description of the past (into which analysis enters almost invariably) and narrative history properly so called. The distinction between higher and lower forms does not arise from the basic method of proceeding and only in a limited sense from the purpose intended. It arises from the quality of mind brought to the task, the degree to which meaningful questions are asked and penetrating answers given, in short from the intellectual content of the product, a quality really only discernible by its impact on other intellects. Whether a piece of description should be classed as antiquarian or historical, a narrative as chronicle or history, is something that only the reader can tell; but in most cases he has little enough difficulty in making up his mind.

Antiquarianism exists in its own right but also where it has no business to be. It may be recognized by a devotion to detail for its own sake : the antiquarian wants to know, not to understand, and it is of little consequence to him what knowledge he is acquiring. One fact is virtually as good as another, and in the event a kind of galloping inflation takes place until the most tinsel facts are treated as at least as good as gold. The proper home of the antiquarian is parish history, local archaeology, genealogy, lawyer's history of the law—the areas where many facts can be accumulated without straining the reasoning or synthesizing capacity of the student. In its proper place it should not be despised, but it should be seen for what it is. The man who thinks the boundaries of the three-acre field as vital to knowledge as the frontiers of empires, who rejoices in the find of a Roman coin as though he had discovered the arms of the Venus de Milo, is an antiquarian. His work has value of a kind because the facts he collects can in the proper light contribute to the answering of real questions, that is intellectually challenging questions.

It is when antiquarianism pretends to be history that doubts must arise. Too many supposedly 'real' historians seem to think that their work is done when they have completed the finding-out part of it. Among such historians, the taint appears in their attitude to others. They are likely to niggle, to suppose that a striking,

novel and imaginative piece of historical writing can be
demolished by finding a few errors of detail; they are
liable to write reviews full of petty corrections and
noting the number of misprints.[14] The antiquarian
believes in accuracy. So should we all : inaccuracy and
error are faults. But a standard of judgment confined
to this one criterion is puny and unintelligent, and a
willingness to discard others because they fail in this one
particular is ungenerous and unwise. Accuracy is the
beginning of the work; to the antiquarian kind of historian it becomes its sole end. The well-trained historian
who lacks imagination, enterprise, and the courage to
make even mistakes speedily lapses into a kind of
antiquarianism which has not even the excuse that its
preoccupation with the multiplicity of facts makes no
pretence at being anything but a harmless end in itself. A
good deal of historical study, and a larger part of the
teaching of history, are still troubled by the censorious
attentions of this species of antiquarian; and it is no
answer that at least he avoids and corrects the more
flamboyant, probably more dangerous influence of the
pretentious, superficial, effect-hunting historians whom

[14] Godfrey Davies, a careful scholar devoid of imagination, tried
to resist the new ideas forced upon him by Mr Brian Wormald's
Clarendon (Cambridge, 1951) in a review so full of petty detail
that it quite ignored the real insights of the book attacked
(*Eng. Hist. Rev.* lxvii, 1952, 271-5). Even a good historian like A.
F. Pollard fell into this trap when, happily without success, he
tried to destroy S. B. Chrimes's *English Constitutional Ideas of
the Fifteenth Century* (Cambridge, 1936), one of the most important
investigations of an obscure period to appear in forty years, however disconcerting some of its details may have been (*History*,
xxii, 1937-8, 162-4). On the other hand, the seemingly niggly
review is justified when it demonstrates that the large conclusions
of some book are baseless because they rest on consistent error of
detail; for a good example see J. E. Neale's review of C. H.
Garrett, *The Marian Exiles* (Cambridge, 1938) in *Eng. Hist. Rev.*
liv, 1939, 501-4.

he conceives it his duty to expose. Two evils do not add up to any kind of good. The way to combat the bogus is to do better that which the bogus do badly, not to deny the validity of the creative mind in the study of history.

Chronicle is the narrative expression of antiquarian fact-collecting, a setting down of events one after the other, without considered discrimination or any discernible purpose except merely to record. By no means all the writings called by that name are chronicles in this precise sense; some men traditionally called chroniclers did apply art—purposive selection and interpretative comment—to a degree which makes them a sort of historians.[15] At its purest, the chronicle is really no more than a list, under each year, of supposedly major events; such, for instance, are the city chronicles of medieval London which give a mingle-mangle of civic officers, public events, natural disasters, deaths and executions, without any application of a considering mind. Even less crude productions bear the hallmark of indiscriminate collection rendered at one single level of expression.

No one, of course, would nowadays dream of writing precisely this sort of stuff. But the chronicle—the largely mindless narrative—is not dead; its modern descendant is the university textbook, provided it is sufficiently textbooky and uninspired. What makes a book of history into a historical textbook is, I suppose, in the first instance, the reason for which it was written: it means to offer an aid to teaching rather than deal with a complex of historical questions. There then results a book which is carefully stuffed with often undifferentiated

15 Cf. e.g. V. H. Galbraith, *Historical Research in Medieval England* (Creighton Lecture: London, 1951).

facts, neatly plotted out in assimilable and usually sub-headed sections of very modest length (so that they can be easily 'assigned' for study), marked by that desire to get everything in which produces in the reader an overwhelming feeling that there is nothing in it, and offering its credentials in unclassified book-lists that are as a rule well out of date. Books of this kind come about because they are written for a particular audience rather than for any reason connected with intellectual enquiry. In addition, they are troubled by a convention of comprehensive coverage which forces them into a steady jog-trot through paddocks marked political, economic, art and literature, and so on. Even good textbooks, like some of the contributions to the *Oxford History of England*, suffer from this diffusion of focus which in the worse examples amounts to the absence of any intellectual centre of gravity. Real narrative history therefore differs from this modern example of chronicle-writing by being composed because the historian wishes to say about history something that is to him important (rather than provide a balanced teaching aid) and because he has in his mind a pattern, a scheme of his bit of the past, which is articulated around a central problem. To this point I shall recur.

These inferior forms of historical writing have been discussed at such length because they are far from rare and can, by the inexperienced, be confused with the higher forms of which they are pale and unintelligent reflections. In looking now at the higher forms, I do not propose to consider whether they are always well-executed or successful; I shall assume that they are, since they are capable of being.

6 *Length*

We have already noted one set of categories into which
real historical writing can be fitted—description/analysis
(for at this point it becomes impossible to keep them
apart) and narrative. That is a division by method and
purpose. Another set of categories applies size and scale :
the learned article or essay, the particular monograph of
book length, and the sometimes multi-volume comprehensive synthesis and account. The differences in
both sets of categories impose special demands on the
historian, and since they do not coincide the writer's
problem is affected by various combinations from among
them. He may write a narrative article or a large
synthesis composed of purely analytical parts, though
no doubt he is more likely to embark upon an analysis of
article length or a large narrative book.

The differences determined by the mere size of the
work consist, naturally enough, in the scope of the
enterprise—the number and extent of the questions
asked. An article cannot deal with as much as can
a 500-page book (though some 500-page books turn out
on closer inspection to be inflated articles). But because an
important corollary is often forgotten, the consequences
of this obvious fact are not always observed. Each
piece of work, whatever its length, must still have its own
proper unity. Though an article may be of the same
length as a chapter in a book, it is not by any means the
same thing, and the frequent practice of publishing
unaltered parts of a doctoral dissertation in learned
journals has nothing to recommend it. Every piece of
historical writing should be self-contained, should set
itself a specific task and discharge it completely; and it

is the particular task to be discharged, not the possibilities of publication, which determines the category to which the piece belongs. This also means that length alone does nothing to affect intensity : the short piece which deals with only one or very few questions is not for that reason less governed by the need for depth and completeness than is the long study, nor is length to be achieved by padding and dilution. The nature of the question rules all.

It is, however, true that certain kinds of question demand answers at article length and others call for books. And here a somewhat paradoxical situation arises. The more particular the question and the more restricted the purpose, the shorter will be the answer. So much is obvious. But it is less obvious that the concern with detail, the attention to the evidence, will also be more intensive as the view is narrowed. Thus one valid distinction introduced by differences in length lies in the growing distance from the primary material that increasing size brings with it. An article, to be soundly done, must deal exclusively with the problems set by the historical evidence at its most particular.[16] As the work expands to include more questions and more ranging answers, derived conclusions rather than analysis of the evidence itself increasingly, and rightly, take their place by the side of the use of sources. The historian is perfectly entitled to build not only from the raw material of history but also from the smaller units created out of it by other historians, or by himself in another place, and the larger his view gets the more he will have to do this. One purpose of the learned article, therefore, is to

[16] This applies to creative and original work. Commentary— writing about other people's work, by way of summary or criticism—is a perfectly legitimate activity in itself, but it does not here concern us.

resolve specific and detailed points at issue so that only the answer, not the argument, may be absorbed into a larger whole. This is not to say at all that writing an article is somehow less worthy than writing a book, nor that this contribution to bigger units constitutes the article's sole service in life. Some questions, independent and interesting in themselves, call for no more than twenty or thirty pages to answer them. Description and analysis of a class of evidence, for instance, or the clarification of a judicial or administrative process, belong to this type; their usefulness to others does not involve inclusion in a bigger building but instruction in the use of that building's components. Nor are articles necessarily easier to write than books, though no doubt they take less time to produce and make fewer calls on the historian's ability to construct an argument and hold a great variety of detail and thought in his mind. Too many articles betray an inability to construct by being clearly chopped off at beginning and end. All historical writing must be complete in itself—must argue a case which seems to arise naturally from the evidence and is concluded with the last full stop. Writers of articles need, by and large, to think rather more about what they are trying to do. The institutional demand for published work explains but does not excuse the frequent appearance of dull or somewhat pointless pieces. The man who has nothing to say cannot disguise the fact by putting down his notes in a sort of connected sequence. That, once again, is antiquarianism—history without a mind in it.

These conditions—the restricted range of the point to be made and determined concentration on the real evidence—are likely to mean that a learned article will appeal to fewer readers, or at least will be read by fewer. But this does not absolve the historian from his obligations as an artist. Good writing, clear exposition, wit and life should no more be missing from an article than from a book enshrining a man's life's work. Dullness can never become a virtue, and dullness produced by (as so often it is) mere caution in the face of possible criticism is the proper reward of cowardice. No one wishes to encourage brilliance for mere brilliance' sake, and a sound regard for difficulties expressing itself in well-guarded statements deserves respect. But no one should write until he has achieved a clear view of the answer to his question, and when he has that view he must not allow professional fears to inhibit free expression nor haste to override his concern for lucidity and precision, any more than he must let a childish desire to startle lead him into spurious liveliness. The composition of a short piece, dealing with a real issue, is the best training that the beginner can have in the practice of his craft, but it will serve this purpose only if all the rules of the craft are observed as they would be for a 'real' book—depth of research as well as range of imagination, full exposition as well as living language. Even a technical article should be a pleasure to read and hold interest for the non-specialist.

Still, a technical article is technical and therefore makes demands on knowledge and interest which will restrict its attraction to those who possess a measure of both. As the scope of the work enlarges, as the questions range wider and the issues multiply, that restriction will, or should, progressively disappear. Yet increasing appeal should grow naturally from the subject and its treatment, not be achieved by additions (self-conscious art, unorganic brilliance, stucco decorations) or omissions (avoidance of the difficult, simplification of the complex, concessions to the reader). However large the work and however universal its content, it must still fulfil the demands made of even the smallest good article: it must ultimately and provenly rest on valid interpretations of valid evidence, it must be organized around an intelligent and intelligible argument, and it must be written with clarity and vigour. It should embody a sort of sober pride and sound conviction of professional craftsmanship.

7 Analysis and Narrative

This means that once the difference between an article and a book is passed little is to be gained by looking further at mere length. What matters now is the distinction between analysis and narrative, between the dissection of a topic and the telling of a story. An article or essay can, as has been said, be used for either of these tasks, though in the nature of things questions restricted enough to be exhausted in less than thirty pages are likely to call for analysis. Books can do both, and obviously do do both, sometimes inside one set of covers. Which is the method to be preferred? The nature of the question must determine the choice: this needs no labouring. But (as seems sometimes to be held) is one method 'better'—more serious, more distinguished, even more respectable—than the other? And are there rules to be observed or pitfalls to be avoided in either?

It is a fairly common error to suppose that narrative and analysis answer, respectively, the questions 'how' and 'why'. Those questions, together with 'what' and 'when' and 'who', underlie all historical discussion, no matter what form it may take. Nor can analysis overlook the fact of time, or narrative ignore the simultaneous occurence of divers events; otherwise the former would not be history (it might be something like sociology) and the latter would be chronicle. The real question to which analysis in the main addresses itself is 'what was it like', while narrative concentrates on the question 'how did it happen'. The analytical method takes a problem, or a complex of problems, and investigates them by dissecting them into their component parts and their relationships. Narrative, of course, tells the story. The first, therefore, requires a table of topics; it organizes its subject matter under headings and deals with each head in turn. The second arranges things in a series of happenings and divides its matter in the main into chronologically consecutive segments. Both are legitimate methods and both must consider significant questions. However, fashion supposes that analysis is superior; narrative is at present under a cloud. The historian who tells a story is supposed to be a little undemanding at best, superficial and ignorant at worst. To study problems not periods was Lord Acton's much-quoted injunction, and those who cite him approvingly fail to note that it is now some seventy years since he uttered those gnomic words, and that in actual fact he proved incapable of studying either problems or periods to a practical conclusion. The historian, working in the records and meeting one unresolved problem after another, quite naturally persuades himself that the real work consists in tackling these dark entities, and nearly always it is perfectly true that they will yield only to the analytical method. But that does not mean that one should pin a special medal on analysis. Since history is the record of events, and of problems, proceeding through time, narrative must be not only legitimate but also urgently called for.

Once again, the only point which determines the choice is the historian's purpose, the questions he is asking. The complete historian must ask both what it

was like and how it happened, and he can ask this
either at different times (that is, in different books) or
occasionally at one and the same time; he must not
think of the method of ordering his thoughts as something imposed on him from outside, by training or
convention; and he must cultivate both techniques in
equal measure. Thus he must thoroughly acquaint
himself not so much with the peculiar characteristics
of each—these are not obscure—as with the dangers
and difficulties which beset them.

The main danger inherent in the analytical method
is that it fragments the unity of the historical process.
I am not here thinking of Professor Hexter's 'tunnel
history', the use of categories like political, economic
or intellectual history to circumscribe the work done.[17]
Nobody can write universal history—everything that
happened or has been thought—in one piece; the
processes of writing will not permit it. These 'tunnels'
are necessary mechanisms, and history so divided up can
in each case yield to both the analytical and the narrative
approach. The point is that, within the necessarily
circumscribed section of history which the historian can
manage, analysis still runs the danger of fragmentation.

Up to a point, this is inescapable. Topics do not
occur in isolation, but if they are to be discussed in turn
they are liable to give that impression. The first rule to
be observed is that an analytically organized book
must still be a book, not a series of articles. There must be
a common theme to hold the topics together, and
chapters must appear to run on naturally one from
another. The order in which these more or less parallel
topics are introduced is vitally important : it should
have a discernible logic in it. Every device, however

[17] See above, p. 28.

superfluous it may seem, should be employed to underline coherence and continuity. Each new topic should be linked to its predecessor by lead-over and pick-up sentences, and the general question of the book should be kept constantly in mind and frequently before the reader. Thus, suppose one were to write a book on the Industrial Revolution in England (a not uncommon thing to do). This is a theme which cries out for the analytical treatment, as all the various elements in the story (agricultural reform, technological advance, changes in population and labour force, capital market and rate of interest, and so on) pass before the historian's mind. No one could possibly assemble them into a useful single narrative. But a mere series of chapters on these topics would be neither a good book nor a real exposition and explanation of the phenomenon studied. If the task is to be properly discharged, each element, as it is analysed in turn, must contribute directly to an understanding of a major movement which must at the same time become comprehensible in its passage through time. This suggests that the historian should isolate for himself a main thread in a story he does not propose to tell as a story. He may choose what thread he pleases— for instance, increase of production, or the role of the entrepreneur. Having chosen it, he cannot profitably abandon it : he will have to write each section not as a self-contained account of that part of the panorama he happens to be dealing with, but deliberately as part of an account of his main theme. Swapping horses in mid-book destroys books. The analytical historian is composing not a mosaic but a painting in which the canvas is covered several times over with different pigments and patterns, until an amalgam of colour and design emerges from the repeated process. This metaphor has its dangers because it does not permit the introduction of a movement through time which should also be apparent from the book, but it will give a hint of the right idea.[18]

Analysis can be very static and prevent an understanding of change: this is one major danger to guard against. In the example I chose, of the Industrial Revolution, the danger is not great because each element in the story clearly calls for some progressive treatment. But analytical books, even good ones, often fall into this trap which is sprung by failure to realize that evidence taken from a given period of time must be evaluated against the background of change involved in temporal progress. To use, for instance, evidence from the beginning and end of a long period as though it necessarily belonged to one and the same order of fact is to run into trouble. How seriously this can affect the best work is demonstrated by Christopher Hill's fine book on *The Economic Problems of the Church from Archbishop Whitgift to the Long Parliament* (Oxford, 1956). Its arrangement is entirely analytical: four topic-chapters on 'The State of the Clergy', six on the financial problems, four on the work of Archbishop Laud. No other arrangement could have brought out so well the condition of Church and clergy or the situation faced by them, and no other could have provided such thorough discussion of problems like tithe or

---

[18] Two recent books illustrate the point. T. S. Ashton's concise study of *The Industrial Revolution* (London, 1948) is held together by the author's conviction that the clue to the story is found in the fluctuations of the rate of interest. Though he was probably wrong in this, he was able to write a well-articulated book. On the other hand, Phyllis Deane's *The First Industrial Revolution* (Cambridge, 1965) is really a collection of separate essays on various aspects, held together by no single line of argument; and it reads like that. The work grew out of a course of lectures, always a difficult thing to turn into a real book.

pluralism. But a treatment which collects its facts indiscriminately from a period of sixty years, as though in that time such things as Puritanism or the complaints against the hierarchy had not passed through profoundly changing attitudes, purposes and ambitions, creates a very misleading air of sameness by the simple device of assuming that nothing changed. The analysis itself is distorted because the transformations of the historical situation are ignored; people's thoughts and actions are seen in unreal isolation from changing circumstances. This is by no means an indictment of the analytical method (though it forms a legitimate, if limited, criticism of this book), but it constitutes a warning to remember the story when dissecting components. To be satisfactory, analysis must incorporate narrative. That is to say, while the fundamental organization of any book asking 'what was it like' should be by topics and sections, each topic must not only be organically linked to the rest but must also run through time and remember change.

However, if the question obviously posed by the purpose of a book is 'what happened', then analysis must not be allowed to usurp the place of narrative. It is here that the present dislike of story-telling as a historical method introduces real perils. The historian faced with the task of writing an account of some large piece of history—the history of a country, a continent, or an age—cannot avoid a basic structure which concentrates on the chronological, even chronicle, element, the passage through the years. Otherwise he cannot possibly convey the essential feel of time passing, men succeeding each other, lives being lived and deaths being died. He may well come to the conclusion that of some topics he has to treat separately; he may require analytical chapters, though whether he should surrender to this supposed need is something to be discussed in a moment. But he cannot allow himself a mainly analytical structure. To take, once again, by way of example, a book good enough to stand such critical regard : Christopher Brooke's *Europe in the Central Middle Ages* (London, 1964). This is one volume in a general cooperative history of Europe and covers the years 962 to 1154. Nearly two hundred years, a time of much change; and Europe is a sufficiently large area. There can be no question of a single main problem being here dissected into its parts. Yet of Professor Brooke's eighteen chapters, no fewer than ten are strictly analytical and the rest, embodying sections of narrative, follow in the main an analytical approach. The difficulties of narrating the confused and multiple history of those years are indeed formidable; yet it is hard to be satisfied with a treatment which by some 100 pages separates chapters on certain emperors and certain popes whose lives were spent in conflict with each other. The result is that the book lacks a main thread. Quite possibly the feeling that things happen higgledy-piggledy, here, there and everywhere, reflects a reality; it could well represent the feelings of such contemporaries as were alert enough to think of their world at all. But the historian's task is to explain—to make plain—and in order to do so he has to discover and elaborate his theme. I am not expert enough on that age to suggest one with confidence, but one can imagine a book working out the emergence of a particular civilization, dominated by a reformed and aggressive Church on the one hand and locally ascendant monarchies on the other, which would firmly organize its narrative of kings, popes, emperors and thinkers to that end.

To say this, however, is at once to call up the retort that to write a narrative of emperors and popes is to do very little justice to the realities of history. The current

preference for what is called social history demands a
progressive analysis and account of societies (politically
and socially identifiable groups of people) at all their
levels and in their multifarious appearances, not only as
agents of political action but also as producers of wealth,
harbourers of internal conflict, promoters of intellectual
enterprise; and it is not perhaps much of an answer
that hardly any such books in fact exist. How can
narrative possibly manage to render the complexities of
such a story, and is it not therefore inevitably condemned
to superficiality, for ever recalling the simple chronicle
from which it grew? While history confined itself to
the doings of governments, so runs the argument, narrative was a proper and satisfactory method, but we have
left all that behind. The long ascendancy of Ranke,
primarily concerned with international relations and
diplomacy, themes thoroughly amenable to the narrative
method, has been replaced by such influences as that of
the French *Annales* school which wishes to understand
a whole society in every detail, in all its interrelations and
activities, and therefore insists on analysis. Compare a
work like Prescott's *History of the Reign of Philip II*
with Fernand Braudel's *La Méditerranée et le monde
méditerranéen à l'époque de Philippe II* (Paris, 1949),
and the change becomes very apparent. The second book
offers some splendid understanding of the circumstances
which contributed to the shaping of policy and action;
the only things missing are policy and action. There is
a clear and admirable sense of life, but how those
lives passed through history is much less clear. To me, at
least, the *Annales* method—certainly until it lost itself in
rhetoric and self-adulation—represents a valuable, perhaps necessary, stage in the development of historical
writing, one which attacked genuine deficiencies and
did a good deal to remedy them, but it must not be

regarded as in some way the sole consummation of the historian's duties. In many fields of history it is either clearly insufficient or has already done its work. Legitimate in itself, and in such hands as Bloch's or Braudel's remarkably successful, it can no more answer all the important questions of history than can any other method.

Unhappily, any attempt to restore narrative to a respectable place in the historian's armoury runs into the reformer's most awkward problem : the friends he makes and the unwanted allies that surround him. It cannot be denied that a good deal of the occasional clamour against 'technical' and analytical history, or the sort of praise for story-telling one encounters in the worthier lay periodicals, arises from intellectual indolence and a desire for popular success. It is perfectly possible to feel respect and liking for the writings of the serious popular historians without believing that theirs is the highest form of history or the model to follow. Among them are notable practitioners of a far from easy skill; it would not be difficult to bias the argument by looking at the lesser lights; but even the best lack the searching depth of investigation, the establishment of solid truths, and the accumulation of fruitfully illuminating explanations which professional history must and can provide. However hard it may be to write flowing narrative or to evoke people and places, it should not be doubted that the intellectual effort involved in real analysis and its presentation is markedly greater. In addition, much narrative history helps itself by ignoring unsolved questions, accepting ready-made explanations, repeating stale argument at second hand; and narrative that depends on art superficially imposed on simplicity or ignorance does indeed merit the strictures of the austerer scholars. The question is whether other forms of narrative are possible, and I think they are.

The defender of historical narrative as a profound form of writing history faces one further handicap in the prevalence of biographies. Though biography is really a separate art, with rules and problems of its own, most people seem to think of it as simply a form of history; yet, in so far as it is history, it tends to underline the potential weakness of narrative. It is certainly historical, and it is bound to be narrative in its main structure. Since it deals with an individual's life it possesses a given beginning and a known end between which the sequence of events runs clearly in one direction. The biographer thus has his first problem solved for him : neither the limits of his study nor its basic structure are open to choice. Now in England, at least, biographies are innumerable; their production forms one of the country's most flourishing industries, and they are well liked by readers. Whatever may be true of the bulk of them, quite a few are admirable. What matters here is that even at its best biography is a poor way of writing history. The biographer's task is to tell the story, demonstrate the personality, and elucidate the importance of one individual; he should not be concerned with the history of that individual's times except in so far as it centres upon or emanates from him. In measure as he deserts his proper subject for what concerns the historian, that subject's age, he fails in his own task. Very occasionally, a 'great man's' life may prove a tool useful for opening a problem of history—some kings or statesmen can serve this purpose—but even when the tool is useful it is not the best available. The limits of one man's life rarely have any meaning in the interpretation of history; even if his death marks a period (and how rarely this happens) his birth will not. However influential he may have been, no individual has ever dominated his age to the point where it becomes sensible to write its history purely around him. And, above all, those parts of his career that may carry the greatest historical significance are not likely to be those on which a biographer should mainly concentrate. He should give much weight to those private relationships and petty concerns which have little to tell the historian; in particular, if he is to understand his subject's personality, he should deal thoroughly with those formative years during which the history of the age is likely to be quite unaware of the growing man. None of this speaks against biography as a form of writing, but it does mean that biography is not a good way of writing history. The historian should know the histories and characters of many men, as he should know much else, but he should not write biography—or at least should not suppose that in writing biography he is writing history. The low esteem in which biography is often held—not without reason—therefore offers no argument at all against narrative history : the two are different things.

What, then, should narrative do to avoid the charges of superficiality, intellectual weakness, inability to deal with the real questions—charges that are often raised against it by professional historians? If a narrative form could be found which would enable the historian to offer real explanations of problems and to accommodate more than the traditional political story, the genre would again become respectable, especially if at the same time it could preserve its special distinction as literary art. In this endeavour, the narrative historian confronts two technical problems : the definition of a theme, and the discovery of a structure which amalgamates with this theme historical points and problems not directly arising from it.

In defining his theme, the historian must first of all establish meaningful limits, points in time which give to his narrative a true sense of coherence. Any old bit cut out of the interminable flow of time will still be history, but it will not be good history because it will lack purpose and so will not enable the writer to create a work of thought and art. In practice, the limits may well be provided by the main theme chosen. The narrative historian necessarily decides to tell the story of something—of a nation, a political organization, a Church, a government, a business, or whatever may come to mind among the activities of men, or of some phase in that story which interests him. When he has chosen his theme, its limits should come to him as a matter of course, but it is still worth saying that he should from first to last be aware of the need to have real limits and should so construct his story that it naturally runs from one to the other. Few themes do in fact run from one clearly defined point in time to another, but this does not permit the writer to delay the opening of his narrative with long scene-setting chapters or to drag it out into lengthy perspectives and forecasts at the end. If scenes are to be set and consequences be made plain, this should be done inside the narrative; narrative history at its most effective demands that no clearly defined sections be blatantly analytical.

The kind of theme chosen may also pose serious problems. If the history is to deal with a restricted body of men, things may be easy. A history of the East India Company or Imperial Chemical Industries, of the king's Chancery or the Methodist Church, will naturally be written along a main line defined by the fortunes of those organizations. But narrative history often has to deal with groups of men expressing themselves in different ways or living side by side in entanglement and separateness, as it might be a nation which has a political, social, economic, religious and intellectual history; or it deals with an age in which a number of such societies can all claim to have lived such varied lives. Here the historian must choose a main theme, often a very hard choice but not one to be avoided by running a number of themes alongside each other in separate chapters. The historian may suppose that his choice depends on his own preference, and to some extent this enters into it. But there are two chief considerations that really determine the main theme : the availability of evidence, and the need to find a theme sufficiently dominant to carry the others along with it.

In practice, it has to be admitted, this means that the main theme even to-day will be nearly always 'political' : it must consist of the actions of governments and governed in the public life of the time. For all ages before about 1800 the vast bulk of the surviving evidence bears on such topics, and even thereafter that kind of evidence predominates. And secondly, since narrative is necessarily a record of events succeeding each other, it is necessarily the record of action (and suffering); and the most manifest, continuous and purposeful action is that which guides a community through its life and its relations with other communities. Thus political narrative—the doings of the rulers and the reactions of the ruled at all levels—still stands out as the probable main thread of any narrative. The history of Tudor England can be written as the history of sheep-farming, or of vernacular poetry, or of maritime enterprise, or of doctrinal debate; other themes could be found. But none of these lines runs clean down the middle because they do not involve a large enough part of the people living at the time nor a large enough part of the evidence. None of them make it easy to accommodate the others in the same story. As main themes they are therefore inferior to politics—the activities of government—for which the evidence is thickest and to which other themes most readily relate.

However, it is perfectly true that mere political history is not enough. A plain tale of wars and treaties, elections and reforms, the fortunes of the great, however well it may be told, can no longer satisfy our conception of history or accommodate our knowledge of it. In order that action may be understood, its setting, circumstances and springs must be made plain, and these are found not only in the psychology of individuals and crowds, but especially in the details of administration, the economy, the intellectual preoccupations of the time, and all other so-called 'factors'. The narrative historian comes up against separate problems that either have been solved and must be absorbed, or that have to be solved by him, before he can continue his story. It is his task to accommodate such matters, which require analytical treatment, in such a way that the narrative seems hardly to be interrupted at all. This means that he should not treat of them as plainly separate entities, in separate chapters or sections clearly marked off. Rather they should be erratic boulders carried along in the glacier flow—paragraphs, sometimes sentences, which seem to come naturally at some point of the narrative and slip readily into its continuation, so that the reader is barely aware of the change of pace. (In itself, a change of pace is desirable in any prolonged account.) To be satisfactory, and in order to avoid the charge of superficiality, historical narrative must, as it were, be thickened by the results of analysis. This requires the historian to gather together every aspect and every turn of the subject matter, digest it comprehensively in the mind, and use it to elaborate the points of his narrative.

While it would help to illustrate these probably obscure

prescriptions, I feel unable to do so without displaying the conceit involved in citing my own example. This kind of narrative is what I attempted in my *Reformation Europe* (London, 1963). The book avoids the customary scene-setting at the start. Instead it goes straight into the story of Luther's rebellion, whch naturally calls for some description of the man; this introduces, as a matter of course, the points of theology over which he rebelled. Once the narrative is well under way, it demands some understanding of Luther's success in the circumstances of time and place, which necessitates a long—possibly by these rules too long—discussion of 'the state of Germany'. Because this comes after the narrative has begun, and not by way of introducing Luther's action, it seems to me to avoid the appearance of a separate and unintegrated chapter, though in this I may, of course, be quite mistaken. Smaller problems are more easily accommodated. The account of Charles V's wars with the French can be arrested for a couple of paragraphs to analyse the military practice of the time; his involvement with the Turks can be used to slip in a description of that despotism. And so on. It is perfectly true that those aspects of the age which yield best to thoroughly analytical treatment will not come across in such detail as another approach might provide; the point is that I was trying to write the kind of narrative in which analytical chunks are somehow embedded without destroying the sense of action, movement, time passing, across the whole range of problems. Certainly I did not succeed completely : if I had, I should have been able to do without a chapter on 'The Age'—parts of which, it now seems to me, could have been treated in the course of the narrative. There are some other passages where analysis seems to me to threaten the narrative, or at least to hold it suspended for rather too long. I cite this example only because I did try to practise what here I preach, and I think I had some measure of success with it; I managed to discuss topics and argue points not usually encountered in books treating narratively and concisely of controversial and intellectually complex periods. The method is possible, but it still needs a great deal of thought and work to improve it.

In actual fact, it need not be doubted that the ideally pure form of this sort of narrative can never be written. The complexities of every story are too great, and the historian must lose his worth if either through ignorance or by design he solves his problem by leaving out the awkward things. To some, a traditional method, alternating narrative and analytical chapters, may seem preferable, because it is more easily done and less likely to omit matters, but I do not like it so well. I am, however, inclined to think that large-scale history cannot be written without *some* patently analytical sections which I regard as inescapable setbacks in a battle that must on balance be won. If the question is 'what happened', the answer must tell a story, and however 'thickened' or interrupted that story turns out to be it must continuously keep the reader moving through the years. People must palpably be born, grow up and die; institutions, organizations, societies must be seen to change and vary; events must clearly follow one upon another. Everything must most manifestly be taking place in time. And yet the deeper insight into problems, the discussions of unsettled or doubtful points, the hard intellectual digging which analysis alone can provide must also be ever present as the tale proceeds: not only present to the historian, but by him also communicated, integrated in the flow of time, to all who read.

Narrative of this sort, however short of the ideal, is

not, of course, easy to write. It challenges the constructive skills of the writer as well as his ability to hold together a great number of traces that keep pulling apart. It is much harder to do than analytical history which, in turn, may well require more concentrated and intensive thought. Neither is, however, superior to the other, and he who dissects problems need not look down upon the narrator as a mere teller of tales, nor need the story-teller despise the concerns of his analysing colleague as absence of imagination. The complete historian, in any case, is both. Both are truly important forms of intelligent and intellectual activity, proper to be reckoned among the more respected occupations of the human mind. Within the single task of understanding and recreating the past, they serve different and complementary purposes. Still, I confess to a personal hankering after the sort of narrative I have described. I find it more difficult to accomplish than the analysis of historical problems, and therefore more exciting to do. It needs even more art, more transformation of the raw material. But personal preferences should not be mistaken for general rules, even by him who holds them.

It should be plain by now that though I believe in the independence of history and the possibility of discovering a right truth by the techniques of scholarship, I do not hold that these facts result in historical writing independent of the writer. Quite often this dependence does not interfere with the statement of manifest and incontrovertible truth; there are a good many problems in history, large and small, for which nobody now manages to work up any bias or prejudice. At other times it does interfere. Add the uncertainties of historical writing—the gaps in the evidence, the frequent obscurity of what does survive, the need to read and interpret

with a controlled imagination, the demands of order
and sense—and it is plain enough that no work is free
of the tentative, the doubtful, the correctable. Yet what of
that? Why should this limit the historian's desire to
know and to write, or his claim to be listened to? Only
those to whom the insufficiencies of the human existence
are anathema could ever suppose that it should, and
people of that cast of mind have no cause to concern
themselves with men or their history.

The historian fulfils his function properly if, aware
of the unsolved and insoluble problems, conscious that
he is not a machine and can be moved by love, anger,
contempt and vanity, he concentrates on honesty and
integrity. He must become a scholar, which is to say
that he must add a dimension to his humanity, not
remove one. And he will be wise to cultivate the sceptic
mind, a reserved and questioning attitude to all claimed
certainties, for as long as he can. He needs to be
learned, balanced, imaginative, able to see all points
of view and yet to assess them from one of his own.
Imagination will give life to his learning, learning will
direct the sweep of his imagination. Over all should
rule a searching intelligence, asking that fundamental
question of the sceptic : just what do you mean by that?
And if that question is asked with a real desire to
know and understand, if the imagination is centred upon
people—dead people once alive—and sympathy and
judgment are controlled by scholarship and by a mind of
quality, the work can be done. All the deficiencies
of knowledge and writer notwithstanding, the historian
can rest assured that he can fulfil his ambition to know
and tell about the past. His can never be the last word,
an ambition in any case bred out of vanity, but he
can establish new footholds in the territory of truth.

IV

Teaching

The vast majority of professional historians nowadays earn their living as teachers. Though there remain a few whom private means or successful books enable to dispense with employment, and though historians can be found on the staffs of archives, libraries and museums, the typical member of the profession divides his time between his researches and the instruction of the young. The whole training scheme, built round the much abused Ph.D., is designed to produce teachers who use the mould they have stepped from to fashion more men (and women) in their own image. The expansion of university education all over the world has in the last twenty years altered the proportions in which these men divide their time: teaching takes up more of it than once it did, and those professors who use their eminence and effrontery to redress the balance in their own lives only succeed by placing more of the burden on others. For that it can be a burden is true enough and need not be denied; anything is that interferes with lotus-eating. Everybody at all acquainted with these matters has heard the frequent laments about the way in which teaching interferes with a man's 'own work', and nobody, however dedicated a teacher he may be, can have passed through even a few years of his career without feeling at times that these complaints are justified.

It is therefore worth stressing—as the great mass of

competent and conscientious university teachers know
perfectly well—that the two sides of the work are equally
necessary and mutually complementary. Teaching not
only enables a man to eat and therefore live in the
pursuit of the truth; it also makes him a better historian.
And the teacher who has ceased to take part in the
work of exploration, discovery and restatement is very
unlikely to remain a useful instructor. Only continuous
first-hand experience of the way in which history
should be studied and written maintains the ability to
convey it to others with a sense of purpose and inspiration. This would probably be readily agreed to by most,
and recognition of the fact justifies, to some extent, the
demands for 'production' which university administrators
so often make on their professors. (Not that they demand
it for this reason: though blind, they may sometimes
tread well.) What is less widely realized is the truth of
the reverse: that the constant experience of teaching
is at least a very important preserver of scholarly
energies and standards. It would be possible to adduce
examples to show how able historians have deteriorated
as they have abandoned teaching. The man who has to
explain himself to others and to excite their excitement,
and who has to do this in inescapable conditions of
personal contact, finds that he is thereby controlling
and improving his performance as an historian no less
than as a teacher. I remember many occasions on
which attempts to explain something to a student suddenly brought into focus the components of a problem,
for the first time showed me where accepted interpretations had been too easily accepted, or by making
me think afresh made me reorganize a mass of material
of which the student, the stimulus to it all, could not
even be aware. Teaching of necessity creates its own
form of arrogance; the position of preceptor, the

claims of seniority, contain strong elements of assured superiority, and instruction must at times be didactic. But teaching also provides an opportunity for humility and a discipline in precise thought and even more precise expression, and the historian who never has to try his knowledge and ideas on an audience physically present and able to interrogate him misses one of his most useful experiences.

Thus the double existence of scholar and teacher is not only an economic and sociological necessity but a convenient and profitable thing for the working historian. This means that he would do well to give some thought to what he is doing not only as an historian but also as a teacher. The necessary association of his two activities, research and instruction, in fact itself reflects the fundamental difficulty involved in teaching, a difficulty much greater in history than in some more precise subjects. Can history be taught at all? Teaching is conventionally supposed to be a process of instruction, whether by the simple transfer of knowledge from one mind to another or by the evocation in the mind taught of the learning and understanding present in the mind teaching. Yet history is a subject in which the learned dispute as much as they agree; progress in it comes as often through an argumentative study of old problems as through the solving of new ones. Certainly there is an agreed body of knowledge to be transmitted, but no one supposes that such transmission constitutes the teaching of history. On the one hand, it is much too big a task : in the few years that a man can set aside in his life for his student days, no one can 'teach' him all that is firmly known in history. On the other hand, it is perfectly obvious that instruction which confines itself to expounding some knowledge and demanding its absorption by the student does not deserve the name of teaching because nothing of value is done to the student mind. The study of history consists of debates— between the historian and his evidence, between different students of history, between the historian and his own society—and if the teaching of history is to be successful it, too, must rest on debate. All teaching requires the active participation of both the teacher and the taught; in history, this is made more necessary as well as more difficult by the fact that the mere conveying of knowledge runs up against both the enormous and unorganizable quantity of that knowledge and the debatable uncertainties which alone give meaning to that knowledge.

In this discussion it will therefore be taken for granted that, though all teaching involves some straight infusion of facts and figures, history cannot be taught in the sense that any student can, by teaching, be made to possess a sufficient, coherent, self-satisfactory body of knowledge. No doubt this is true of all fields of study, but in the natural sciences, for instance, or in engineering and medicine, teaching must aim at instilling a grasp of agreed knowledge which, as it is added to by research, also sheds points proved erroneous and thus continues to be a teachable entity, namely the subject in question. Just enough of this happens in history, where also elements once thought true can be removed by the process of research, to justify a large measure of normal teaching activity; but here one important consequence of new knowledge is to put old knowledge into new light, not to destroy it, so that what might at one time be a manageable entity soon becomes too large, too subtle, and too diffuse to be taught in this sense. A subject in which no one can rewrite the standard textbook—in which, indeed, there can be no standard textbook, no Gray's *Anatomy* regularly renewed through the generations—obviously poses problems of a very different order.

If 'history', not being a subject like anatomy or molecular chemistry, cannot itself be taught, the purpose of teaching history must be different from that of teaching medicine or law; the end in view cannot be simply assumed but needs thought. In the main, that end differs with the class of persons taught. I shall not concern myself with the teaching of schoolchildren, though I have practised it (rather badly) in my time. Perhaps because I have tried to do it, I have developed serious doubts about the wisdom of doing it at all. History deals with the activities of men, not of abstractions, and a measure of maturity is really necessary before the student can understand what is before him and is being said to him. The intellect may well be at its brightest before experience comes to tarnish it and confuse every issue : chess players and mathematicians do well to register their achievements young. But in history only experience and insight can save the intellect from its characteristic fault of over-simplifying and over-organizing every problem, and even at eighteen, when mankind is most certain that it knows everything, it is easy to mistake absence of understanding for clarity of vision. In a very real sense, history is not a good subject to teach to children, or rather, the 'real' thing—academic history— is the wrong thing for them. What may be right shall not be enquired into here. I must confine myself to the academic teaching of academic history, which means that I shall consider the problems of teaching history at a university. These naturally divide into the teaching of undergraduate and graduate students, not only because the two groups differ in age, attainment and the particular knowledge they seek, but more fundamentally because the purposes of teaching them are quite different.

1 Undergraduate Teaching: What?[1]

In the history departments of British universities, at least, 'syllabus reform' is a game played in an atmosphere heavy with suspicion and ambition; the rolled logs, clattering by, at times drown the very voice of the teacher, and instead of pursuing 'their own work' scholars draft memoranda to one another. The more enterprising and less scrupulous publish their pet schemes in the press and on the air, gaining a reputation for advanced thought and an exclusive hearing for one side. The motives behind the turmoil vary a good deal. There is fear : history is losing students to such other disciplines as English or the social sciences and must be made more attractive. (This fear is sometimes voiced by those who complain most loudly of the burden imposed on them by excessive student numbers.) There is self-interest : the man who has specialized in something not prominent in the syllabus understandably enough wants to change that sad state of affairs. There is resentment : to judge by the feelings entertained by many professional historians, especially of advancing years, for medieval studies, medievalists must in an earlier generation have been most unwisely arrogant.

[1] Nearly all my experience has been with English undergraduates with their high level of specialization at school. This naturally colours what follows, but I believe that the principles which I shall try to distinguish have a wider application, and that the practice which I shall describe can be readily adapted to students who have passed through a different pre-university career. Though there are special difficulties in teaching mass audiences or those for whom history is only part of their course, I think that at heart the problems remain the same and that the answers, while they may vary a little, do not change in essence.

But the main body of the clamour arises from genuine doubts about the value of existing methods and subjects: those who would wish to widen studies by the inclusion of various parts of the world hitherto obscure, or who favour 'interdisciplinary' courses combining history, geography, philosophy, literature, and so forth, are often imaginative and enterprising as well as sincere. Whether they are also wise is another question. New universities, with at first small departments and few students, offer opportunities for experiment, and though not all the experiments have avoided the taint of gimmickry many sound interesting and some are striking.[2] Still, sincerity can be an overrated quality and is assuredly no guarantee of sense. The value of all these experiments and the justice of all these complaints must depend on a more rigorous analysis of the purposes pursued than one commonly encounters. Just what are we trying, just what should we be trying, to do when we teach history to undergraduates?

I have already said that in my view we neither can nor should try to convey a knowledge of history in the sense of simply acquainting the student with a given body of facts or interpretations. We need to do a certain measure of this because our courses must have content, but we cannot restrict our purposes to so low-grade an exercise. If we really had nothing better to do than present a history of England or China, of political thought or economic practice, and afterwards to elicit that same information again by means of examinations, we might as well resign our students to more intelligent disciplines. Yet the frequent demand that insularity

---

[2] At the newly founded University of Warwick, history students are to spend one term away from base, in either Italy or the United States. This is not only nice for them but nice for their relieved teachers, too.

be replaced by global concerns (or some such phrase)—
that the student should know about Russia or know the
facts of African history—seems to suppose that the
purpose of teaching history is just instruction in information hitherto unknown. A subtler argument starts
from the axiom—which happens to be true—that the
purpose of all university education is to equip men and
women for their lives in the world, and then draws the
conclusion that the contents of the course must therefore change as the place of a man's country changes in
the hierarchy and importance of societies. Thus to
Professor Southern, the predominance of English constitutional history, which has long characterized the
Oxford school, was justified while Great Britain was top
dog and Oxford graduates in history might commonly
expect to employ themselves variously in the government
of an empire. That condition has vanished : therefore,
constitutional history should be replaced by a study of
what alone now gives Englishmen influence, namely
culture and ideas.[*] Does one have to be a crude
imperialist to question the logic of this reasoning? More
straightforwardly, the many who argue that the study of
history should teach the young student to understand
his own time hold that the syllabus needs to be restricted
to recent history, or that it should include compulsory
study of the history of science. It should be said, with
regret, that there is no proof that a knowledge of history,
recent or distant, at B.A. level succeeds in giving a man
much understanding of his own time.

What, to me, seems wrong with all these pleas is that

[*] R. W. Southern, *The Shapes and Substance of Academic
History* (Oxford, 1961). I do not think I misrepresent the argument
of this inaugural lecture which seems to me an unacceptable
plea for the superiority of the study of the mind over the study of
matter.

they look for entirely external conditions to which their programmes must answer. I cannot accept that the study of history should be justified only by such incidental consequences as additions to a man's memorized knowledge or an understanding of this or that situation. As was said earlier on, anyone concerning himself with historical studies in any form should seek their purpose in the intellectual training they provide and in the augmentation they offer to the life of the mind. That greater proposition surely includes this lesser: if the historian may justify his existence by reference to the contribution he makes to the human intellect, the teacher must similarly consider that the purpose of his teaching is to turn out men with improved intellects at their disposal. Three or four years spent at a university cannot teach a man to know history; they cannot train him as a politician or publicist or publisher; they can at best begin to lay some foundations for a view of the world and (universities being what they are) are likely to lay foundations which, as later experience shows, need to be broken up. None of this invites blame: the impossible need not be attempted. But if those years do not produce an effective conditioning of the reasoning mind, if they do not teach a man to think better than otherwise he would have done, they may justly be condemned as a waste of time.

It follows that the purpose of teaching history to undergraduates is to equip them with the special intellectual training embodied in the study of history at any level. This intellectual training consists of two elements: a sharpening of the critical analytical faculty, and a deepening of the imaginative and constructive faculty. Since these are the qualities required in the successful study of history, they are the qualities which the teaching of history is most competent to instil. The study of history involves the analysis of problems in an extensive setting, both temporal and spatial; the student needs to be capable of close reasoning and the sceptical assessment of evidence, but must perform this common scientific duty in such a manner that the surrounding circumstances of his problem, antecedents and consequences, concomitants and contrasts, affect the solution of the specific details of the problem itself. That is what one means by an understanding of history, and it seems only reasonable to suppose that the undergraduate reading history should be instructed in just this kind of understanding. Inasmuch as these abilities are essential to the professional historian, it might be argued that all academic teaching of history concerns itself with the training of professional historians; and I myself believe that in approaching the student one should indeed treat him as a potential scholar of one's own kind. Of course, few of them will in fact choose that career, but that is not the point. The point is, firstly, that the professional scholar teaching others will do best if he stays within his professional competence; he may by all means try to enlighten his pupils about humanity at large, but he will be really successful only if he employs the techniques of his own craft in the elucidation of the subject matter of his teaching. Secondly, it need not be doubted that the special intellectual qualities developed in the scholar and for the potential scholar have a much wider usefulness: no man is the worse for having acquired an ability to analyse problems and to grasp larger wholes imaginatively. Where he applies this ability is of no importance; what does matter is that he should have it, that it rather than the acquiring of a body of knowledge is the proper end of education, and that the study of history is exceptionally well qualified to teach it.

A teaching syllabus must, therefore, be so constructed as to give an opportunity to develop these qualities of the mind. Since all history, properly deployed, can do this, it matters in essence very little what particular sections of it are taught. A course of study should concern itself less with the question whether this or that bit of historical knowledge will be 'useful' to the student than with the more difficult problem of finding topics which, on the one hand, teach the analysis of problems and, on the other, encourage imaginative vision, provoke comparisons, and range through time.

In practice, this means selecting two types of subject. There should be both the particular and the general, the narrow and the wide. Both kinds have their obvious dangers. The particular and narrow can lead to pedantry and immersion in the minute; the wide and general can result in the parroting of superficial, second-hand opinions. Teaching both kinds side by side is probably the best insurance against the dangers inherent in either. All undergraduate courses therefore need to include the study of some large area over a considerable stretch of time, as for instance European history from the first days of the Renaissance to the Enlightenment, or the history of the United States (still short enough to resist subdivision for this purpose). But though the subject may be large, it should still have a coherence of its own; any old lump carved from the body of history will not do. Since the purpose is to train a man in the taking of comprehensive views and the understanding of massive interactions, the subject of his study needs to convey a sense of meaning and singularity. Thus those familiar topics, medieval and modern European history, dividing conventionally round about 1450, are ill-designed for the task, whereas the student who is asked to study the manner in which European intellectual development, reflected in politics and economics as well, took up the influence of Renaissance thought and practice and worked it out until the temporary eighteenth-century synthesis emerged, is faced with a specific defined problem which happens to be large in extent and implications, and instructive in the way in which it compels the student to follow lines in all directions while holding a meaningful interpretation in the mind. A large and general subject should not be diffuse; rigour of a kind, provided by the fact of coherence, must still be sought.

Admittedly, some good judges hold that, since history is a whole which, for purely practical purposes, has unfortunately to be cut up, the knife should be inserted at some totally meaningless point, some date of no significance. In this way, so runs the argument, the student is saved both from the prearranged meaning given to an historical problem by his teacher and from the false supposition that terminal dates are fundamental realities. If the dates of his subject manifestly begin and end nothing, he will the more readily remember that the problem he studies reaches back and continues further than he has time to take it, so that he will get a more positive grasp of the continuous flow of history through time. Also, he will be able to see things in a fresh light, whereas meaningful terminal dates themselves condition the answer to be discovered. There is a good deal in this argument, and my only reason for preferring the possibly more old-fashioned construction of a teaching subject coherent in itself is that in practice it is likely to work better. To the trained historian, the moving, or removal, of conventional landmarks is one of the most fruitful exercises in the rethinking of historical problems, but here we are concerned with the beginning student who has to be taught to think historically at all. He, it seems to me, needs a framework, an interpretative scheme, of manifest meaning, however much he may ultimately come to progress by rejecting that framework and that interpretation. After all, the teaching and learning of history consist in great part of such iterated breaking-up, but before a thing can be broken up it has first of all to exist.

One of the best 'large' subjects for undergraduate study is the history of political thought. Politics—the problem of political organization and action—must always constitute a large part of any undergraduate history course; to attempt a study of other ways in which society expresses itself, as for instance through art or agriculture, without some understanding of political events and conditions is to encourage only woolliness and pretence. But to go on from what happens in political life to what, over the long ages, great minds have thought and said about it, is to most students a highly illuminating experience. They learn to think on a new plain of abstraction; since they deal with people who often read each other they get a feeling for continuity and interaction; and at the same time they learn to distinguish the permanent from the occasional, the universal from the particular. Probably all well-constructed intellectual history can serve this purpose : one might choose the history of science or of economic thought or of religion. The advantages of political thought are purely practical : it has long been studied and many good books on it exist; it has been exceptionally continuous; it bears directly on a main part of the student's 'hard' history; and it deals with problems which require little specialized or technical knowledge. I should always make it a main subject in any syllabus, especially if it were accompanied by other 'large' subjects more specifically directed to an understanding of what happened rather than what people thought.

The other kind of subject—that which teaches analytical reasoning—must even more obviously have its own coherence. Since, by definition, it will have to be much more restricted in time and space, there is no problem here. The kind of topic to be looked for is one in which at least some primary evidence is available to the undergraduate, and which casts up precise and narrow questions for him to consider. As against the 'large' subject, which preferably should compel a man to consider every aspect of a given age and society, the 'narrow' subject should be 'tunnel history'—should specifically concern itself with, say, the constitutional or economic or military history of one country over a relatively short stretch of time, perhaps a century or two. I prefer constitutional or economic history to such other possibilities as general political history or the history of ideas for three main reasons: because they throw up the more clearly defined problems, because as a rule they contain more solved problems a study of which will show the student how such reasoning is done, and because they involve him in learning some technicalities (the structure of law courts, the power of the executive, price mechanism or the labour market) which force him to think with precision. Of course, I am here concerned entirely with the student who is taught, with a man who must essentially take all his information at second hand. Unlike the student who pursues research of his own, he will find the solved questions much more instructive than the unsolved ones, provided it is understood that in history 'solved' is a relative term: the student should always be kept aware of the dark patches and the debates. In addition, it is necessary that the good teacher should combine the pedagogue's necessary dogmatism with the fellow-scholar's free exchange of ideas, even when dealing with undergraduates.

One kind of subject, growingly popular, seems to me unfortunate. There is an increasing interest in historiography, the study of historians, and there is no doubt that it can be a fascinating study, especially when it is treated properly as a form of the history of ideas. But when, as too often, it becomes only a confrontation of conflicting views, it is not a good way to teach history because it directs the attention away from what happened to what was later said about it. Students are only too ready to absorb and present 'rival views' of a problem rather than come to grips with the problem itself, for the discussion is ready made and easily creates a spurious impression of learned depth. This fashion for discussing historians rather than history helps to destroy any sense, tenuous enough at the best of times in most undergraduates, that what they are reading about actually once happened, actually is life. A special historiographical topic is as legitimate as the study of any form of human thought, but it is also exceptionally difficult, insufficiently explored, and liable to be a little precious. Good historians are not primarily men of ideas, and to make them shoulder the burden of carrying the thought of an age is to overload them; if treated with a sense of proportion, they cannot, in honesty, appear so important or exciting as more theoretical thinkers. Anyhow, the infiltration of historiographical methods into the study of straight historical problems should be kept to a minimum: it leads to a misunderstanding of what history is about and to a false sense of profundity in the student. All those booklets and pamphlets which treat historical problems by collecting extracts from historians writing about them give off a clear light only when a match is put to them.

Subjects of both the types distinguished—wide and narrow—are plentiful, nor, from the point of view of intellectual analysis, does it matter which are selected. In practice, however, it does matter, if only because some choice has to be made. There are certain considerations which can assist in the choice, apart from that most commonly applied, which is established usage. Why should one not simply continue to teach those parts of history traditionally taught in a given university system, provided they offer a sufficient range of both types, since one satisfactory subject is as good as another? Why not, indeed—except for two things. In the first place, fashions change as well as interests, and established subjects can become bores to teachers and taught alike. Since there is no virtue whatever in boredom—only an ass justifies any form of study on the grounds that it is a distasteful discipline and therefore good for the soul— historical subjects can lose their usefulness and should be removed before they rot. Secondly, historians themselves change their approach to old problems often enough to necessitate a change also in the teaching of them, although as a rule such changes can be made without altering the ostensible description. While, for instance, English constitutional history was for long taught as a series of legal issues and problems (an approach which often provided an excellent training in rigorous analysis) it is nowadays regarded much more as one form of 'social' history in which the particular problems of government are related to social structure, personal relationships, and the distribution of wealth. There is here a very real gain in insight and depth, nor need this necessarily be accompanied by the loss of rigour which in practice has often resulted. But the alert teacher, himself a working historian, should be able to re-define the contents of his subject without having to devise a new label, provided the subject is still alive. And nearly all historical subjects are in fact immortal, metamorphosing internally, sometimes out of recognition, while wearing the same suit of clothes to the casual eye.

Still, the search for proper subjects to teach is an unending one, and at the present time, when historians' own interests have everywhere expanded to take in more parts of the world and additional regions of human activity, the pressure to bring in the new just because of its novelty is great. It is a double pressure, for the desires of the teachers in command of novel subjects are matched by the desires of lively young minds to find new things to think about. Neither pressure is always legitimate; we have all met the determined builders of empire and the addicts to frivolous mutability. Yet at heart the arguments are serious and proper: historical studies must renovate themselves not only by filling old bottles with new wine but on occasion also by buying in some new bottles, sometimes unhappily filled with some rather ancient and vinegary stuff. It is therefore to be hoped that in constructing courses of study academic teachers will observe some general rules. If in their search for specific subjects that satisfy the need for narrow and large topics they keep in mind something like absolute criteria, they may hope to avoid the disaster which strikes a school of history when things are thrust in all anyhow, just because someone wants them and has a loud enough voice.[4]

The criteria I wish to put forward may not look

---

[4] Of course, in some universities, especially smaller ones, what is to be taught must depend on the skills of the limited teaching staff available. But in an era of expansion this is a diminishing problem; and in any case, teachers' interests can be directed by the teaching syllabus.

very impressive, but they seem to me exhaustive. They are two pairs of opposites. There are advantages in the familiar and the unfamiliar, and there are advantages in coherence and in variety. If the student is really to learn how to handle evidence, weigh up conflicting views, and analyse problems, it seems unwise to train him on subject matter with which he has no previous acquaintance. Furthermore, all historical understanding involves some grasp of the conventional attitudes and behaviour of another age and, possibly, place. The student has to become aware of how the people he reads about commonly thought and acted, in a manner so obvious to themselves that they rarely made it explicit but far from obvious to other ages and societies. This is a very difficult thing to do, and more difficult in the face of unfamiliar pieces of history. On the other hand, a familiar piece—for instance, a period already studied in some depth at school—will start the undergraduate off a little way ahead of the baseline, so that he will have more time available to learn the practices and benefits of serious study. However, familiar subjects may unquestionably become very tedious. This is particularly true in the English educational system which ensures, through premature specialization, that people anticipate university work in their last two years at school. If on arriving at the university they find themselves faced once more with a topic which they believe themselves to have studied already, they are likely to become frustrated and resentful. There are ways of overcoming this (of which the best one, naturally, is really first-class and exciting teaching) nor is it invariably the case that a student does not want to go more deeply into something that he has already become quite well acquainted with, but no one will deny that the introduction of a new and unfamiliar subject can have the most stimulating effect, provided it is treated in an intellectually respectable fashion.

The rival advantages of coherence and variety are equally difficult to balance. By coherence I mean a scheme in which the various subjects bear upon one another. For instance, the student of ancient political thought might also be required to work on the general history of Greece and Rome; the study of Australian history might be accompanied by work on both the history of British expansion and the problems of the Pacific; the history of England would be read together with the history of Western Europe. A special and specially useful form of coherence is provided by continuity. Since one of the services of history to the human mind consists in enlarging the imagination and understanding through time, in giving a sense of things happening in a rational and interlocking sequence, there is much virtue in a fairly intensive study of one area through long periods. If the study is to be intensive this means not a single large outline but a series of topics taking over from one another : the study of the whole of English history, for instance, might be demanded, divided into three or four manageable sections. On the other hand, such concentration on one region or nation can prove stultifying : it can limit the vision quite unduly and can lead to intellectual lethargy in the student. Therefore the course should include variety, that is subjects not manifestly connected with each other, so as to restimulate interest at intervals, to provide new openings for the mind, and to apply the spur of unexpected comparisons and contrasts. Thus a historical syllabus which includes only political topics, or only topics related to England and Europe, is seriously deficient; one need not fall for the present fashion which seeks salvation from the urban congestion of Britain in the steppes and pampas to believe that no course is well designed unless it provides for the teaching of diverse and unfamiliar bits of history.

The problems posed by these pairs of opposites, all desirable, cannot, in the conditions of a three- or four-year course, be resolved without compromise. In choosing subjects to teach, the teacher will be wise to avoid the visionary and to remember the capacities of the student. I suggest that a good course will provide familiar and coherent topics in order to teach analysis and rigour, while it will seek to train the historical imagination by means of unfamiliar and various subjects. Of course, this does not mean that the former section needs to be devoid of imagination or the latter of rigour. It does mean that the overriding necessity of training the student in both these mental aptitudes will be served most successfully by assigning the chief part in one task to the familiar and coherent subject where concentration in depth becomes possible, and in the other task to a ranging series of less obvious options. The kind of course here advocated would, in fact, consist of a compulsory backbone with a free choice among additional members. The backbone should be composed of a familiar subject studied in depth and designed to train the intellect by means of the study of primary sources, historical controversies, and specific problems. In practice, I suppose, this is likely to mean that a student would have to work on the history of his own country, and despite a good deal of opposition to this principle I cannot see what may be wrong with it. True, excessive insularity and chauvinistic prejudice can lie in wait there, and in the illiberal or aggressive countries of the world such dangers are real. I should probably hesitate to recommend my scheme in Russia or Indonesia, countries where the historian ought to do his best to redress the patriotic balance. But in Britain, the older Commonwealth countries, and up to a point the United States, where most historians (like most intellectuals) are only too likely to regard their own country's history with feelings that range from critical scepticism to blatant cynicism, the danger of producing yet another generation of chauvinists seems pretty remote. On the other hand, when it comes to the training of the reasoning faculty, the advantages provided by a longish period with the main outlines of which the student is familiar, and by the fact that he knows the country and language in question, are so overwhelming that I find the frequent attacks on English history in English schools of history hard to understand; or rather, I should find them hard to understand if I thought that the attackers were pursuing intellectual ends rather than political and social—were concerned to train reasoning intelligences rather than produce supposedly desirable beings—worthy citizens of the world, admirers of the United Nations, or even Friends of the Soviet Union.

The other parts of the scheme will have to take account of what can be taught; new subjects, however striking, must prove that they rely on a sufficient range of serious scholarly work, that neither their problems nor the treatment of them need be trivial, and that the reason for teaching them lies in their ability to stimulate the imaginative and coordinating powers of the trained intelligence. Here some liberty of choice should be given to the student, though experience proves an excessive number of options to be more of a burden than a joy. Advice on this is pointless; circumstances and available talent determine what can be done. For myself I should always like to offer something to the man who wishes to opt for coherence rather than variety, as well as to the other kind of student; I see little advantage in compelling a student to collect a number of detached topics if he does not wish to do so, but also no justification for pushing everybody into the single straitjacket of a narrowly conceived course. The student whose backbone subject is English history can have his imagination trained very well by crossing the Channel; he need not cross the oceans, though I should hope that he would wish to do so, and I would naturally give him the opportunity. The boundaries that he should really be encouraged to cross are of another kind : if his intense study concentrates on the political, economic or social problems of society, he should be guided in his choice of options to range into fields of intellectual history as well.

One thing, however, needs stressing once more. The undergraduate reading history should be taught history, not the medley called inter-disciplinary studies which is increasingly fashionable in reformist circles. Since it is the intention to train his mind, there have to be a specific content and a hard outline to what he is doing. Bits of history mingled with bits of philosophy and literature, taught by different specialists with quite dissimilar intellectual concerns, may seem a good way to provide what is known as a broad education; but in terms of a genuine university experience, it is in fact a bad way. The university must train the mind, not fill the untrained mind with multi-coloured information and undigested ideas, and only the proper study of an identifiable discipline according to the rules and practices of that discipline can accomplish that fundamental purpose. Certainly, teachers of history should concern themselves with their charges' broader education; they should want them to know some poetry and art, have some idea about philosophic or theological concepts, understand a bit of the teaching of economists, lawyers

and natural scientists. However, this is nothing to do with
the framing of courses for study and examination,
with the real work of intellectual training. There is no
greater heresy in the teacher than the familiar conviction
that students will learn nothing in which they are not
examined. Should our thinking really be determined by
the student who will never read a poem unless he
has to sit a paper in English literature, or even by the
eminent scholar (*absit nomen*) who has told us that
it took the battle of Stalingrad to open his eyes to the
existence of a world and a history beyond the confines
of medieval Germany? The historian should regard his
subject as capable of training and equipping reasoning
intelligences and should use it for that purpose; his
concern for the wider interests of a civilized mind he
should express in the manner and method of his teaching.

2 Undergraduate Teaching: How?

Teachers and students—especially teachers—differ so
widely that it may be quite pointless to offer any personal
views on methods of teaching. On this topic, instruction
of any kind, however well meant or well disguised,
would certainly be resented. If I nevertheless go on to
consider these matters, it is because I am convinced that
whatever may be done must be controlled by thinking
in principle, because I believe that I can offer certain
considerations which amount to a principled set of conditions, and because it may be useful to describe from experience how these considerations work out in practice.

In the first place, if history is a subject (as has been
argued) in which to teach cannot mean merely to
convey information or instruct in techniques but must
mean to assist in the formation of a given type of trained

mind, it follows that in a sense it cannot be taught at all but only learned. At least—and this is the more accurate as well as less absurd way of putting it—the process of teaching must be quite exceptionally two-way, must involve a most active participation from both workers in the operation. Subjects like law and engineering, the sciences and classics, in which a great deal of factual knowledge and acquired expertise must be transferred to the new practitioner, can and should teach a lot by straightforward instruction. History has just enough of such matters in it—for no one can work on it without some factual knowledge and some mental techniques, such as summarizing and paraphrasing texts or computing and analysing figures—to maintain a solid core of instruction in its teaching, but if there were nothing else it would not even begin to be the teaching subject 'history' that we know. Its main purpose requires something different: a dialogue, sometimes a dispute, in which the superior knowledge and equipment of the teacher calls forth the student's active creation of his own knowledge and equipment.

Before teaching methods are considered, one point needs to be made. It is fundamental to a successful course of study in history that the student should read widely, thoroughly and purposefully for himself. Any teacher who confines his task to what in the jargon of the educational civil service is called 'student-confrontation hours' deserves to have his labours classified in that kind of language. More important: any student who thinks that his time divides between the hours of work when he sits in class and the remainder when he does not—the 'on-parade, off-parade' attitude which is becoming distressingly familiar—had better be rapidly disabused of such nonsense. All this may seem too obvious to need mention, but is it? Administrators refuse to recognize that the teacher is not necessarily dissociated from teaching when he meets students casually, when he reads to keep up with the work of his colleagues, or when he pursues his share in the discovery and display of new knowledge and interpretations. And bitter experience shows that undergraduates increasingly conceive their task in terms of attendance at somebody's formal instruction. Both teaching and learning are full-time, day-long activities, a fact which justifies the rather long breaks in immediate contact conventionally called vacations which in fact are commonly filled with a continuation of the teaching scholar's activities, slightly transformed by the temporary absence of instruction in the limited sense. The student, too, needs to think of vacations as times for a change in his work rather than a cessation from it. These may be counsels of tediously traditional perfection, and university systems with long terms and short vacations no doubt have to find other ways of adjusting the relationship between periods of direct contact and periods of separation, for instance by calling professors into the presence of students only two or three days each week.[5] Nowadays students must also find time to earn the money which, sometimes, is used to see them through college. Yet though practice will always fall short of the ideal, I remain convinced that it would be very wrong to replace the old ideal by a new and more realistic one. At least we must never cease to work towards a situation in which the active labours of teaching and study fill the year and every day of it.[6] And for the student this means

[5] I prefer the system under which I work: very heavy direct teaching duties in short terms, followed by comparatively long periods during which the concentration can shift to reading, research and writing. Or it could if the world were properly organized.

[6] When I was first a research student, my supervisor said to me,

much reading designed by himself and carried out on his own, an activity which results only indirectly from the specific teaching work done by the instructor, but which distinguishes the true student from the counterfeit.

However, we must turn to the ways in which the instructor specifically teaches. I am aware of the many discussions concerning so-called teaching aids and so-called new methods, sometimes involving teaching machines, closed-circuit television, or 'practicals' like undergraduate research projects. In the main, however, these are only variations on traditional methods, intended to adjust the situation to new mass audiences. In the study of history, the printed book remains the best 'teaching aid', and nothing can replace a trained ability to read. Similarly, it may be enterprising to present one expert to more people by means of television, but he is still giving a lecture, though he will be hampered in effect by his lack of physical contact with the class. When all is said, methods of teaching remain traditional, and there are basically three of them; since all three are in use in my university (Cambridge) I have had some experience of them all. They are firstly the lecture in which one teacher addresses a variable group of students, sometimes (but outside the United States very rarely) replying to questions and interjections; secondly the class or seminar, a gathering, preferably round a table, of a group with a presiding teacher in which individual students present views or even papers for guided discussion by the group; and thirdly the meeting of one or at most two students with an instructor in which written work by the student is discussed and criticized (super-

---

quite seriously, at the end of the first term: 'Now don't work every day of the vacations; do take Christmas Day off.' I fear that I took Boxing Day off as well.

vision, tutorial). It is my belief that a good history school will make full use of all three methods because they complement one another; each does something that the others cannot do.

The lecture, possibly, needs defending to-day; some newly founded institutions are trying to do without it. Certainly, as a teaching method it has its dubious side. However, in some places the ancient reliance on teaching by lectures only still prevails, though everywhere in England, at least, teachers are trying to introduce the other methods in which discussion rather than instruction predominates. Oxford cherishes an old-established prejudice against lectures, not unjustified, if reports are true, by the standard of lecturing encountered. On the principle already stated that the teaching of history should rest on a two-way traffic of debate, the replacement of lectures by group or individual supervision must be welcomed. Nevertheless, it seems to me too early to abandon lecturing as a method of teaching, but a great deal depends on the place assigned to the use of lectures. The invention of printing put a term to the lecture's necessary predominance in teaching and at least called for a reassessment of its purposes, though too many university people—students as well as teachers—seem to be unaware of this. The lecturer has no business to attempt that which the book can do better. Thus it is wrong to use the lecture in order to convey information either on facts or arguments which is available in print. The lecture should not 'cover the syllabus', that is to say, supply the student with what he needs to pass examinations. It cannot afford to be dull, inaudible, incomprehensible; it must not yield a set of student's notes reading like the abstract of a textbook.

What, then, can it do? The chief purposes for which it remains uniquely useful are two. In the first place, it

can communicate new knowledge not yet found in
the books, a function of no little importance but
in history not likely to be called frequently into use.
More important, it can and must provide the stimulus
of a live contact with another intelligence wrestling
with the problems of history. This means that the
lecturer *must* endeavour to be new, even original, even
wild, at all costs. It is his task to bring to the student,
especially the not uncommon student reared on books
that suggest a kind of complete and finished quality in
historical knowledge, a real sense of the fluidity inherent
in enquiry, debate, disagreement. Reading books, even
reading many books, is always liable to leave the beginner with the impression that history can be learned by
absorbing other people's words : the lecturer must shock
him out of that state. Of course, he should be lively
and vigorous and deeply concerned; why should any
listener be interested in what appears to bore the lecturer
himself? But this liveliness is by no means to be confined
to manner; I am not advocating a mere theatrical
playing to the gallery or that search for popularity by
such means as blue jokes, contrived paradox, rhetorical
device which one sometimes encounters. The life of
a lecture should come from its contents, and it comes
from them if the student is confronted with new ideas,
new interpretations, new associations, new comparisons,
if the surprise stems from the unexpectedness of the
intellectual attack, not from the decorative dressing.
Wit, humour, savagery, even obscenity can all be justified
at times, but none for their own sakes; they are only
the means to wrest the student out of stupor, uncork
his ears, and alert him to the real message, which is
that history is never done, and all he has learned
needs to be called in doubt, that he himself is a member
of a band jointly engaged in trying to disentangle the

truth about the past. The lecturer should disseminate a sense of a scholar at work, and he should occasionally demonstrate how that work is done : few things enthral an undergraduate audience more than an exposition of the technicalities of research, provided the dosage is not too large. In general it is less important for a lecturer to be 'right' than to be alive—alive as a working scholar—for it is his function to cast doubt upon the possibility that in historical studies anyone will ever be finally 'right'. The necessary redressing of the scepticism so engendered can be left to the other occasions of teaching; let the lecturer stick to the task of destroying overfamiliar landmarks and boundaries, of building new structures to be tested by the student, of removing the school-produced, book-confirmed shell of acquisitive learning which can guard the critical faculty like a carapace.

Therefore the best lecture courses are quite brief, perhaps some twelve to fifteen lectures long. The matter to be handled does not affect the issue; if a lecturer is required to cover really long periods of history in detail, he is being asked to do the wrong thing, to take the place of books, but he can and should contribute also to the study of large and long subjects. Thus suppose a university offers a course on Europe since the Renaissance, a common enough thing. To ask any lecturer, or even several in sequence, to utter comprehensively on this sprawling monstrosity of a subject from the rostrum is quite absurd, which does not at all mean that the course itself is absurd. Some forty or more lectures on such a subject, going steadily through the years and countries, can serve no purpose except to supplant the printed book. On the other hand, three or four sets of ten lectures each, taking a section or a topic, tearing it apart and building it up again, organized around a theme and determined to shake if not to shock, can restore meaning and excitement to what at first may well appear to be a worn-out subject. Lectures should be arranged either to do this for the large and familiar subjects, or else they should be used to treat of some (unpublished) specialist matter; in either case, quite short runs will do much better than weeks on end plodding through time.

There is no need to discuss the technical skills required. No two people lecture alike : at least, none should, for in a lecture a man must stand forth, must impose and display himself. He will naturally avoid the obvious faults : he will not read a script, mumble to himself, address a blackboard or some high corner in the far end of the room, walk about too much. He must establish contact with the audience, which means that he must physically and visibly address them, be constantly aware of them (for instance, catch their yawns), and be careful of the tedium promoted by too even and unmodulated a delivery. For the rest, whether he speaks fast or slowly, uses notes or none, constructs a work of art or runs off at the mouth, it will be up to him to choose what suits him best. Provided he keeps before him the duty of doing what the printed page cannot do, he will do well.

It may be argued that this task of disturbing set notions and stimulating the student's interest is better performed by methods which rely on discussion rather than discourse. Though, of course, all teaching of history will seek to some extent to call forth new thinking, the lecture has advantages of its own. For one thing it is economical. The lecturer can get at scores or hundreds of students at a time, and since the sort of lecture here described must be given by experts still at work in the labour of discovering historical truth, much is gained by enabling all students to hear them. For another, a lecturer can take risks not open to the man conducting a discussion group. He need not feel obliged to stand by every word he says, he can be rash, he can be flippant, he can be passionately serious, all attitudes which sound quite false in the intimacy of a seminar but often work efficiently from the platform. Above all, some people just are good at lecturing and not so good at handling a discussion. Of course, if the lecturer is good at answering impromptu questions he can add this to his technique, though if he does he must always remember one golden rule : be as sharp as you like about books and scholars and even history, but never show the faintest trace of contempt for or impatience with your audience.[7] The question may be stupid : it must still be treated with total seriousness. Of course, if it is malicious the case is altered. The student who refuses to accept that the process before him is a joint enterprise deserves the hard answer.

The other methods of teaching history are generally accepted as good and need no defence. On the other hand, it may be useful to distinguish between them, for the seminar and tutorial differ in more than size. The class or seminar should provide a genuine discussion among the students themselves, neither a lecture from the chair nor a dialogue between the teacher and one undergraduate. Everybody must be involved, though to achieve this is one of the most difficult tasks for the teacher who has to combine some of the qualities required in the conductor of an orchestra, Speaker of the House of Commons, and lion-tamer. Although it will be necessary to assign specific tasks to individuals—to appoint probably two 'reporters' on an assigned theme—

---

[7] This applies to all teaching. Sarcasm is out.

the rest of the class must on all accounts be prevented
from just listening or possibly going to sleep, or doing
a crossword puzzle. This means that, as a rule, the
topics to be discussed cannot be too particular and
narrow, or at least that they must be of the kind that
is central to the whole historical subject being studied by
the class. Thus everybody will feel stirred to come in.
Ideally, an undergraduate class should have some of the
feeling of the graduate seminar, which is to say that
the participants should have a sense of sharing in the
discovery of historical truth. In practice this makes
for some difficulties well worth watching out for. It is
quite unlikely that an undergraduate class will in fact
be operating on the frontiers of knowledge, nor is it
particularly desirable that they should. As the teacher
will probably be taking the same sort of class year by year
he will become excessively familiar with all the possibilities contained in the material and the limits set by
undergraduates' knowledge and experience. The tempta-
tion to replace discussion and search by instruction
and information increases every year. On the other
hand, the students are necessarily aware that their class
debates things often debated before; given half a chance,
many of them will seek the short-cut of receiving a
lecture. Keeping a class at its proper level of multiple
discussion tests the teacher severely, but the rewards
are worth the labour. No other method so readily
produces a development of ideas, a working out of
problems, and a genuine interaction among several
minds. A good class probably gives the student the
clearest idea of what the study of history is about.

Lastly, the individual supervision or tutorial, or if not
individual then at least never larger than two students
with one teacher. This is the special pride of the old
universities of England, and it certainly can be a most

effective way of teaching. Of course, it is immensely
uneconomical; a teacher charged with ten students will
have to go over the same ground five or ten times.
When the student is silent, very slow, or idle the tutorial
can be sheer pointless agony; and if the teacher becomes
bored or indifferent—a danger greater in this method
than any other—the purpose of the whole operation
collapses. This can happen especially if the teacher does
too much of this kind of work; the normal maximum of
twelve hours a week permitted at Cambridge is probably already too high, and the horror stories coming
from Oxford, where, one hears, tutors are likely to be
doing twenty hours or more, testify to an imbalance
in the teaching system.[8] But the good supervision deserves
the praise given to it. Its essence consists in the analysis
and consideration of a specific circumscribed topic in
a dialogue between teacher and pupil. No doubt the
customary essay, written by the pupil on a subject
given to him (with a reading list) by the teacher, forms
the best foundation for this. It compels the student
not only to study a problem but to understand it and
formulate his own answer; it enables the teacher to
guide the student's mind into proper attitudes of analytical rigour, comprehension in depth, and adequate expression. In other words, he teaches him to think and
react like an historian, and (hopefully) to write like a
good historian. By its intimacy and intensity the super-

[8] There is also the question of how many supervisions a student
should have; at Cambridge, some scientists undergo up to four
a week. Such practices are bound to turn the supervision hour into a
period of mere instruction, concerned perhaps with the solving
of set problems with finite answers, a method which may be suitable
in some subjects and is widely practised in the teaching of law,
too. In history it is out of place, and one supervision a week is
probably right, even if this means that many issues are left
undiscussed.

vision creates, at its best, a genuine scholarly link between the partners in the enterprise, but even when it falls short of that (as commonly it does) it is bound to elevate the student above the role of mere receptacle. Since he has had to do real productive work, the vital element of his active share is secured.

Trouble arises if the supervision is used to do the work properly performed by one of the other methods. One hears of tutors who employ their time to replace lectures or even to 'cover the ground', that is to replace private reading. Any useful discussion of the student's essay will naturally range beyond its particular problem, though this must be clarified first, but that is not the same thing as giving general instruction. More insidiously, quite a few people seem to think that the class can take the place of supervisions and should do so. They argue that the class is less wasteful of man-hours, and that a class held by an expert will profit the student more than supervisions by a man who of necessity cannot be expert in everything he has to teach. But cogent as such arguments are, they overlook a difference in functions and potential. I do not think that the supervision can do the work of the class in starting genuine debates and cooperative enquiry; but neither can the class give that sense of sitting together with a trained mind and actively interested teacher, concerned (for the moment) only with oneself. It is also possible to get away with things in a class—with imprecise thinking, slipshod expression, bad writing, and an unconscious lack of understanding—which the direct and relentless questioning of the supervision exposes and corrects. Quite possibly, among the three methods described the tutorial may be thought the 'best', but I see no virtue in such hierarchies. By itself the tutorial is no more sufficient or satisfactory than any other method. Each contributes its own special gifts to the tasks of teaching and study; each can be used well or badly; between them they are capable of training minds to a clear understanding of problems, a right use of reason, a passion for intellectual exercise, and an ability to frame answers in convincing ways.

I do not propose to touch on the question of examinations. Methods differ widely, from the constant grading common at most American institutions, to the once-for-all ordeal, after three years' work, of the University of London. I like none of them particularly well, but I recognize the necessity for something of the kind. At any rate, the three methods of teaching history here described will work within any arrangement of syllabus or examination. The student who has passed actively through a course using all of them in competent hands, and who in addition has found his way to the library, will know at the end why he came to university to read history.

3 The Graduate Student

The graduate student needs teaching very different from that given to the undergraduate; it would be a serious mistake to suppose—though a mistake which I think is quite often made—that he is merely a somewhat enlarged version of his earlier identity. Should he, indeed, be taught at all, in the sense that the undergraduate unquestionably is?

It must be said that this question can probably be asked only in England, the only country known to me where a happy, gentlemanly, even dilettante attitude can still be found here and there in the universities, where B.A.s sometimes think that they have learned all they need to know, and where research students are still too frequently left to their own devices. One still meets dons who hold that a man who cannot make the grade (that is, obtain the Ph.D. degree) on his own is not cut out for a scholar's career. On the other hand, I once met a student who in a discussion of training courses declared that the research student's inviolate soul rejected all such things as interference—though admittedly he was a New Zealander.[9] At the other end of the scale we find the American graduate school, with its schematized demands of general study and 'comprehensive' examinations in varied subjects, a system in which the dissertation, so vital in England, almost takes second place. I will say at once that I take my stand somewhere between these extremes, believing that graduate students are indeed students and therefore should be taught, but that their work should be very definitely, even excessively, concentrated upon the specialist study they have undertaken. If these issues are to be raised above the level of personal taste, it becomes again necessary to ask precisely what purpose those years spent in graduate study are meant to serve.

While one does well, as I have said, to treat the undergraduate as though he were a future scholar even though only a very few ever will be, the graduate student has no end in mind except to equip himself for a career of scholarship. His life is that of an apprentice learning a craft, and his dissertation represents proof of his claim to have learned that craft, to have become fit for membership of a profession.[10] And the profession is that

[9] He is now an eminent professor, and I wonder if he has changed his opinion. It has to be conceded that he made himself into a very fine scholar, without courses of instruction and with not too much assistance.

[10] There is therefore much to be said for what is usually a gibe: the Ph.D. *is* a union card because it proves the owner to have been fully trained. Or rather, that is what it ought to prove.

of the working scholar rather than of the teacher; despite some rather desperate attempts here and there, no one has yet succeeded in training academic historians as teachers, and that accomplishment is left to be acquired by natural aptitude, imitation of exemplars, and experience. I am not myself persuaded that this is a bad thing, or that formal teacher-training courses would be profitable. But the craftsmanship of historical scholarship can be tested, and therefore it can and should be taught. The young man who has obtained his doctorate has proved only one thing : that he has the basic equipment to pursue a life of scholarship. He may claim credence for his work because he has convinced experienced elders that he has absorbed the canons of rational research and controlled judgment. Whether he is an historian, or what sort of an historian he may be, he will, one hopes, go on to show thereafter. His dissertation is not, or should not be, the same thing as the books he will presumably go on to write, any more than the tool-chest made by the apprentice carpenter for his masterpiece represents the norm of his later production.[11]

The teaching of research students must therefore concentrate on the competences which a newly fledged historian is supposed to possess. I suggest that these are : a thorough knowledge of the materials, primary and secondary, available for the study of his chosen area of operations; ability to use these materials, both in the sense of discovering and understanding them, and in the sense of being able to evaluate them critically; ability to formulate meaningful questions and relevant answers; ability to present a sound reconstruction of a

[11] A masterpiece, in defiance of the usual metaphorical usage, originally meant something that lay at the foundation of a man's life's work; it did not crown it.

piece of history, founded with painful accuracy on the evidence; ability to present this reconstruction according to the conventions of historical writing, as for instance in the proper drafting of footnotes and references. I do not believe that at this stage of his career he should be required to prove a wide knowledge of history in general or a superior ability to write on the grand scale. These are skills that come with further learning and experience; a technically competent standard of scholarship is a sufficiently demanding test for the apprentice; and in any case, it is the craftsmanship rather than the art which the young historian must learn first and must prove himself possessed of if he is to be taken seriously as a scholar.

Therefore the form of instruction follows naturally from these ends in view. It is wrong to subject the graduate student to further courses of general history at second hand. Of course, in order to produce a worthy specialist study he needs to have a sufficiently general knowledge of his chosen area, and whether he should be made to study this further depends on the standard of knowledge he has attained with his first degree. This standard differs in different university systems, and I concede that most American or Australian bachelors of arts need to do some more work of the type associated in England with undergraduate studies before they are ready to embark on research.[12] Nothing, however, it seems to me, justifies the imposition of further study outside a man's chosen field. Concentration on the one task in hand, the bane of undergraduate studies, is the

[12] This is not intended as an insult. The English B.A. usually lacks the breadth and variety of knowledge (especially of languages) that distinguish his American and Australian counterparts, but his previous experience happens to have fitted him more completely for the one further purpose of research.

only proper attitude for the research student. If he wants to work in Tudor history, he should have a good working knowledge of England in the sixteenth century; he need not, at this stage, be required to show a knowledge of sixteenth-century France or Renaissance culture; and he must not be troubled with any other more distant bits of ancient, medieval or modern history, as he is in some American graduate schools. His labours are determined by the one consideration that he is training himself in the craftsmanship of history by means of the one successful method known, the practical method of writing an original piece of work.

The teaching for this purpose falls naturally into three stages, more or less consecutive though there may be overlaps. At the introductory stage, the student needs to be equipped with the technical skills required of him. He must be taught to survey the area of his concerns and its material, guided to the bibliographical and archival aids, made to learn any languages likely to be encountered in the work, taught to read the handwriting of his manuscripts (supposing it represents a problem), and led to a proper understanding of their meaning. He is thus given the foundations of scholarship in the abstract, as it were, though of course the solidity of these foundations depends on the manner in which he renders them concrete by his own labours in research. These matters can be taught in classes, by a mixture of lectures and discussion, though this depends on there being enough students with allied interests to arrange group teaching. If there are not, the individual teacher must see to it that his individual student receives this instruction. If the skills required are technical in the narrow sense—for example, medieval palaeography, statistics, economic theory—proper organized courses should be available, and the student should preferably be compelled to attend them—perhaps even face examinations in them. Two or three months of this kind of instruction (the student's first term) should ordinarily suffice, but much time is saved, heartbreak averted, and certainty created if this stage of the training is as systematic and organized as possible.

Having laid such technical foundations and roughly defined his proper subject, the student will now start on the research itself. That is to say, he will begin to study his potential material and attempt to ask useful questions of it. The sooner he gets to this stage the better; months spent in generalized preparation sound all very fine and systematic, but in practice they prove disheartening. It is important that the research student should quickly grasp how very different his existence and concerns are from those of the undergraduate, how more intensive and continuous his labours, how more precise and narrow his interests. I like to send my students to their sources within four weeks of arrival, and the longer one waits the harder it becomes to change the undergraduate into the graduate student. From the moment that he begins to read his sources, the student is in some ways on his own. He can learn his craft only by practising it himself, and, in addition, he is about to become the world's leading expert on some small part of history. However, his being on his own does not mean that he can or should be left to himself. The serious business of teaching the graduate student really begins when the stage of formal or organizable courses is over. The teacher must now devote himself to instilling in his pupil the right methods of research, right standards of criticism, ability to see points and connections—in short to helping him become a working scholar. I know no better way of doing this than the individual supervision. If the teacher has to guide a

sufficiently large number of students he may well organize them in a seminar, but he should still see them
individually to discuss their work, answer their questions, criticize their deductions, argue their views, and
keep abreast of their scholarly development. Such supervision should be regular; the custom sometimes current
in England by which the teacher leaves it to the student
to ask for a meeting when he thinks he needs one is at
this stage unfortunate. How frequent these meetings are
depends on individual men and the kind of work they
are doing; some may need to bring particular problems
of the evidence at frequent intervals, while others may
take weeks of solid work to accumulate enough matter to
make a discussion with their supervisor fruitful. However, for myself I do not like to allow more than three
weeks between supervisions, at least in the first two years
of research (and excepting the summer vacations).

The usefulness of the seminar as an instrument of
graduate teaching depends on the particular meaning
given to this protean concept. In its original form, in
nineteenth-century Germany, the seminar consisted of
a group of students, working under the direction of one
man on a variety of closely allied topics, usually assigned by the professor. Such a seminar takes research
problems shared by the group and discusses them
round a table, in common. It is probably the best kind
of training school ever devised for the scholar, but it
has disadvantages. In particular, it constricts choice
of subjects and interest, can inhibit new lines of enquiry,
and—since the best teachers tend to be the most
formidable personalities—is liable to produce disciples
rather than fellow-scholars. In any case it cannot exist
unless there are at least six or eight men whose subjects
of study touch or overlap. If one is faced with a group of
students working in roughly the same area but not

able to tackle single problems jointly, one may still organize a seminar at which individuals present problems or conclusions arising from their own work for discussion and criticism by the rest, under the teacher's guidance. This is valuable to all concerned, but it is much less like teaching and must not take the place of the individual supervision. I have known seminars which were more like multiple supervision, and I do not think them very useful. Going round the table and asking students briefly to put their questions or state their problems may cut down the labours of supervising, but it is an inefficient and insufficient form of teaching. The German seminar, in its own peculiar circumstances, can cover most of the teaching needed, though even in that system individual confrontation of teacher and student is very desirable. Individual teaching really comes first, to be supplemented by group meetings if they are feasible and so organized as to meet the needs of any given set of people. I do not think that there is an ideal form of seminar; it is a flexible method, adaptable to circumstances, though some forms of it (in which no effective teaching takes place or the teacher is really seeking assistance in his own work) are plainly unsatisfactory.

The third and last stage of the training begins when the student turns to write up his findings. I have known professors who would read no part of a man's dissertation until he had submitted it for examination, on the grounds that the work was to be his, not theirs; and I have known others who regarded the reading and criticizing of written work as practically their sole teaching duty. Both attitudes seem to me rather needlessly extreme. If the student has been thoroughly and properly trained during his researches, it is probable that he will prove competent enough in the use of his material, but the actual task of putting in order a lot of detail and argument is not one that can be learned by instinct. At this point the student needs quite a lot of help in thinking out the scheme of his dissertation, and he should receive every necessary criticism of the product. At the same time, it would be wrong for the teacher to write the dissertation himself, in any sense. Supervisions will probably become fewer at this stage; on the other hand, every time there is a piece of writing in hand it should be gone over thoroughly from the point of view of both content and style. The task of teaching now becomes concrete : the student at last comes to understand fully what may be required of him. But if he was worth admitting in the first place and has since then been properly supervised, he ought to have the ability and equipment which now entitle him to opinions of his own; the teacher must be more careful than before not to impose himself but to act the part of an older colleague whose advice has been asked.

Of course, this description of the various tasks involved in teaching and training graduate students embodies simply a personal experience and a personal attitude. I am very far from claiming universal validity for it, though I admit to thinking it the right way for myself to go about things. It will be seen that I put a lot of weight on teaching, that in my view the supervisor of research students should work very hard. Others may well regard this as too much like direction and even intrusion; some men of experience argue that the teacher should confine himself to guidance and suggestion. But if the practice of history requires aptitudes that can be learned (as well, of course, as aptitudes that are born in the man) then they should surely be taught consciously and with determination. What point is there in leaving such training to chance? Of course, the intensive teaching here advocated has its dangers. One must beware of creating anything like a master-disciple relationship: the student must be kept aware both of his own liberty and of his duty to think and work for himself. It is a good idea to encourage one's students to learn from each other, and an even better one to make them consult other scholars. However much it may please the ego to preside over a 'school' or to dispose of the futures of clever young men, such temptations are really wicked. There is no sadder sight than the young man who knows that all his prospects of a career are bound up with one man's good favour; such things are bad for the character of both teacher and student. The point does not need elaboration; it needs brief mention only because the situation occurs more often than is comfortable to contemplate.

But while this abuse of a teacher's place and duty may lie in wait for the unwary or conceited, it remains true that it must not be avoided by running away from the duty to teach the apprentice historian. Even more than the undergraduate he must be instructed, guided, and trained. In teaching research students, we prepare the next generation of scholars, and this is responsible work, perhaps the most responsible we have, not to be skimped. If we honestly think that the study of history is a proper pursuit for civilized man, that it amounts to a sincere and intense search for the truth, then we must take seriously the task of maintaining this study and this search in future generations. In the end, all depends on what we pass on to others.

Index of Historians

Acton, John Dahlberg Lord, 30, 76f., 137, 161
Ashton, T. S., 164n.
Aydelotte, William O., 51n.

Bacon, Francis, 13
Beale, Howard K., 60n.
Belloc, Hilaire, 134
Berlin, Isaiah, 63n.
Bloch, Marc, 87n., 97, 168
Brady, Robert, 13
Braudel, Fernand, 167f.
Brooke, Christopher, 166
Bruni, Leonardo, 13
Butterfield, H., 13n., 133n.

Carr, E. H., 25ff., 33ff., 56ff., 62ff., 75ff.
Chrimes, S. B., 153n.
Clarendon, Edward Hyde Earl of, 14
Collingwood, R. G., 79
Crump, C. G., 87n.

Danto, Arthur C., 70n.
Davies, Godfrey, 153n.
Deane, Phyllis, 164n.
Douglas, D. C., 13n.
Droysen, J. G., 87n.

Elton, G. R., 53n., 125n., 141n., 146n., 147n., 174
Erikson, Erik H., 39n.

Fisher, H. A. L., 56f.
Fox, L., 13n.
Fussner, F. Smith, 13n.

Galbraith, V. H., 13n., 98, 154n.

Gallie, W. B., 8n.
Gardiner, P., 8n.
Garrett, C. H., 153n.
Gasquet, Francis Cardinal, 134
George, Charles H., 142f.
Geyl, Pieter, 53n.
Gibbon, Edward, 14, 61, 135
Guicciardini, Francesco, 13

Heimpel, H., 52n.
Herodotus, 12, 16, 39
Hexter, J. H., 28, 129n., 162
Hill, Christopher, 40n., 125n., 164n.

Ibn Khaldoun, 13

Johnson, Samuel, 14, 108

Kitson Clark, G., 87n.
Knowles, David, 13n., 99n.

Langlois, C. V., 87n.
Livy, 12

Mabillon, Jean, 13
Macaulay, Thomas Lord, 14, 135
Machiavelli, Niccolò, 13
Maddox, Thomas, 13
Maitland, F. W., 14, 135f.
Makkai, L., 54n.
Mansfield, Harvey C., 133n.
Merriman, Roger B., 99
Mink, Louis O., 42n.
Momigliano, Arnoldo, 16n.
Mommsen, Theodore, 26, 33, 35

Namier, L. B., 14, 132f.
Neale, J. E., 32, 153n.

223

The Secrets of
Grindlewood

Dedication

For Tommy

The Secrets of
Grindlewood

JACKIE BURKE

LINDON BOOKS

First published in 2013 by
Lindon Books
www.grindlewood.com

Paperback ISBN: 978 1 909483 125
eBook – mobi format ISBN: 978 1 909483 132
eBook – ePub format ISBN: 978 1 909483 149

Produced by Kazoo Independent Publishing Services
222 Beech Park, Lucan, Co. Dublin
www.kazoopublishing.com

Kazoo Independent Publishing Services is not the publisher of this work. All rights and responsibilities pertaining to this work remain with Lindon Books.

Kazoo offers independent authors a full range of publishing services.
For further details visit www.kazoopublishing.com

Cover design by Andrew Brown
Cover and internal illustrations © Fintan Taite 2013
Printed in the EU

About the author

Jackie grew up with her sister and three brothers in South Dublin. She has dreamed of becoming a writer since she was a little girl, but other things (like work, sport and baking cakes) kept getting in the way. So she sat down one day and started writing *Grindlewood*, and she hasn't stopped writing since (except for tea and chocolate cake).

Jackie loves thinking up new adventures for the animals of Grindlewood garden, but when she's not doing that you might find her out hill walking in the Irish countryside, reading a good book or trying out a new recipe for chocolate cake. She and her husband live in Bray, County Wicklow, where they share their home with a big fluffy cat called Millie.

Contents

Prologue

THE FINAL FEUD

'I must hurry, I must hurry,' thought the frightened little witch. She tore through the forest, her long black hair blowing behind her, and her purple dress stuck against her body. Wanda was in grave danger. She knew the evil warlock was gaining on her. She could hear him, sneering and snarling, promising to catch her. He would be looking forward to this moment. She could smell him, too. His stench was foul from years of drinking his disgusting potions. Fear was starting to grip her, making her legs go wobbly. She stumbled and fell, trembling all over. She had to reach her house and secure her magical treasures. She got up and ran on.

She was almost there when a dreadful thought went through her mind. 'What if the boy has come to visit today? He is so often in the garden during the summer months. What if he is there when the warlock comes for me?' Despite these worrying thoughts about her young friend, Wanda kept running as hard as she could. She had no choice.

The path through the forest seemed so lonely and long, and soon Wanda's legs began to tire. She was breathing hard and she felt weak. The warlock would catch up with her soon. She had to run faster if she was to stand any chance of escape.

When she reached her little house, she rushed inside and slammed the door behind her, jamming it shut with a wooden beam. 'Will that keep out such a powerful warlock?' she wondered. She looked anxiously out of the crooked little window. Her young friend, Luke, was indeed in the garden, watching the frog hop about the pond. She knew the warlock wouldn't spare the boy if he got in his way.

She hurried to the little hiding place under the floorboards and took out an old wooden box. Her hands were shaking as she lifted it. She closed her eyes briefly and whispered to the little box in her hands. She threw it out the side window of the house, just as the warlock stomped onto her porch. Despite the clever cloaking spell she had used to conceal her little house, the wicked warlock had figured out where Wanda was hiding. He had finally caught up with this plucky, but annoying, little witch. He was glad that he had left her till last, the last of a long list of powerful opponents whom he had destroyed.

Worfeus stood at Wanda's door, his hands on his hips, his head held high. Then he pulled out his wand and waved it about his head. He called out the words of an ancient spell and blasted away the knobbly wooden door.

The tall and wiry warlock had to duck to enter the little house. He marched inside, looking certain of victory. He sneered at Wanda, his deep set eyes glowing red with evil. He fired his wand and blasted away some crockery to scare the witch even more. But he was in for a surprise. Wanda was well prepared and ready to defend herself. The witch stood calmly in the corner. She was calm again and in full control of her fear. She met the warlock's gaze and held it. She would not give in as easily as others had. There would indeed be a duel this time.

'So you want to fight me, then, witch. Well, let's see what you've got. Come on!' the warlock taunted her.

He prepared for the duel, whipping his wand back and forth, staring at her.

'You rotten, wicked warlock, Worfeus! No matter what happens today, you will meet a horrid, nasty end, just as you deserve. Mark my words, and mark my wand!'

Then the duel began. The two enemies fired spell after spell at each other across the little room. Each one flashed like a bolt of lightning as it tried to find its target. The witch and the warlock ducked and dived, trying to avoid being hit by each other's curses and fireballs. The contents of the little house were smashed and thrown about by the force of the spells, sometimes exploding on impact.

Wisps of smoke rose from singed hair and clothing, stinging Wanda's eyes. The warlock's eyes just looked redder and meaner. Strange smells filled the air as Wanda's display of potions popped and exploded one after the other. Wanda shrieked and Worfeus roared as the final feud became fierce. Their wands glowed as they became hotter and hotter with every killing spell they fired. None had hit their target dead on – not just yet.

As Wanda jumped sideways to avoid another spell,

she caught a glimpse of Luke in the garden. She knew he had heard the noise of the duel, because he stood up and looked around. Her heart was thumping loudly, as if it would jump out of her chest. She was very worried about her friend, but she was powerless to help him.

After dodging another few spells and firing a few more of her own, Wanda glanced outside again. She knew by the look on the young lad's face that he couldn't quite make out what was going on, but he was curious. The cloaking spell on the little house was keeping Wanda and the warlock invisible, but the boy could hear their shouts and the crackle and fizz of the spells as they shot from their wands.

As Wanda dived and lurched about her little home, trying her hardest to beat the evil warlock, her thoughts about Luke distracted her. She had to protect him somehow. She was horrified to see him walk slowly towards the house. At the next glance, she saw the boy stop. She was so relieved that she lost concentration for a moment and almost got hit by one of the warlock's shots. She jumped and rolled to one side and hid for a second behind her baskets of logs and ferns.

Worfeus roared at her, stomping around the room to get a better shot. Wanda was watching for the warlock's next move so carefully that her thoughts left Luke, who was now walking more quickly towards the house, following the noise of the duel again. Wanda desperately hoped that he wouldn't come any closer. For although the house was made invisible by the spell, Luke might just be able to see them through the open part of the window. And he did. He stood there, outside, looking at them. He was absolutely horrified.

As Luke stood frozen to the spot, he saw the warlock point his wand directly at Wanda. She was trapped in the corner. Worfeus looked very angry. He clearly didn't like how long this duel was taking.

'How dare you try to defeat me? You should surrender to one as powerful as I – Worfeus, greatest leader of the Worfagon people,' he bellowed.

He screwed up his bony face, concentrating hard on this final shot. He roared a spell and fired his wand, and this time a dark purple blast shot out and struck home. As she spotted Luke approaching the window, Wanda tried to dive out of the way. But she wasn't quite quick enough. She was hit. She screamed and fell to the floor, rolling over in terrible pain. It was clear that it was a fatal blow, but she wasn't going to give up just yet.

The warlock laughed his crazy laugh. He bent over her, watching her wince, waiting for her to die. His eyes flickered with hatred and delight.

'You are dying, dear witch, you are dying. At long, long last, it is over,' he sneered.

'Not yet, Worfeus, not just yet,' she croaked back at him.

'Ha, ha! Not yet, you say. Well, in a few moments you will be gone, and everything you have died trying to protect will be mine. Oh, I will find what I want my dear, I will find it all,' he roared.

The evil warlock was relishing his moment of victory. Wanda knew he was proud of himself and of all his wicked deeds, but it was clear that defeating her gave him the greatest pleasure of all. She had been the last hope of the gentle Wandelei clan, the magical people who had suffered for so long at the hands of the evil Worfagons. Worfeus was the Worfagons' leader and it was said that he was the most wicked warlock to have ever ruled. That much was certainly true, and Wanda knew it. She had learned a lot about this evil warlock – dreadful things, frightening things.

Worfeus was looking very pleased with himself. He believed he was so much cleverer than everyone else, and even more so now that he had defeated Wanda. But the witch guessed correctly that he did not know so very much about her. This was her last advantage, and she had one or two tricks to play on him yet, if she could just hold on a little longer.

Worfeus straightened up, watching her closely and waiting for her last breath. A sickly smile spread over his bony face as he saw her become weaker. Outside, Luke had shaken himself alert. Wanda heard him call to her as she struggled to stay alive. She needed just one more minute. The warlock heard the boy too. He swung around, annoyed at this interruption.

'Well, what have we here?' he snarled, moving to the doorway. He stood tall and menacing, blocking the entrance. Luke had moved towards the door when he heard the warlock's loud footsteps inside the cloaked house. When Worfeus reached the doorway, Luke stood quite still for a moment, staring at him, then at Wanda. He was shocked to see her lying so badly injured on the floor. He stepped back a bit, not really knowing what to do. How could he get past the warlock to help her?

Seeing the smoking wand in the evil warlock's hand, he reached down by his side, grappling for something, anything, that he could use to defend himself. As the warlock leaned forward and took aim, Luke's shaky hand finally gripped the little bugle that was tied to his belt. As a very small boy he used to blow on the bugle if he was in trouble, but before he could blow it this time, he took fright and ran.

'No, no, nooooo!' Wanda shrieked from the floor.

The mortally wounded witch reached out with her burnt and withered arm, and struggled to pick up her wand. In great pain she rolled over to grab it, and with all her might she fired a counter spell. It shot from her wand as the warlock fired a killing curse at the boy. As the purple jet from the warlock's wand zoomed towards its target, Wanda's jet of bright yellow light raced beside it. The two spells crashed and fused together, locking in mid-air. An explosion of coloured light and millions of sparks lit up the surrounding space. Stardust burst from the jets of light, fizzed and then sprinkled all around.

Luke turned his head to look back as he heard the spells shoot towards him. But he couldn't outrun them.

He was blasted off his feet, upwards and backwards to where he had been earlier, near the pond. He had been hit by both spells, joined together in a mixture of magic – good and evil, ancient and powerful. And then he vanished, before he had even hit the ground.

The warlock looked furious. He turned on the witch once again. 'Not dead yet, Wanda?' he roared, screwing up his face into an ugly frown as he prepared to fire again. The witch made one last effort to lift her wilting arm. They both fired directly at each other and once again two jets of light exploded on collision and then hurtled on towards their marks. This time, both of them were hit.

Wanda collapsed in a smoking heap. Her broken wand fell limply from her delicate hand. The warlock sneered, wobbling on his feet from the impact. He was still in one piece, if a bit singed and smoking, and a peculiar shade of green. He looked around for the boy. From where she lay on the floor, Wanda tried to look around for any sign of Luke too. She hoped he was gone. That had been her intention, and the only way to save him.

Wanda's sight was fading and soon she couldn't see much at all, except for Worfeus stumbling about, searching her little house. There was nothing she could do to stop him now, but she knew that he wouldn't find what he was looking for. She smiled weakly as the warlock rummaged through her cupboards impatiently. In his frustration, he ransacked the house, smashing and throwing the witch's belongings without a second thought. Finally, his patience ran out completely and he gave up his search.

The warlock straightened up and brushed himself down. 'Never mind those little trinkets of yours, Wanda,' he bellowed. 'I've done it. I have finally defeated all my opponents, including you. There is no one of any importance left to stop me now. I am the Supreme Warlock of all time! Bah!'

The little house shook at his bellowing and it began to crack.

The sound of a barn door banging in the yard silenced the warlock. With an irritated little snort, he slipped away and returned to the forest.

Later, in the darkness of the night, the brave little witch was carried away by the forest nymphs and fairies to her clan, to be mourned and later buried. That night, a new star twinkled brightly in the sky above the garden. The little house became visible again after the duelling had broken the cloaking spell, but it was little more than a pile of rubble. The curses and spells had almost destroyed it. Creepers and ivy quickly smothered the remains of the house.

As the years passed, the untended plants and shrubs grew thickly over and around the ruins. It was soon covered completely, keeping Wanda's secrets safe and her story untold, at least for a while.

Chapter One

NEW ARRIVALS

Four big blue eyes opened wide with amazement. What they saw was incredible! The view from the top of the driveway was so vast, wild and free. There were many oak trees and horse chestnuts, their long branches swishing high above them. There were overgrown bushes bursting out all around, and an acre of long wild grass blowing in the breeze. Lots of different birds and animals were chattering too, but most of the wildlife was hiding.

Jamie and Jemima looked around, waiting for their parents. Timber, their big dog, plodded softly up beside them and sat down. His wet nose rubbed against the children's knees. The young boy and girl liked to have Timber beside them, especially in such a strange yet wonderful place, their new home. Their little cat peered out from the safety of his carry-box.

He wouldn't be let out just yet, but Jemima wanted him to get a quick look at his new surroundings. In fact, the pets were just as curious and excited as the children. With a little gasp from Jemima and a loud 'Wow' from Jamie, the children entered Grindlewood for the very first time.

'Even the gate is huge,' cried Jamie, looking up at the great iron gateway arching over their heads. 'Look, Dad, this place is enormous!'

'Just look at it, Jamie! It'll take months to discover everything in here. It's so beautiful,' said his sister Jemima. The children were dying to explore it all.

Grindlewood had always been a special place. The big old house stood in the middle of a couple of acres of gardens. The house itself had fallen into disrepair while it lay empty for over five years, but it still had a fairy tale feel about it. The children stood at the gateway to the grand estate, at the bottom of a long tree-lined avenue that curved and twisted all the way up to the big house.

'My, that does look lovely,' said Gloria, as she stood looking at the view. 'And look in the distance, there's a big forest higher up, across a field or two, behind the house. It looks very dark, even from here.'

'Yes, so there is. It looks quite dead and dark in there,' said Greg, gazing into the distance. 'Well, our new house and garden are certainly as big as it said in the letter,' said Greg. 'OK everyone, now that we've had a quick look, let's jump back in the car, and we'll drive the rest of the way. Come on, then, in we go.'

The Grindle family and their pets piled back into the car. They set off down the lovely winding driveway.

Jamie and Jemima were brother and sister, which meant that they were often quite alike – and they were also very different. Jamie was nine years old and Jemima was almost eight. Jamie was a very sporty and energetic boy and he was tall for his age. He had a cheeky freckled face and light brown hair that was always untidy. He loved playing football, bows and arrows, climbing trees and mostly getting wet, getting dirty and sometimes getting into trouble! And he loved his big dog, Timber.

His sister, Jemima, was a very pretty girl with curly blonde hair and a shy, sweet smile. Although terrified by large spiders and other ugly creepy crawlies, Jemima was fearless when it came to witchcraft and magic and anything spooky. This sometimes annoyed her brother, but the older she got, the more interested she was in the sorts of things Jamie liked too. And this meant they could have great fun together.

No doubt, Jemima expected to find some magic or enchantment in their big move to Grindlewood. Jamie, on the other hand, was always very practical. If he could see it and touch it, he believed it. Both children loved the outdoors and they adored their pets.

Finally, after many twists and turns, the car came around the last bend and Greg pulled up right in front of the house. Gloria looked at the long letter in her hand. Their solicitor had sent it to them with information and a description of the house and land that they had inherited from Greg's Great Uncle George.

'That's it,' she said. 'A big red brick house, with five steps up to the grand white front door and large stone pillars either side. It is just as it says in the letter and you can see it all clearly in the photograph too. Yes, this is definitely it. Isn't it fantastic?'

The whole family were beaming from ear to ear. This was such an exciting and unexpected journey, moving all the way from Alaska to a wonderful new home.

'This is like a fairy tale. I just love it,' said Jemima, in her dreamy sort of way.

'This is so cool. It's really huge. We have so much exploring to do. When can we start? I want to make a swing on one of those big trees, and maybe a tree house too. And we'll need a huge kennel for Timber,' said Jamie, who was about to burst with excitement. Timber was wagging his tail furiously. He was just itching to get out of the car to sniff and explore.

'Right, let's go and have a look around,' said Greg, laughing at the children's happy faces.

As the house and garden had been empty for a while, Greg and Gloria knew it might need some work to make it a comfortable home, but even they could see that living there would be a lot of fun. And, as Greg was a fine carpenter, and his wife Gloria was a wonderful interior designer, they also saw it as the perfect project.

'Hey, kids, before we go into the house, let's take a look around the back, shall we?'

'OK, Dad,' said the two children and they raced ahead with their dog.

They were so excited that they nearly knocked over the two large blue flower pots that stood either side of the front door. Surprisingly, they were still bursting with dazzling, pink geraniums. After narrowly avoiding the pots, the children ran back down the front steps and raced along the crunchy gravel pathway which led all the way around the house. They stopped abruptly at the tall side gate and waited for their parents, who had the big bunch of keys.

'Look, Dad, there's a huge yard, with stables I think,' cried Jamie, peering through the bars of the gate.

'You're right, Jamie, but there are no horses here any more, not for a long time I'd say. Hmm, I will definitely convert one of those barns into a workshop. Yes, that should do nicely.'

'Oh look, there's a rather battered chicken coop, and it's still full of chickens. Isn't that a wonder?' said Gloria, finally finding the right key to unlock the gate.

On three sides of the yard there were large sheds and barns that had been used for the old master's horses and hounds. They looked to be in quite good condition, despite not being used since the house was last occupied. The family went through the side gate, had a quick look at the barns and then continued right around to the back of the property. Behind the house was the greatest surprise of all.

'Oh, this is absolutely wonderful!' said Gloria.

'Wow! WOW!' said Jamie, again and again. Jemima was speechless. Timber let out a few soft snuffles and barks. His nose was sniffing hard, picking up lots of new smells and information. Teddy, the cat, was scratching to get out of his carry box.

The garden was spectacular, wild and absolutely enormous, even bigger than the acre or so of garden out front.

Over to the left side was a small apple orchard, and on the other side there was a long curved pond. In the middle of the pond sat a little grassy island with bushy reeds and a few scruffy nests. Farther down, and just about visible from the house, stood a large, stone water fountain with a trumpeting angel rising up from the centre. The fountain was smothered in moss, and very weather beaten, but it still looked beautiful.

The children couldn't wait to explore every inch of the garden. Their pets seemed to feel the same. Just like every curious cat, Teddy was keen to check out his new surroundings. Jemima opened the door on the carry box, and Teddy hopped out, keen to get a better look. Then suddenly from over his head, 'Woo-woo-wooooo, Woo-woo-wooooo!' rang out across the garden, loud enough to reach beyond the neighbouring fields. It was Timber howling loudly, making sure everyone around knew he had arrived!

The residents of the garden got a terrible fright when Timber howled, and they quickly ran to hide, if they weren't already well hidden. Teddy never minded Timber's big howls – he was used to them. Jamie and Jemima were used to them too, and they laughed at all the fluttering, squawking and splashing as the wildlife quickly took cover. The dog was simply saying hello.

'Timber the Super-mal,' shouted Jamie, and he hugged his beautiful dog. Timber was an Alaskan malamute, big and strong, all white and silvery grey. He had a bushy, curly tail and dark-grey markings like a mask on his handsome white face. He was a loyal and brave dog, and a trusted member of the family.

Teddy was Timber's best animal friend, even though he was a cat. He was very cute, and also mostly white, with black patches on his head and ears (which resembled a little hat) and a long black tail. Teddy loved to be with Timber. The dog was his hero.

With the 'danger' seemingly over, the garden residents slowly peeped out of their hiding places. They were careful not to be seen. They just wanted to watch and listen and try to find out what was happening.

'There hasn't been anything like this for years. What on earth is going on?' asked a very concerned hedgehog, who was hiding under a bush.

'I don't know. We'll simply have to wait to find out. And keep your voice down!' the fox replied.

'Humans can't hear or understand us, remember,' said the hedgehog.

'Yes, yes, I know, but keep quiet anyway, and stay hidden!'

'Wait a minute! Didn't the butterflies say something about a great change coming? Is that what this is? Where are you going? Hey, wait for me!' There was a shuffling in the bushes and the conversation stopped.

'Come on you two, it's time for tea,' Gloria told the children.

'But Mum, there are loads of animals and birds here. We want to go and find them, all of them. We think they're hiding in the long grass and the bushes,' cried Jemima.

'I want to check out the pond. Is it deep? Can we swim in it?' asked Jamie.

'Not now, please,' replied Gloria. 'You can spend all of tomorrow exploring the garden. We all will, but it will be an early night for all of us, tonight.'

While the children ate their sandwiches, their parents went back out to the garden for a quick look around. They wandered through the long grass, past the overgrown flower beds and came at last to the pond.

'Here's the famous pond then. It really is as big as the letter described.'

'And look further down there, I think I can see a statue on a fountain. There was no mention of it in the letter, and there's no sign of it in the photograph either. I wonder when they put that in,' said Greg.

'It doesn't say,' said Gloria. 'The photo does look quite old, though.'

They both looked around, looked at the photograph and looked all around again, taking it all in.

'You know, the kids are going to love exploring this garden, Greg. We probably shouldn't do anything to it for a while. Tidying up the house and building the new kennels should keep us busy enough for the moment.'

Some of the residents of the garden were hiding quite close by and they were listening carefully. They would report back to their friends later. Grindlewood garden was home to lots of wildlife, along with great uncle George's cat and dog, both of whom had been left to fend for themselves when he had passed away. Life in the garden was good for the birds and animals, and they were happy living there undisturbed, all getting along very well with each other. They were understandably worried about any newcomers.

'Well, it's been a long day. I think that's all we can decide on for now. Let's go inside, shall we?' said Greg.

Gloria nodded and yawned. It had been a very busy day for all the family. Just after they got back to the house, there was a loud knock on the door. It was their nearest neighbour, Farmer Finlay.

'Hello, everyone, Arthur Finlay is my name. I just wanted to welcome you all to Grindlewood. I thought you might like some information about the area, so I brought over this book for you. It has been in my family for ages. We go back years in this neighbourhood. In fact, this was my son's favourite book. It's called *The History of Grindlewood*. I haven't actually read it myself, but you might find something interesting in there, if you like that sort of thing,' said the farmer, as he placed the book on the hall table.

'That's very neighbourly of you, Arthur. Thank you very much,' said Greg.

'I should tell you that there are a couple of pets that come with this house,' Arthur said, chuckling. 'I'll bet nobody told you that before today!'

'Well, no, actually they didn't,' said Greg, surprised.

'Don't worry, they're no trouble at all. One is a nice old beagle and the other is a little stray dog that arrived quite recently, a black spaniel sort of thing, nice dog too. They're probably out somewhere in that huge back garden, hiding until they're sure it's safe. There's an old grey cat too. She often sleeps in the house as she likes her comforts. She could be anywhere, indoors or outdoors, at this time of day. No one came to take them when the last owner died, so I came over and left some food out for them each morning. Oh, I see you've got pets of your own. He's a fine big dog. Hello there, boy!'

Timber woofed back as Farmer Finlay petted his ears.

'Right, well we haven't found the pets yet, but I'm sure they'll turn up when they're hungry,' said Gloria.

'No problem,' said Greg. 'We're used to cats and dogs already.'

'Yes, so I see,' said Arthur. 'My wife, Alice, and I live on Meadowfield Farm, just down the road a little way. If you need any help with anything while you're settling in, just give me a shout. Oh, and by the way, there's a fine bunch of chickens in the yard. You've probably found them already. I've been keeping an eye on them, giving them some grain and taking the eggs. I hope you don't mind. They're your chickens now, of course.'

'No problem, and thanks for looking after them for us,' said Greg with a smile.

Arthur chatted on for a while and explained how old Mr Grindle was the last known member of that family to live in the neighbourhood. When he died, no one seemed to be in a hurry to find new occupants for Grindlewood House. That was five years ago. Greg told him how he had never known his eccentric great uncle, and that was probably why it had taken such a long time to find a legitimate heir to the Grindlewood estate. He had been very surprised when the letter arrived from their solicitor. The new friends talked over some tea and scones before Arthur said he should go. Arthur said goodnight to Gloria and the children, then stopped again at the hall door for a quiet word with Greg.

'Just before I leave, Greg, I really should tell you about the forest out the back. It rises up onto a hill, starting at the edge of a field behind your garden. I'm sure you can see it quite clearly from upstairs, and maybe even from inside the garden, depending on where you are standing'. Arthur sounded a little uncomfortable.

'Yes, we noticed the forest as we were driving up to the house earlier,' said Greg.

'Well, Alice and I had a son, Luke. I say had, because he disappeared five years ago, just before old Mr. Grindle died. We never found him, but we think he must have wandered into that forest and got lost. We still hope, of course, that he'll be found some day, but the more time that passes, well, we just don't know.' Arthur looked very sad.

'I'm very sorry to hear that, Arthur,' said Greg, 'I really hope Luke will be found, and if there is anything we can do to help, just let us know.'

'I will, I will, thank you,' said Arthur. 'Now, I had best be off. Good luck with your new home. Don't forget to give me a call, if you need any help, anything at all.'

'Thanks Arthur,' said Greg. 'See you soon then.'

Arthur strode down the winding driveway, back to Meadowfield Farm. Greg went back to join his excited family. He would tell them about the forest tomorrow.

Chapter Two

SECRET MEETINGS

Biggles was a lovely thoroughbred beagle. He considered himself to be the natural leader of the garden and all its residents, as he was the master's oldest pet and therefore the most senior resident of Grindlewood. He preferred to be called the Brigadier, the nickname his old master had given him. He did his best to keep everything in the garden running smoothly.

Sylvie, the cat, was a real beauty. She had sleek silver-grey fur, glistening green eyes and a bewitching purr. She had belonged to the mistress of the house since she was a very young kitten. And then there was Dougal. He was the stray who had wandered into Grindlewood, lost and alone.

He was a nice little dog, nearly one year old, and he liked to follow the Brigadier around. His coat was shiny black, and he had soft brown eyes and floppy spaniel ears. These three pets had been particularly excited about the arrival of the new owners, but they were also a little nervous. The Brigadier called a residents' meeting that same night.

'Settle down everyone, please, settle down,' said the Brigadier. The meeting was being held in amongst the long bushy reeds at the end of the garden, well away from the house. All the resident groups were represented, including the pond dwellers.

'We all knew the day might come, when people would move into the house. Try not to panic. Their rather large dog, Timber I think his name is, is a malamute. They are very nice dogs as far as I know.' The Brigadier was finding it hard to reassure his audience quickly. 'And that little cat isn't afraid of him, so that is a good sign. Then there are the children. Well, they seem very pleasant. I heard their parents say they would not be doing too much to the garden for the moment, so hopefully our homes will stay largely undisturbed.' He smiled around at his nervous friends.

'Maybe they will like you, Dougal and Sylvie,'

squeaked Norville the hedgehog, 'but what about the rest of us? Maybe they won't think we're good enough to have in their garden. I was turned out of many gardens before I came here.'

'Or they might think that we're not beautiful enough,' muttered Ernie the frog, who was suddenly feeling very conscious of his warts.

'Yes, that is a possibility,' said Eldric the fox in his deep, serious voice. 'Though I too heard them say that it would be best to leave the garden just as it is for the children to explore, at least for now. I'm sure they will want to control the weeds, maybe tame the long grass, prune shrubs and replant the flowerbeds, but hopefully that will be all. No bulldozers, and shotguns, I hope. I've seen too many shotguns in my time.' Eldric rolled his eyes thinking of the angry farmers and excited hunters who had chased after him in the past.

'No need to panic, friends,' purred Sylvie. 'The Brigadier, Dougal and I will introduce ourselves to Timber and Teddy in the morning. We'll let them know how nicely things work around here. So let's not worry ourselves too soon.'

'Yes, quite right, Sylvie,' said the Brigadier cheerfully. 'This might be a stroke of luck, you know, having nice owners again. Let's hope for the best and put our best paws, eh, wings, yes, and eh, whatever, eh, forward. Goodnight then everyone, and good luck tomorrow.'

The residents went on their way, hoping all would be well in the morning.

There was another meeting going on at about the same time. It was taking place inside the house. After everyone had gone to bed, Jemima crept into Jamie's room. She was carrying the heavy old book their neighbour Arthur Finlay had brought over earlier that evening.

'Jamie, are you awake?' whispered Jemima.

'Of course I am. What is it?' asked Jamie, suspecting that Jemima wanted to tell him about something magical she had read about, again. And he was sort of right.

'Jamie, I think magical people used to live around here,' said Jemima in a whisper, holding the book closely, turning the pages to find the piece she wanted to read to him.

'No they didn't. It's just another story, Jemima. Not everything you read is true, you know,' said Jamie.

'But Jamie, this book is the history of Grindlewood – it has to be true. Listen to this.' Jemima began reading from the book:

> Her decision was made. The brave young witch requested permission from the Forest Queen to leave their secret home and search for new and powerful magic.

That's a witch, Jamie, a real witch they're talking about, and a queen!'

Jamie sighed. More magic stuff from Jemima. But his little sister was eager to continue.

'Oh, go on then,' said Jamie, too tired to have a row.

Jemima was very excited about the next piece. She continued reading to her brother.

> 'Your Majesty,' said Wanda, bowing low before the Forest Queen.
>
> 'I know why you are here, brave Wanda,' said the queen, 'and I am not pleased that it has come to this.' The queen looked very sad.
>
> 'My queen,' replied Wanda, 'you know I must leave. There is no way I can find the

right magic here. We have nothing left to help us create a spell that can break the curse on you, or destroy the wicked Worfeus. The Ancient Book of Magic is gone and most of our experts are either dead or have left us for town and village life. I must leave right away and begin my search for more powerful, and perhaps even darker magic.' Wanda's voice trailed off as she thought about leaving her tortured queen and the only home she had ever known.

'And where will you begin your search, dear Wanda?' asked the queen.

'In the forests, Your Majesty. They have always been the keepers of secrets and dark magic. I will begin my search there, and go from one forest to the next, and beyond, until I have the killing spell complete.'

'Very well,' said the queen, 'a wise choice, made by a wise witch.'

'Jamie, don't you think it sounds like it might be true, even some of it?' said Jemima, 'and did you see the forest out at the back, Jamie? Maybe the witch went into that forest, once upon a time.' Jemima was really hoping that Jamie would believe her this time.

'Well, kind of,' said Jamie, reluctantly. 'Read a bit more.'

Jemima returned quickly to the story.

> 'My dearest Wanda, I will miss you, but you are indeed our brightest star, and the only one who can save us. But take great care, my dear. Even with your brilliant mind, this will not be an easy task. The warlock is extremely dangerous. Go now, with my blessing.'
>
> The Forest Queen bowed her head in sadness and shame, unable to do anything more. It was up to Wanda to save her people now.

'Jamie, when do you think all this happened?' asked Jemima.

'Probably hundreds of years ago — it is a history book after all,' he replied, though he felt a little uneasy because it did sound much more convincing than he expected.

'I think we should read the whole book, as quickly as we can. This is really exciting! There could be ancient magic here, all around us, Jamie! Just think of it!'

Jemima squealed with thoughts of finding magic.

She hugged the book close to her chest, jumped off the bed and crept back to her bedroom. It was a long time before either of them fell asleep.

Chapter Three

INTRODUCTIONS

The next morning, Jamie and Jemima were full of
excitement. They were so keen to run out to the
garden that they spilled half their cereal. As soon as
they were allowed, they raced out the door with
Timber and Teddy in tow.

'Be careful at the pond, please!' cried Gloria as
the two excited children ran down the path. They
headed straight for the pond, just as their mother had
expected, and stopped abruptly when they saw it. The
pets had so much sniffing and exploring of their own
to do that they didn't follow the children all the way
to the pond. Too many scents distracted them along
the way.

'Wow!' said Jamie. 'This is more like a lake!'

'Look at the ducks sitting on that little island,' cried
Jemima. 'I hope there are some ducklings too.'

'And look over here! We have fish in our pond, lots of goldfish!' cried Jamie excitedly. After watching them circle for a minute or two, the excited children followed the goldfish as they swam down to the fountain, where every morning they would hold a swimming race. Jamie and Jemima were delighted to see the fish whizz around the fountain. As they watched the race, the fountain suddenly sprayed a few spurts of water high in the air.

'That's funny – the fish swim so fast the fountain starts to spit!' giggled Jemima.

'Yeah, I wonder if Dad could make it gush out lots of water like a waterfall, and we could dive under it?' asked Jamie.

'I don't know, it looks quite deep around the fountain,' said Jemima a little nervously. She didn't like water quite as much as Jamie. The children looked up at the statue, waiting for more water to spurt out. They noticed three butterflies sitting motionless on the statue's wings.

'Look at the lovely big butterflies!' cried Jemima. They watched as the butterflies rose and hovered over the statue, their rainbow wings working hard just to keep them in the one spot. They flew over to the children and gently landed on their hair. Jemima squealed with delight, but Jamie just felt awkward. After a minute or so, they rose up from the children's hair, did a little twirl in front of them, and then flew off towards the wild flowers.

Ernie the frog also lived in the pond. As the butterflies departed, the children spotted him hopping around the water lilies.

'Look over there. I can see a big chubby frog,' said Jamie.

'Oh, he's a really green and warty frog, isn't he?' said Jemima.

'Listen, Ernie is talking. Listen,' said Jamie.

'Yes, I can hear him ribbit,' squealed Jemima.

After a minute or two, Jamie asked his sister an awkward question.

'Jemima, how did I know the frog's name?'

'The butterflies just told us,' said Jemima, as if it were the most normal thing in the world.

'Oh, OK,' said Jamie, needing to think about that a bit more.

Ernie was indeed a big, blobby frog, rather fat, and a very bright shade of green. Unfortunately for Ernie, he also had several warty lumps all over his bright green skin. He had big bulging eyes, a really wide mouth and a long sticky tongue. He loved his pond and was generally a happy fellow. He also knew he was a rather ugly frog and there was nothing he could do about it. But unknown to Ernie, he had been touched by magic. Just like the butterflies, Ernie had been enchanted with a very special gift. He didn't know what it was yet, but he would find out very soon.

Up nearer the house, hiding under a few bushes, the Brigadier, Sylvie and Dougal had been waiting for their moment. Timber and Teddy had paused on their tour of the garden and were quickly eating up their morning feeds.

'Remember, stay calm everyone,' whispered the Brigadier, trying to reassure his friends, especially young Dougal, who hadn't met many people before. In fact, the spaniel wasn't quite sure what all the fuss was about. The three peered out from the bushes.

'Look, Gloria, there they are,' said Greg softly to his wife.

'Oh, they look so scared, but so cute,' whispered Gloria.

Greg called to them gently. The pets looked nervously at each other, but their instincts told them it was safe. The dogs walked slowly towards Greg and Gloria, eyeing Timber and Teddy, who were still at their bowls. Greg held out his hand so the dogs could have a sniff and relax a bit. He patted them both on the head and rubbed their ears in welcome. Sylvie sat down nearby and watched. Gloria walked slowly over to the beautiful cat and gently rubbed her forehead and chin.

'They seem OK,' thought Dougal, his eyes darting from one to the other.

'I wonder what Timber and Teddy think,' thought Sylvie, purring at Gloria.

'Woo-woo woo-woo,' howled Timber, turning around, as if he could read her mind. He trotted over to greet the trio with a few sniffs, woofs and a slobbery lick or two. Teddy joined them and all five sat in a row, looking at Greg and Gloria, as if waiting for a decision. Would the Grindles keep them all?

'Well, I think all our pets will get along just fine,' said Greg, looking pleased.

'Yes, I think so,' agreed Gloria. 'We must give them

names. What did Arthur call them?'

'I don't think he did, Gloria, let me see now …'

The children had heard Timber's howl and ran back over to see what was happening. They saw the pets still lined up as if for inspection.

'Oh look, it's the other pets! Oh, they're lovely,' cried Jemima, as she and her brother petted each one in turn.

'This is great,' said Jamie. 'Now we have five pets, and I bet we'll find lots more in the garden.'

'We probably will, Jamie,' said Greg, looking around, wondering just how many more might be lurking in the bushes.

'So what do you want to call them?' asked Gloria.

'We already know their names,' said Jemima.

'This is the Brigadier,' said Jamie, pointing to the beagle. 'And this is Dougal the spaniel, and this is Sylvie,' he said finally, stroking the cat.

'I see, well, Jemima, are you happy with those names?'

'Oh, yes. Anyway, those really are their names, Mum. I can't change them,' said Jemima. She was very sure of what she said, but her mum and dad seemed a little confused.

'Well, that's fine then, I guess,' said Gloria, looking at her husband, who looked just as puzzled. The children and their three dogs bounced off through the long grass for more exploring, while Sylvie offered to show Teddy around in a more cat-like way, slinking quietly around the garden.

'See you later, guys,' called Teddy, as he disappeared into an overgrown flower bed.

'Have a good time, cats,' woofed Dougal softly, as he trotted down the garden with the Brigadier and Timber. The dogs were keen to start sniffing.

'What was all that about the names?' asked Greg.

'I don't know, perhaps they had thought of them earlier,' suggested Gloria.

Greg still looked a bit confused.

'Don't worry, Greg. The children are happy and so are the dogs and cats. Thank goodness they all like each other. They have managed very well here on their own, haven't they, even with some help from Arthur?'

'Yes, I guess so,' agreed Greg. 'Come on then, let's finish unpacking, and then we can concentrate on building the new kennels. I might ask our friendly neighbour to give me a hand after all. At least one of the kennels will need to be very big, now that we have three dogs!' said Greg as he marched off to the yard to check out the tool shed.

Chapter Four

NORVILLE'S HEDGEHOG HUNCH

Nosy Norville was a quirky little hedgehog. He lived in a small, cosy home, tucked under the thick protruding roots of a large oak tree at the end of the garden. He had always been a curious fellow and he had become intrigued by rumours he had heard about the garden and the dark forest behind it. He was convinced there must be a real mystery about the neighbourhood, and he wanted to be the one who uncovered it.

Norville ventured out of the garden now and again, wombling through the back field that led right up to the forest, hoping to hear more gossip or find some clues. One time, after snuffling around, he returned to the garden all in a dither. His instincts, or perhaps his very sensitive nose, told him something was wrong. He decided to seek advice from the clever foxes, and in particular, his friend and neighbour, Eldric the red fox.

Eldric shared his den with Freya and Fern. The three foxes lived under a big, thick clump of bushes close to Norville.

'Now look, Norville, telling me you have a hunch just won't do. I can't help you if you don't give me all the facts. Facts please, Norville, facts! What is this mumbo jumbo about witches and warlocks or whatever?' said Eldric, having listened to a short but confusing description of Norville's latest hunch.

'All right then, Eldric, I'll start again, but please try to be a little patient and let me get to the end of it,' replied Norville, nervously twitching and rubbing his pointy little nose. Sometimes his nose would itch when the weather was about to turn nasty. What type of storm was coming this time, he wondered?

'When I lived outside Grindlewood garden, I used to hear other birds and animals talking about the history of the place. Apparently, the area around Grindlewood was rumoured to be magical, enchanted – a favourite place for the magical people to live.'

Eldric rolled his eyes upwards as he always did when he thought he was about to hear silly talk.

'Hear me out, Eldric, there's a lot more to this,' said the agitated hedgehog.

'I hope so,' muttered the impatient fox.

'The story goes that a bitter feud broke out between supporters of the Wandelei Forest Queen and her jealous rivals. There were many battles and feuds, Eldric, and eventually the evil warlords got the better of the gentle people. The Worfagons – they're the evil ones – continued the fighting for centuries. They cursed the Forest Queen and they stole her most prized possession, the W.A.B.O.M.'

'The what? Oh dear,' Eldric sighed.

'Wait, Eldric! W.A.B.O.M stands for the Wandelei's Ancient Book of Magic – the W.A.B.O.M.' Norville paused to make sure that Eldric was still paying attention.

'Go on then,' said the fox.

'Well, the story then jumps forward to quite recently, though I'm not sure exactly when. Anyway, two of the last really powerful magical people – one from the Wandeleis and one from the Worfagons – fought a fierce duel, to the death.'

'Really? Who won?' asked Eldric. He was becoming interested after all.

'Well, it's complicated,' replied Norville.

'Of course it is,' said Eldric, a little disappointed.

'The evil warlock had used a powerful killing spell on the good witch. But she was able, in her dying moments, to cast her own spell at the warlock. Her clever spell turned the warlock into a scrawny grey wolf, after he had returned to his home in the forest. The wicked warlock was cursed to remain like that and stuck in the forest until he could find a powerful potion to turn himself back into a warlock and escape. Are you still with me, Eldric?'

'Yes, go on,' growled the fox. The story was definitely interesting him now.

'Good. Pippa, our friendly garden ladybird, has been trying to collect information for me as she flies about, and sometimes she goes into the, eh ... the, eh ... forest.'

'Does she indeed?' said Eldric, raising a bushy eyebrow. 'Wait a minute, you mean *our* forest, the one behind the field, behind the garden?'

'Well, yes. I know it's a bit, well, strange, but Pippa flits about unnoticed, you know. She is so small no one really notices her. She can watch and listen as if invisible,' replied Norville nervously, as Eldric was frowning.

'And what did she find out, Norville?'

'Well, she did say that she saw a wolf in the forest,' whispered Norville, waiting for a reaction.

'Really,' growled Eldric. 'That's not good, not good at all.'

'No, it's very worrying, but it does tie in with what the butterflies said last week, about the wolf,' squeaked Norville. 'You remember their latest prediction, don't you?'

'Hmm,' said Eldric, but nothing more. He was deep in thought.

Norville glanced anxiously around, and then continued. 'One day, Pippa saw an ugly vole scuttling around. Indeed, he was quite close to the edge of the forest, and Pippa saw him talking to the wolf. I would have expected the wolf to eat the vole, rather than stop and have a little chat, wouldn't you, Eldric?'

Norville rubbed his nose again. The itching just wouldn't stop. He looked at his friend for a few moments, but the fox was giving nothing away. He was as cool as a cucumber.

'So you're saying that the wolf in the forest might

really be this evil warlock character?' asked Eldric, fixing Norville with his beady stare.

'He might be. Oh, I'm not sure, Eldric. I hope not, but I do think something is up. There can't be that many rumours without some of it being true. And what about those nasty magpies and that awful heron? They have been annoying us a lot lately. The magpies keep swooping in, attacking all the little birds, especially the blackbirds. And the heron keeps trying to catch the goldfish in the pond. Poor Ernie is very upset by all the attacks on his home – the pond, that is. And on top of that, so many of my forest buddies, as you call them, keep muttering on about dark magic and spells that are connected to this place. I just don't know what it can all mean. It seems weird, though, all this stuff happening at the same time. Oh dear, it doesn't sound good, does it?' said Norville.

'But you just said that the wolf can't leave the forest, according to legend or spells or something,' said Eldric.

'Yes, that's true, I think. Well, it's so hard to know what is true and what isn't. But there are even stranger rumours about this garden Eldric – more rumours of spells and magic. I was just hoping Pippa and I might be able to get to the bottom of it,' said Norville rather sheepishly.

'Hmmm, I don't know. Let me think about it. There might be something in all those rumours you and your forest buddies have heard. I'll speak to the Brigadier. We should hold a residents' meeting and talk about it then.'

'Yes, yes, good idea. Let's talk to the others. I'm glad that big malamute Timber is here now,' said Norville. 'He is such a big, strong-looking dog, and he seems like a smart fellow too. He wasn't a bit shy or nervous of his new surroundings, was he?'

'That's true,' said Eldric.

'I must say, though, magic, spells and all that stuff might explain some of the stranger things that happen around here. It might explain why the butterflies have visions, why Sylvie and the Brigadier never get any older, and why the fish speed around the pond. Yes, maybe there is some magic around this place after all.' Norville scratched his nose with his front paws, and then continued worrying. 'Maybe the witch isn't dead after all. Maybe the evil warlock has come back, or never even left. Or maybe the wolf can actually leave the forest. Oh dear!'

Norville was rubbing his nose frantically. He was having so many scary thoughts he was in quite a state.

'Steady on, Norville. We're not sure of anything yet. We'll figure it out. We always do,' said Eldric confidently.

But Eldric was not at all comfortable with what he had just heard. With eyes of steel and jaws tightly clenched, he trotted off to find the Brigadier and Sylvie. He was worried. The fox had heard something about a wolf legend before. He also knew that Sylvie had seen something scary in the distance when she was up a tree some months ago. She wasn't sure what she had seen, but, not wanting to frighten everyone, she told only the Brigadier and the fox. Eldric was fairly sure now that she must have seen a wolf at the edge of the forest, and he was beginning to think that there might be something to the hedgehog's hunch after all.

Deep in the forest, Worfeus had greatly improved his potion to return himself to warlock form, and soon he wouldn't keep turning back into a wolf at all, unless he wanted to. But to his great annoyance, he still couldn't magic his way out of the forest. This time, he was in a tyrannical rage. His latest spell to release himself from the forest had failed. And he so desperately wanted to get to Grindlewood garden.

He fired spell after spell and curse after curse at every dead tree around him, trying to blast his way out. Purple bolts shot from his wand as he blew up more trees and bushes, boiled over his cauldron and practised killing spells on some of his magpies.

'I must get to that garden!' he bellowed. 'I must, I must! I will make those rotten little animals pay for all my troubles. How dare they keep what is mine from me! How dare they! I will make them suffer. I will eliminate them all! And I won't stop there. I will destroy the place – that garden!'

As he roared and ranted in frustration, all living things within several miles looked in the direction of the forest. They wondered what sort of creature could have let out such a dreadful shriek of rage into the night.

Chapter Five

DISCOVERING A WONDERLAND

A great pile of storage boxes had been dumped in the kitchen after all the unpacking. Gloria wanted to move them all to one of the sheds in the yard. As she reached down to pick up some boxes, she saw a little movement in amongst the paper packaging and assumed the worst.

'Aaahhhh!' she screamed. 'A mouse! There's a mouse in the kitchen! Greg, quick, I think it's a mouse, or maybe a rat!'

Greg raced into the house, hammer at the ready. He checked around the kitchen. He certainly didn't want to find mice or rats in the house. That would be a dreadful nuisance. He heard some paper rustle in one of the boxes. 'Ah ha,' he thought, 'there's the culprit.' A little more rummaging and 'Ow, meow' was heard. Then another squeaky little meow came from the bottom of the box. With a rustle and a fumble, a lovely fluffy kitten tumbled out, all muddled and confused after getting lost in some packaging.

'It's OK, Gloria, look what I found!' called Greg. Gloria peeked around the door and saw the cutest little kitten bouncing around the kitchen floor.

'Oh, look, Mum, that must be Cindy. She's so cute,' cried Jemima, as she pushed past her surprised mother. She picked up the little bundle of fur and stroked her gently.

Cindy was a very small kitten, with grey and white stripes on a lovely fluffy coat of white kitten fur. Only a few weeks old, lost, hungry and frightened, she had run up a tree in the garden and got stuck. Sylvie had come to the rescue, climbing up the tree, picking up Cindy by the scruff of her neck and bringing her all the way down to safety. After that little adventure, Sylvie had brought the kitten into the house through the old cat flap and looked after her until she recovered.

'Listen, Cindy's purring!' shrieked Jemima, as she ran outside to show her to Jamie.

'That's another new pet for the household,' said Greg, relieved it was only a kitten.

'Yes, indeed,' agreed Gloria. 'And another pet name, just like that.'

The pet count was up to six. Greg returned to his kennel building and Gloria to sorting the boxes, while the children played in the garden and the yard. There was a lot more to explore, after all, and lots more residents to meet.

Gloria had let the chickens out of the coop earlier, so that she could clean it properly, count all the chickens and collect the eggs. While Jemima tried to catch a chicken, Jamie made chicken clucking noises behind her, flapping his arms like a big silly chicken himself. The chickens ignored him. They had been in Grindlewood a long time now and had seen many chicken imitations before.

The rooster emerged from the barn and gave the children a hearty welcome.

'Cock-a-doodle-do,' he hollered, as he flapped his way out of the barn where he had been waiting to hear from the chickens that everything was OK.

Roosevelt was a big, fat, jolly rooster who had lived in the yard with the chickens for years. He was very proud of his magnificent cock-a-doodle-do song, which woke all the residents in the garden without fail, until this particular morning. He strutted about showing off his brightly coloured feathers of red and orange, yellow and brown. He also had fluffy, feathered feet which made him look very clumsy as he patrolled the chicken yard. Roosevelt liked to believe he was in charge of the chicken run, but he usually ended up being bossed about by the chickens.

'Hello, Roosevelt,' called out Jamie. 'You are a jumbo rooster! Mum, Jemima, just look at the size of him!'

'Yes, he is a big fellow, isn't he?' said Gloria, laughing at the sight of the huge rooster.

'Roosevelt is a great name for a big rooster.'

'It sure is, Jamie. You two are very certain about all these names. It's great that there are no arguments! If only everything was so simple.'

'Let's explore some more, Jemima,' Jamie shouted over his shoulder as he took off down the winding path that led from the yard right around the side of the garden.

As the children approached the boundary hedge at the side of the garden, the rabbits were bouncing around, in and out of the hedge, to and from their burrows on the other side. The bees were out and about, following their leader, Balthazar Bee. Big, fat and friendly, the bee was so chubby he looked like he should hardly be able to fly.

He was in charge of all the bees in the entire neighbourhood. While the queen bee was busy in the hive, Balthazar led his troops in Operation Pollination, visiting all the blossoms and flowers. Now, in the middle of summer, Balthazar was a very busy bee, but he always found time to be friendly. He flew over to Jemima and landed on her shoulder.

'Well hello, you two,' buzzed Balthazar, forgetting for a moment that people cannot hear the garden residents talking. Jamie peered over Jemima's shoulder to look.

'Wow, he really is huge. I'm not touching him, and you shouldn't either. Let's hope he flies off soon or you're stuck here,' teased Jamie. Luckily, however, Balthazar could understand the children. He smiled and flew back to the hive where the bees were buzzing merrily and the honey was coming along nicely.

Deep in the forest, something else was doing very nicely – at least Worfeus the wicked warlock thought so. A thick, smelly, yucky brew was reaching boiling point in a big black pot. A miserable little vole was stoking the fire underneath it, working the flames hotter and hotter. The contents were very nearly cooked, which could only mean trouble. But Worfeus was still in a rage.

'This brew will do the job. Yes, yes, it will. That cosy band of do-gooders will get such a shock! Yes, they think that Wanda has protected them, charmed them even. Bah! I'll show them and I'll show Wanda – even if she is dead! I'll pick her friends off one by one, and make them pay for all the curses that little witch put on me. Me! Worfeus! How dare she! And how dare they!'

Worfeus chanted another spell over the bubbling cauldron, causing more purple smoke to rise and more strange and noisy gurgling, as the magic pot cooked its evil brew.

The children were unaware of any dangers that might be hiding in the nearby forest. They ran and played through the long grass, enjoying their garden wonderland. They soon made their way over to the pond again.

'Let's see what else is in the pond,' said Jamie. They knelt down at the edge of the pond and looked around. The ducks were about to swim by.

'Look, there's Delilah and her ducklings!' Jemima tried to whisper so she wouldn't frighten them.

'And that must be Danville over there, preening his feathers,' said Jamie, pointing to the other side of the pond, where Danville was waiting for Delilah and the brood.

The ducks had a new brood every year. Delilah minded her flock very carefully on the little nesting island. She always fussed over her ducklings, a very attentive and devoted mother. But sometimes she would get a little tired of all this mothering stuff. In fact, just like the chickens, Delilah had a secret. On certain nights, she would sneak out of the nest, paddle across the pond and, crouching in the thick rushes, she would spy on the chickens. Their dancing was a big secret, and Delilah was the only one who knew about it. She would love to join the chickens for their dance rehearsals. But would her husband approve? She thought not.

Danville was a quiet fellow. With his wide yellow

paddle feet, he could swim around the pond for hours on end. As the children watched the ducks, Jemima suddenly spotted something tiny and red sitting on the top of one of the rushes at the edge of the pond.

'Look, it's the ladybird. It must be Pippa. Over there,' she cried.

'Oh yes, I can see her,' said Jamie.

'I think she's lovely,' said Jemima, leaning forward to get a closer look, almost falling into the pond. Dainty and beautiful, Pippa was a fairly new resident of the garden. She was completely defenceless and the other residents watched out for her much more than she realised.

But there was something else that little Pippa didn't know. Her little world was about to change, and what she had seen and heard in the forest would start to unlock another of Grindlewood's secrets. That secret would be so shocking that life in this wonderful garden would never be the same again.

Chapter Six

TROUBLE, TROUBLE!

The butterflies were the most enchanted of all the garden residents. They were Wanda's special gift to Grindlewood, one of many magical charms she left behind her. Just before the new Grindle family arrived, the butterflies had been in quite a panic. They hurried over to the Brigadier, and landed on his head.

'Brigadier, wake up! The butterflies have a message for you,' said Dougal, nudging him with his nose.

'What, what, WHAT!' spluttered the sleepy beagle. He hated to be woken from his dreams of running with the hounds.

'Wake up, Brigadier. The butterflies will lose their ability to speak to us soon. You must hear their message right now!' urged Dougal.

'The butterflies? What? Oh yes, dear ladies, excuse me. How can I help you?' said the Brigadier, shaking his ears to wake himself up.

'Brigadier, we have had another vision. Great change is coming to Grindlewood, and, and, it looks like a … a … a wolf!' whispered one of the butterflies, almost afraid to say the words.

'A wolf?' cried the Brigadier.

'Shhhh,' said Sylvie, approaching quickly. 'You'll scare everyone.'

'What's a wolf?' muttered Dougal.

The Brigadier was about to answer when the butterflies spoke again.

'And people. People are coming very soon,' twittered the butterflies nervously to each other. 'Lots of people – big ones and small ones. Yes, people!'

'Thank you, ladies, leave it with me. I will let the others know,' the Brigadier replied quite calmly, but he looked anxiously at Sylvie.

'Thank you, Brigadier,' twittered the butterflies as they twirled away on the breeze. They would not speak again until the next vision.

'Dougal, come here while I explain something to you, and don't say anything out loud, not a word.'

'Yes, sir, Brigadier, I'm all ears!' replied Dougal, and the two dogs walked off to a quiet corner of the garden for a quick explanation of wolves.

Now the butterfies had had another vision. This time, they woke up even more startled.

'Quick, quick, we must tell the Brigadier! Quick!' said Beatrice Butterfly to her sisters and they flew over to the dogs.

'Uh oh,' said Dougal. 'Brigadier, I think we have another message.'

'Oh my,' he said. 'Two visions in one week is most unusual. I wonder what it could be this time.'

The butterflies settled on his head and whispered in his ear.

'Oh dear, not again,' said the Brigadier, pawing at the ground. 'The heron and the magpies are up to no good, my friends. We need to prepare for more trouble from those nasty birds.'

'What's going on, Brigadier?' asked Timber, trotting over to the older dog. 'I've never seen butterflies whisper to a dog before. What's all this about?'

The dogs trotted further away from the children, leaving them to play by themselves. The animals needed to talk together privately.

'Well, it's like this, Timber. Strange as it may seem, when the butterflies sleep on that angel fountain – you know, the statue that stands in the pond – well, afterwards, they have a vision, a foretelling of what is going to happen. They come and tell me while they can speak, which is only for a few moments after they wake up, and then Dougal and I, and Sylvie, we run around and tell everyone the news,' explained the Brigadier. 'If it's really important, we will call a residents' meeting to discuss it properly.'

'I see,' said Timber. 'And is it always bad news?'

'Oh, not always. They knew you were coming, for example. They gave us that warning, I mean information, a few days ago. Trying to figure out what their visions actually mean can sometimes be a bit tricky, though today's message was clear enough. Come on, we need to tell the others right away.'

'Yes, I think we should,' said Eldric, coming out from

under the hedge. 'Hello, I'm Eldric. I believe you're the new dog, Timber. Welcome to Grindlewood. I have some news of my own, or rather of Norville's, to tell everyone. Let's call a meeting for tonight, shall we?' suggested Eldric.

'Yes, tonight will do nicely. The butterflies don't expect the aerial attack until tomorrow or the next day,' replied the Brigadier.

'Nice to meet you too, Eldric,' said Timber. 'Did you say aerial attack, Brigadier?'

'Not again,' said Eldric, rolling his eyes.

'Yes, I'm afraid so, Eldric. Spread the word please,' said the Brigadier. Eldric ran off while the Brigadier trotted on with Timber. 'Timber, call Teddy and come with me. I'll introduce you to some more residents and explain the butterflies' message as we go.'

Timber woofed to call Teddy over and Dougal followed too. The four set off to tell the other residents about the meeting.

After talking with Eldric, Norville had been feeling both nervous and guilty. He knew that the rumours he had heard would frighten the residents, and he didn't like to look foolish in front of his friends. But Norville's nose wasn't the only thing annoying him. He had been having a horrible hedgehog hunch for a while now and it just wouldn't go away. He had to do something about it. He decided to pay Pippa another visit.

Norville scratched his way through the thick and prickly hedge at the end of the garden, out into the surrounding fields. He trundled along through the back field and on towards the forest. Pippa was hitching a ride on his head again. It was a long walk for a hedgehog and he was sweating heavily in the warm evening sunshine. But no matter how tired he felt, he was determined to find out something useful before the next meeting. Onward they went.

As they got closer to the forest, the skies darkened quickly as strange clouds gathered. Looking back it was still a sunny evening over at Grindlewood. 'How spooky,' thought Norville, but he said nothing to his little passenger, who was simply enjoying the ride.

When they reached the forest, Norville asked Pippa to fly around and see what she could find, but not to go too far. In the past, he had waited for Pippa at the edge of the forest, but he had never gone in himself.

He had been too nervous. This time he thought he should go in, if only to stay closer to Pippa as she flew around. He didn't want either of them to get into trouble.

Off Pippa flew, drifting from dead leaf to dead branch, finding a few little bugs to munch on as she went. She soon disappeared from sight as Norville decided what to do. He really didn't like this forest much.

'Can I help you?' asked a raspy voice from behind a very sad looking tree.

'Oh, eh, hello,' gulped Norville. 'Um, who are you?'

'My name is Valerius Vole, and you are?' asked the rat-like animal. He was so skinny and sickly-looking, and such a strange colour too.

'I'm Norville. I, eh, think I might be a bit lost. Um, do you know where I could get a drink of water? It's so warm today,' said Norville, swallowing nervously.

'Warm, you say?' sneered Valerius. 'It is never warm in this forest, not today, or any day for that matter. What is your business here, Norville?'

'My business? Oh, no business at all – just mooching around. I think I took a wrong turn somewhere back in the field, somewhere back there. I should really be heading off now. Sorry to disturb you,' muttered Norville.

The vole gripped Norville by the nose, stopping his escape. He pulled Norville towards the heart of the forest. 'Nonsense! You look like you are about to faint. Come along with me and I shall get you a drink. If my master is at home, you shall meet him too. Worfeus is his name, he is quite famous around these parts,' said Valerius, smiling all the while.

Norville wriggled a bit more and then, luckily, he sneezed. It was a most explosive sneeze, causing both the hedgehog and the vole to fall over. This gave Norville his only chance to break free from the vole's tight grip.

'Oh, I really must be off. Goodbye!'

Norville quickly turned and hurried out of the forest as fast as his wobbly little legs would take him. Valerius watched him go, unable to leave the forest himself. He was stuck there just like his master.

When Norville was finally out of sight, the vole turned and ran. Worfeus didn't like interruptions and he had a terrible temper at the best of times. It was going to be very unpleasant, but he knew it would be better to tell his master about this hedgehog's visit before he heard about it from those sneaky magpies. He had to hurry. The birds just loved getting him into trouble, especially if there was a chance that he might be punished.

All this time, Pippa had been flitting about unaware of the danger, munching on tiny bugs. Eventually her tummy was so full that she started to feel sleepy, and she snuggled into some moss to take a quick nap. She knew nothing of Norville's sudden departure from the forest.

Norville raced on and on, his legs moving as fast as they could. He was so scared and his head was buzzing with questions. Why did that nasty vole try to lure him deeper into the forest? What would have happened if he had gone with him? Norville kept looking over his shoulder as he scurried along through the field. Suddenly he stopped. 'Oh no!' he thought. 'Pippa! I've left Pippa behind! Ohhhhhhh! I can't go back now. I'll never make it. I'm too exhausted to go back. I could die in there. I could die on the way back! Oh no, what will I do? What will the others say? I should never have gone. I should never, ever have asked Pippa to come with me. I might even be banished from Grindlewood for breaking the Rules of the Garden and putting her in danger!'

Norville was dreadfully upset but he stumbled on towards the safety of Grindlewood, knowing he would have to face the residents and tell them what had happened. Suddenly it seemed that Norville's horrible hunch might be correct.

Back at the house, Arthur had arrived a little after tea-time to help Greg with the enormous dog kennel and the smaller one for the cats.

'You know, Greg,' said Arthur quietly, 'it was just after his tenth birthday when Luke disappeared – just a young boy. He loved this garden. He used to play in here all the time when he was off school, or after finishing his chores around the farm in the summertime. I still think he might have wandered out the back and into that forest. It's very big and very dark. Some of the villagers think it's cursed. All the trees in there have died over the years and no one knows why. It's a weird place, best avoided.' Arthur looked very serious.

'I'm so very sorry, Arthur. Thanks for the warning. I mentioned it to Gloria last night. We might as well tell the children now, I think,' Greg said, glancing over at Gloria, who nodded. She was having a picnic tea with the children on a patch of grass that had been cut especially for the occasion. The children had overheard a little of this conversation, but they didn't look worried as they were distracted by events in the garden. The butterflies were dancing around Jemima again, and Jamie was rewarding the dogs with scraps of food when they did their tricks correctly.

'Children,' said Gloria carefully. 'Did you hear what Mr Finlay said? You must never go into the forest behind the back field. People have got lost in there. Do you understand?'

The children looked at her, a bit surprised, so she continued. 'Arthur's son, Luke, vanished five years ago, and he was never found,' said Gloria.

'So, no wandering off kids. Understood?' said Greg sternly.

'OK, Dad,' said Jemima.

'OK, Jamie?' Gloria wanted to be sure Jamie was paying attention. He loved exploring even more than Jemima did.

'I hear you, Mum,' said Jamie. 'No wandering off, as usual.'

'Maybe Luke has gone off on an adventure. I like adventures. Maybe he'll come back when the adventure is over,' said Jemima.

'Yes, dear, I hope he will. Now let's tidy up the picnic and bring everything inside. Will you help me please, Jemima? Jamie, I think the dogs have had enough treats. Why don't you help your dad and Mr Finlay with the kennels for a little while? Then it will be time for bed,' said Gloria.

Jamie jumped at the chance. He loved to watch his dad make things and it was even better when he was allowed to actually do something with him.

'Look, Timber, your kennel is going to be huge!' cried Jamie.

'Woo-woo,' replied Timber. He was looking forward to sleeping outdoors again, instead of in the warm kitchen – malamutes don't like to be too warm. With a bit of luck, the kennels would be finished that evening.

Chapter Seven

WARLOCKS AND WITCHES,
STARDUST AND SPELLS

Timber and Teddy were very excited about their first residents' meeting and they arrived early. Like previous meetings, this one would be held behind some dense shrubbery at the end of the garden.

One by one, all the residents, or their representatives, arrived and waited for the Brigadier to begin. The rooster always represented the chickens and he arrived on time to do his duty. Danville represented all the ducks and Balthazar buzzed in on behalf of the hive. The frog hopped in to represent residents of the pond. Serena Swan from nearby Lindon Lake had been especially invited by the Brigadier, as she and her mate Swinford were hoping to move to Grindlewood soon.

'Are we all here, then?' asked the Brigadier in a loud voice.

'No,' said Eldric, impatiently. 'Norville is missing. He's late again.' With that, a sweating, gasping, exhausted hedgehog trundled out of the bushes.

'Goodness gracious, Norville, what happened to you?' asked the Brigadier.

'It's a long story,' gasped Norville.

'Where is Pippa, Norville?' barked Eldric, suddenly noticing that the little ladybird was missing.

'That's a long story too. Let me catch my breath, will you, and I'll tell you everything,' wheezed Norville.

Everyone was staring at him and whispering under their breath. The meeting was getting tense very quickly. And Eldric was snarling.

'Right then, ahem, I shall begin while Norville catches his breath,' said the Brigadier. 'First of all, we know that the butterflies' prediction of last week actually meant that the Grindles, together with Timber and Teddy, would be arriving. And may I say, we are all delighted to welcome you both, eh, all,' said the Brigadier, smiling. There was a collection of noises to welcome Timber and Teddy, who smiled and nodded at their new friends.

'As some of you already know, the butterflies have had a second vision. They predict that there will be another aerial attack in the coming days. This time, the nasty heron will be working with those dreadful magpies. I think we can expect the next attack to be even more vicious than the last one, especially for the fish and the little birds.'

There were many gasps among the audience.

'Everyone should be on alert, and try not to be too far away from somewhere safe to hide when this happens. Luckily we now have Timber and Teddy on our side and this should help us enormously as we defend the garden. All of us dogs, cats and foxes have been practising our plan of attack, or rather defence, and we will be ready when the heron and the magpies swoop in to make trouble.'

The residents whispered and nodded to each other. Everyone knew what they had to do, but some of them were still very worried.

'We have had lots of these attacks now, Brigadier,' said Ernie, the frog. 'When will they stop?'

'I don't know, Ernie, but we will do our best to protect ourselves and the garden, as always. For the first time ever, I am going to allow the use of extreme force,' said the Brigadier. Everyone cheered, except gentle Serena.

'Do you really think we will need to use teeth and claws?' asked the beautiful swan.

'Serena,' said Timber very gently, 'from what the Brigadier has told me, scaring them might be enough. But if not, we will have to get tough to protect the garden and all the residents, especially the smaller ones.'

'Yes, I see what you mean,' said Serena quietly.

'Well said, Timber,' said the Brigadier, delighted with some support from the big dog. 'Unfortunately, we now believe there are other dangers lurking nearby as well. I will hand over to Eldric to explain.'

The Brigadier stepped back to let the clever fox continue the meeting.

'Thank you, Brigadier,' said Eldric. 'Good evening, all. Firstly, earlier today Norville told me about some disturbing rumours regarding our nearby forest. Secondly, Sylvie confirmed that a couple of months ago she did indeed see a wolf in there when she was up one of our trees. Thirdly, the butterflies' earlier message about a wolf, which we thought at first meant Timber, also confirms that there is indeed a wolf in the forest.'

Almost everyone shrieked. Most of them had never had to worry about wolves. A few had never seen or heard of a wolf. Now it seemed there was one living right beside them.

'I was right! I was right! I knew it! Eldric, let me speak, let me speak!' squealed Norville, pushing his way to the front. 'Friends, I foolishly went to poke around the edge of the forest this afternoon, and I met a very nasty fellow called Valerius Vole. He mentioned his master, Worfeus, and he tried to lure me into the forest. I was really scared, *really* scared.' Norville gulped.

'What about Pippa, Norville? Where is she now?' barked Eldric.

'Oh dear, well, Pippa came with me. She flew off before the vole grabbed me and I didn't see her again. I don't know where she went. I had to run for it. I'm so sorry. Oh dear, this is dreadful!'

This time, several of the group shouted loudly. The poor little ladybird was lost in the forest, probably in grave danger, or maybe even dead.

'How could you be so foolish, Norville?' snarled the fox. 'You put our smallest friend in mortal danger. Are you crazy? You have your nasty little spikes to protect you. What has she got to defend herself with?'

The fox wasn't the only one who felt angry. But Timber quickly intervened.

'Steady on, now. It seems Norville was a bit foolish, but a ladybird is so small that she might not have been seen at all. She may be all right. We could try to organise a search party. Or perhaps we …' Timber stopped short. They heard a great whooshing sound getting louder and louder, closer and closer.

WHOOSH! WHOOSH! WHOOSH! WHOOSH!

'To-wit-to-woo! To-wit-to-woo! Good evening, my name is Oberon, and I think I have someone who belongs to you!'

The beautiful snowy owl landed gracefully in the middle of the residents. To their great surprise, Pippa was tucked snugly into the back of his neck, safe and warm amongst the owl's thick white feathers.

'Pippa! Oh Pippa!' cried Norville. 'I am so, so sorry. Are you all right?' He rushed over to nudge her gently with his nose.

'Oh yes, I'm fine, thank you. You look rather shaken, though! Hello, everyone. Sorry I'm late. Oberon found me asleep amongst the dead leaves and very kindly offered me a lift home. He seemed to

know I didn't belong in that forest. That was very kind of you, Oberon,' said Pippa in her dainty voice.

'You are most welcome,' replied the owl. 'I spotted little Pippa when I came out to hunt this evening,' said the owl, looking around him.

'We are very grateful to you, Oberon,' said the Brigadier.

'I would like a moment of your time, if I may, to tell you an interesting story,' said the owl.

'But of course,' said the Brigadier. 'Please do.'

'Actually, I have been watching you all for quite a while now,' said the snowy owl, eyeing each and every one of the group, slowly and carefully.

'Please, please go ahead,' said the Brigadier, bewildered.

The owl had everyone's total attention. He briefly explained the history of the war between the Worfagon clan and the Forest Queen's loyal followers, the Wandelei. He then talked about an evil warlock and a good witch, who had lived secretly for a while in and around the forest and Grindlewood, not too long ago.

'I told you so, I told you so,' cried Norville, glancing at a very cross fox.

'Quiet, Norville!' snarled Eldric.

'About five years ago, the last of the truly good and clever witches lived here in Grindlewood. Wanda was her name – Wanda of the Wandelei clan. Wanda's queen had been dreadfully cursed, and was doomed to live, stuck in the ground and growing like a tree, until someone clever enough could undo such powerful dark magic.'

'After many, many years of failure by the queen's shrinking number of geniuses, young Wanda decided to ask permission of the queen to leave the clan and seek out new magic, even dark magic, to try to find a counter spell to free the queen from the ground. The queen granted her permission, but also asked her to find, or create, a special spell to rid the world of Worfeus the wicked warlock, who was, and still is, the leader of the Worfagon clan. The queen held Worfeus responsible for all the Wandelei's troubles, and the two remain deadly enemies.'

The residents were utterly amazed. They were listening to a story about warlocks and witches, magic and spells, all in their very own neighbourhood, in Grindlewood. But the owl had more to say.

'So, after many years of difficult and dangerous

work, Wanda did create some very special spells, including one that could actually destroy Worfeus. No sword or shotgun could finish him off. He had learned dark and powerful magic over many years, and he practised it often. He had grown too strong and too mad to control. The good witch Wanda knew this and was afraid that if anything happened to her, no one else would know how to defeat the dreaded Worfeus. So she wrote down her spells, on a special scroll of parchment, which she hoped to return to her queen.'

There wasn't a sound at the meeting as Oberon paused and then continued.

'Unfortunately, Wanda ran out of time when Worfeus caught up with her, but it is rumoured that she managed to hide the scroll safely. Once he had killed Wanda, Worfeus had to find and destroy the scroll himself to be absolutely certain that no threat to him remained.'

Oberon confirmed the story of the bitter duel and

Worfeus' obsession with finding not just the scroll, but also the queen's personal treasures.

'After the duel, and to his great annoyance, Worfeus found that he couldn't escape the forest once he had returned to it. The spell Wanda cast as she lay dying had cursed him to remain imprisoned there, stuck in the form of a mangy wolf. He is said to be still there, working on potions to return him to his warlock form, and also trying to formulate a spell that will allow him to leave the forest. Thankfully he has had no luck solving that particular problem – so far. Wanda cast her clever spells to give others the time to find the secret scroll and cast the only spell that would rid this world of the evil Worfeus.'

It was quite a story for the residents to take in.

'But why didn't Wanda cast the spell herself?' asked Dougal.

'Good question, young fellow, good question. Unfortunately, she couldn't. The spell was so intricate, so the story goes, that the creator of the spell could not be the one to cast it. Someone else would have to do that. Such conditions are not unusual when dealing with the darkest, cleverest magic.'

The audience felt nervous as the owl looked

slowly and steadily around the group. Who could be the one to cast the spell? Was it one of them? They all shuddered to think of it.

Chapter Eight

HATCHING A PLAN

Oberon finished his story with great flapping of his large wings and stood back, waiting for a moment for his audience to think about it. The residents were stunned. All this had happened on their doorstep, some of it in their very own garden.

'My friends, any of you in the garden that very day, close to where the final spells were cast, may have been sprinkled with stardust that exploded from the clashing of the spells. This may explain why some of you have some rather special, if unusual, talents.'

The owl looked around at everyone, and everyone looked around at each other. It was true. Some of them did have special abilities. They never had any explanation for this before. They had just accepted it as part of the wonder of Grindlewood.

'How do you know all this?' asked Sylvie.

The owl suddenly looked rather sad.

'Around the time this happened, I was living at the edge of the forest, but I wanted to leave the place immediately on hearing of the dreadful duel. Before I left, I was approached by Worfeus himself.'

'You were approached by the warlock?' cried Dougal.

'Really!' said Eldric.

'Yes, he wanted to enlist me to his cause, to be one of his spies. But I suspected that he really wanted to know all that I had learned about the Wandeleis. I had studied them for many years, you see. I am quite the expert on the history of magic.'

The meeting was becoming darker by the minute.

'After he approached me and I declined, I thought it was best to leave. So I flew away to another forest. Recently I heard through the tree-tops about Timber and Teddy arriving here with a new family, and something in my feathers told me that I should come back. Then when I found Pippa in the forest, I knew the time had come to tell you what I know – the history, the magic, the scroll, all of it.'

The owl looked quite exhausted with all his storytelling.

'What should we do now?' asked Sylvie gingerly.

'Well, Worfeus will keep searching for the secret scroll until he finds it. There's no doubt about that,' said the snowy owl.

'He has searched the area around here for a long time, then he searched the forest, all the time getting closer to Grindlewood garden. He must be very angry and frustrated by now, especially as he is still stuck in that forest. And as he hasn't found it in all this time, I suspect that the scroll may be hidden here in the garden, my friends.'

Oberon listened as the residents chatted together, trying to understand every word.

'So what Norville said about Valerius Vole is true. He must be Worfeus' servant, his slave. I suppose he patrols the forest and reports back to the warlock,' said Eldric.

'Yes,' said Oberon, 'and he sends the magpies out to spy for him too.'

Timber stepped forward. 'This Worfeus fellow must be stopped, and it sounds like the only thing that can stop him is Wanda's special spell. It seems that we, the residents of Grindlewood, will have to continue what Wanda started. We live here, so this is our quest now. We must find that scroll, cast that spell, and rid the world of the evil warlock.'

Everyone looked at Timber. He sounded so determined. The residents were shocked and scared, but they agreed.

'Yes, quite,' said the Brigadier. 'It is up to us now. We are the protectors of Grindlewood after all.'

'I am so pleased to hear you say that,' said Oberon, looking more relieved. 'There is one other thing you should know, though. There was a young boy who was Wanda's friend. He disappeared right after she was killed. He hasn't been seen since and no one knows what happened to him. You may have heard mention of him. His name is Luke Finlay. He is the local farmer's son.'

'Oh, this is not good,' muttered Dougal, wondering if he was up to the task they were faced with.

'So while Worfeus is stuck in the forest, he has to send the magpies and the heron, and whoever else he has working for him, to chase us out of the garden. He must believe then, that we are protecting the scroll, or at least keeping it from him,' said Timber, raising his voice to be heard over all the chattering and sighing.

He was beginning to get a clear picture in his head of the story, including the butterflies' prediction about the next attack.

'Yes, I have no doubt that Worfeus will do whatever it takes to get what he wants,' Oberon replied.

'I don't like the sound of that, and neither will the fish, or the ducks and swans,' said Ernie. He didn't like the thought of telling the goldfish about all this trouble. They were having a dreadful time already, trying to avoid the heron's attacks. Danville eyed Serena. They both wanted to return home quickly to their families.

'Look, everyone, I know this is a bit of a shock, but Worfeus cannot leave the forest, not yet anyway. We simply must find the scroll, and quickly, before he figures out a way of escaping his forest prison. And figure it out he will,' hooted the owl, waving his wings again.

'Yes, once we have the scroll, that evil warlock's days are numbered,' said Timber.

'Yes, quite right. We must come up with a plan to deal with all of this,' said the Brigadier, looking anxiously around, hoping everyone would support the idea. They had one problem to deal with first, however.

'The first thing to prepare for is the next aerial attack. When that is over we must meet again and decide how we begin this quest. So, please go home now and try to get some sleep. I think we have had enough excitement for one night. Thank you again, Oberon, for the safe return of Pippa, and, eh, for telling us all that, ahem, yes.'

The Brigadier leaned closer to the owl. 'Oberon, perhaps you could stay a few minutes for a further chat with me and the cats and dogs, and we'll fill you in on our existing plans. You might have something useful to add. I don't want to trouble the others any more tonight.'

'Yes, of course,' tooted the owl. 'And I would like a quick word with the frog if you don't mind. Ernie, do you have a minute?'

'Oh, me? Sure, Mr Oberon.' Ernie hopped over to the owl, who bent down low and whispered to him.

'I mentioned earlier, Ernie, that some stardust must have sprinkled on a few of your friends and given them a special talent or charm.'

'Yes, I heard you, Mr Oberon.'

'Well, if the fish in the pond can swim at jet-speed as a result of being sprinkled with stardust, and yes, I have seen them, then it is also very likely that some of that same stardust landed on you. You would have been in the pond at the very same time, wouldn't you?'

Ernie nodded with his mouth wide open, and his eyes bulging bigger and bigger.

'This means, Ernie, that you must also have some special charm. You just haven't discovered it yet. Let's hope it's something really special.' The owl winked at Ernie and then turned to go back to the others.

'Are you sure? Me, really?' he croaked.

'Yes, I am quite certain. And make sure you tell the goldfish to be on the alert,' he called back to the surprised frog.

Ernie hopped off to the pond, somewhat bewildered, somewhat excited, wondering what his special talent could be. He had never been special before.

'I'd like to stay for this chat too, if you don't mind,' said Eldric.

'Me too,' quipped Norville, still feeling very sorry for endangering Pippa, but also a bit relieved that his horrible hunch had been right, and not just in his imagination. Those who stayed behind to talk with the owl huddled close together in the bushes. The others said their goodbyes and headed off into the night.

Chapter Nine

THE GOOD, THE BAD AND THE BRAVE

The chickens didn't know how important the meeting would be. They always sent the rooster to represent them. As usual, they assumed that they would hear the details from him later. They had been having trouble organising their dance routine and there was a lot of arguing going on. In fact there was a full-blown row in progress when they were interrupted.

On his way back to the coop from the meeting, Roosevelt spotted Delilah in the rushes at the edge of the pond, peering and straining to see something.

'Hello, Delilah, have you lost something?' asked the rooster.

'Oh, Roosevelt. You startled me,' said Delilah, all aflutter.

'Is someone minding the ducklings tonight? I saw Danville earlier at the meeting. Is everything OK,

Delilah?' The rooster looked at her suspiciously as she shuffled on her feet.

'Oh yes, of course. My cousin Daphne is visiting and I left her in charge, only for a few minutes of course. I'm heading back there now.'

'Daphne is visiting? How nice. Now tell me,' said the rooster, looking her square in the face, 'what are you peeping at through the rushes, hmm?'

On hearing more squawks from the chickens, he turned towards the coop. He could just make out the flapping of wings and a few loose feathers flying.

'Good heavens, what are those chickens doing?'

'I think they are trying to dance,' said Delilah timidly. 'They are really very good, you know, though they seem to be having a few problems tonight,' she said.

'Do you watch them every night? I mean, do they dance every night?'

'Yes, yes they do, and, well, yes, so do I!' Delilah was blushing.

'Oh! Why didn't they tell me?' muttered Roosevelt, feeling left out.

Delilah decided to do something. 'Come on Roosevelt, let's ask them!'

She took him by the wing and marched him to the coop, which was in chaos.

'Hello, everyone, you know me, Delilah, from over on the pond. The rooster and I were wondering if we could help.'

She sounded very sure of herself, but she was very unsure of how they would react. The chickens looked surprised for a moment, and then their rowing began again, each one blaming the other for the breakdown of the dance routine. Then Roosevelt had an idea.

'I might be able to help,' he said loudly, raising his voice to be heard over all the squabbling. 'I suspect you think I'm just a big, fat, silly old rooster, but when I was younger, I could really jive!'

The chickens' beaks fell open, as they watched the rooster demonstrate a few of his dance steps.

'Well, whoopee!' clucked one chicken.

'Are you kidding?' clucked another, trying to stifle her surprise.

'Yes, really, and no, I'm not kidding,' said Roosevelt proudly. 'Perhaps I could help you with some of the dance steps. You seemed a little bit lost in that middle section.'

'Yes, and I had some ideas too. That bit you left out

tonight, the waddling bit, that looked really good last week. You should include that again,' offered Delilah. 'You could try it like this,' and she shook her tail feathers from side to side like a real expert.

'Hmmm, that's not bad, Delilah. Have you been watching us for long?' asked a curious chick.

'Oh, I'm your biggest fan. Any chance I could have a go?' asked Delilah, hoping they would allow her to join in. The chickens all looked at each other, amazed at all this interest from a duck and an oversized rooster. They nodded their agreement. Why not?

'Come on, everybody, let's dance!' shouted the biggest chicken, and Delilah jumped and clucked for joy. Roosevelt beamed with delight and fluttered his great feathers. They all scuttled off to the barn for a chat. Tomorrow they would sort out the new dance routine and begin practising right away. But first, the rooster had to fill them in on what had happened at the meeting.

The next day the Grindles decided to go to the local farmers' market.

'Can we go into the garden before we go out,

Mum?' asked Jemima.

'All right, but don't be long, please,' replied Gloria as she tidied up the breakfast things. Jamie and Jemima dashed outside immediately.

'Oh no, Jamie, look! It's Ruby Robin and she looks hurt!' cried Jemima almost in tears at the sight of the little robin stumbling about, trying to hop under some flowers to hide.

'I think her leg might be broken. I'll go and get the frog,' said Jamie, starting to run. Then he stopped. 'That's the right thing to do, isn't it?' Jamie asked his sister, knowing she would agree, but not knowing how he knew the frog could help the little robin. He just knew.

'Yes, hurry Jamie. Get him quickly. I'll stay with Ruby,' urged Jemima, as she bent down towards the nervous bird.

Jamie tore off towards the pond. He hoped he would find the frog quickly and not have to get wet into the bargain. That would make his mum very cross.

Luckily, Ernie was sitting on one of the lily leaves. Jamie gently stroked the water to draw the lily leaf closer to him. As the leaf came within reach, he leaned over and lifted the frog gently into his hands.

'Hello, Ernie,' he whispered, 'we need your help.'

Jamie ran quickly back to Jemima with a surprised-looking Ernie sitting in his cupped hands.

'Here, Jemima, I have him,' said Jamie.

'Ernie, you must help Ruby. She has hurt her leg,' said Jemima so earnestly that Ernie just stared at her. Then he saw his friend Ruby and hopped over to her.

'Hello, Ruby, what on earth happened to you?' he asked the robin. She was sitting uncomfortably under some flowers.

'Oh, I wasn't looking where I was going,' twittered the frustrated little robin to the frog. 'I was chasing a worm in the grass, you see, and then I saw a juicy beetle in the flowerbed, and when I went after him, I tripped and hurt my leg. Oh, how stupid of me.'

'Don't worry, Ruby, I'll kiss it better for you!' said Ernie, hoping to make her laugh and forget how sore it was.

'Oh, thanks Ernie, that feels much better,' said a surprised Ruby.

'It does?' said the even-more-surprised frog.

'Why, yes, it's absolutely fine! Look! Thank you,

Ernie. My leg is perfect. How wonderful!' cried Ruby.

After testing her leg a few more times, she flew off to tell her mate Reggie the news.

The children watched her fly away safely.

'Well done, Ernie,' said a very pleased Jamie.

'The butterflies told us you were special, Ernie,' said Jemima. 'In fact, they told us lots of things about the residents who live in this garden, just by sitting on our hair,' she said, as she stroked the happy frog on his less warty tummy. Jamie popped the frog back in the pond, before the two children ran back to the house. It was time to go to the market.

In amongst the lily leaves, Ernie marvelled at his newfound ability. He remembered what the snowy owl had said to him the night before. He suddenly thought that he should tell the others what had happened. This could be important. But Ruby and Reggie were already spreading the news. Ernie really had been sprinkled with stardust after all, and they had discovered his enchantment at just the right time.

As the family headed out, Sylvie picked a nice sunny spot to snooze for the morning. Cindy, Teddy and

Dougal were busy chasing another ball of wool, and getting all tangled up every now and again. Timber and the Brigadier were about to do their early morning woof patrol, when Balthazar buzzed over and rested on a bright red geranium near the kennel.

'Excuse me, dogs. I would like a word if you have a moment.'

Sylvie opened one eye and decided to join them. She was curious.

'Of course, Balthazar, what seems to be the trouble?' enquired the Brigadier.

'I reported back to the hive on what was said at last night's meeting.' Balthazar sounded a little uncomfortable. 'Well, you see, some of the elder bees had an idea. Not really an idea, but more of a suggestion, quite an amazing suggestion.' The big bee was finding it hard to get the words out.

'What is it, Balthazar?' asked Timber, suspecting something alarming.

'Well, we don't usually get involved in these things, but we want to help out when this next aerial attack comes.' He took a deep breath. 'To put it simply, the elder bees have volunteered to attack the magpies with their stings.' He waited for a moment for this piece of news to sink in. 'You all know what this means. If they use their stings like that, they will die.' Tears filled the bee's eyes.

'Oh my, that is incredible,' said the Brigadier. 'But why, Balthazar?'

'All of those who volunteered are due to die next winter, you see. They said they would rather die for the greater good of the garden, than simply die off slowly during the cold winter months. I insisted none of the younger ones be allowed to do it, but I just couldn't persuade the elder bees against it. They said they would do it with or without my permission. Can you believe it?' said Balthazar, still surprised by the bees' announcement.

'I think that's the bravest thing I've ever heard,' said Timber.

'It certainly is,' added the Brigadier.

'I'm still getting used to the idea,' said Balthazar.

'Come on, let's sit down in the kennel and talk it through. Hop on my head Balthazar. You look a bit wobbly,' said the Brigadier. Timber and Sylvie followed. Teddy and Dougal joined them too.

After they had talked things over with Balthazar, the bee flew back to the hive to tell the bees of their plans. The cats and dogs were joined by the foxes in the kennel. They had a little time to talk over their plan to find the scroll, while the family was still out.

'If Worfeus is attacking this garden, then he not only wants the scroll, he wants revenge for being stuck in that forest. If he is that angry, he will keep attacking this garden, until he gets what he wants,' said Timber.

'No doubt about it,' agreed Eldric.

'So what do we do?' asked Dougal.

'We need to plan our defence of the garden, and organise a search,' replied Timber.

'Well, I have some ideas about our defence,' said the Brigadier proudly. 'We have teams in the air – the birds – and teams on the ground – the cats, dogs and foxes.'

'Don't forget me,' squeaked Norville as he entered the kennel.

'Yes, of course. Hello, Norville,' said the Brigadier, slightly embarrassed that he *had* actually forgotten him. Norville was always happy to do his bit, but he was a lot smaller and slower than the other animals. He tired quickly too.

'We don't usually include the rabbits, chickens and ducks in any defence planning, as they can panic a lot and that doesn't help,' said Sylvie, feeling a bit mean for criticising some of her friends. 'The insects and pondlife have never been asked to do much either.'

'I understand,' said Timber. 'The Brigadier has explained your recent defence of the garden to me, and I have a couple of suggestions, which I think might be helpful.'

'Excellent,' said the Brigadier.

'And I have a few ideas about the search,' said Teddy.

'Yes, Teddy and I were talking for a long time last night about the scroll and where it could be hidden. We need to break up into search parties and cover different areas of the garden. That way, we can keep looking, and hopefully not be noticed by the Grindles, or Worfeus' spies. There will be times, though, when we have to stop or our searching will become too suspicious,' said Timber.

'Especially to the magpies,' added Teddy.

So the animals huddled close together and worked out who would do what and when and where in the garden. They decided that the search would begin immediately after the next aerial attack was over. Until then, there would be military training so that every resident would know what to do when Worfeus' evil birds swooped in.

Chapter Ten

AERIAL ATTACK

A combined attack by the magpies and the heron hadn't happened before. It had always been one or the other, not both.

The big magpies were troublesome birds with black and white feathers and very long tails. They weren't quite as large as resident Waldorf Woodpigeon, but they had strong, straight beaks that could do awful damage to other birds or even small animals. They especially liked to chase the blackbirds and robins, who they knew would get agitated and squawky. Most of them nested in the forest, close to Worfeus. They were part of his evil army. There was no doubt that these birds were an absolute menace to all the residents of the garden.

Waldorf Woodpigeon was on watch in the tallest tree. A stout and stately woodland bird, he was much bigger than the other garden birds. His feathers were a lovely mix of greys and soft mauve, and he blended in beautifully with the trees. This made him difficult to spot. Waldorf's most important job was to herald in the new seasons with his gentle coo-coo song. Today, however, his woodland song would instead be a warning. It would announce the arrival of the joint attack of the magpies and the horrid heron.

The rabbits, ducks and chickens all had new offspring to guard, so they remained safely hidden in their homes. Waldorf and the blackbirds spread out across the garden, on lookout.

As expected, the woodpigeon spotted the trouble first and sent out his warning signal as loudly as he could. The blackbirds followed, using their high-pitched squawk to further raise the alarm. Then the magpies attacked with speed. They flew in from a height, screeching wildly with excitement. They were almost hysterical. They separated into three groups of four, zooming around the garden in different directions.

Sixty elder bees were hiding in the fruit trees, ready to fly out from their cover. The four feisty blackbirds, Billy, Binky, Barty and Bertram, darted out from the oak trees to try to lure the magpies towards the waiting bees. The magpies fell for the trick. Balthazar was at the ready as the first group of magpies flew by in hot pursuit of the blackbird quartet. At the right moment, he gave the final command to his fellow bees, 'CHARGE! ATTACK! STING!'

The elder bees flew out and surrounded the four magpies, landing on them, clinging on as they fired their stings into the evil birds. The magpies hurtled downwards, twitching, squirming and squawking, unable to fly and not knowing quite what had happened. The cats, dogs, foxes and hedgehog were all hiding in the long grass close to the orchard and the pond. Wherever the injured magpies hit the ground, the animals jumped out and finished them off. As they bit into the magpies' stinging flesh, the nasty birds simply turned into dust. Clearly they were part of the warlock's evil army, made of dark, dark magic.

The other magpies saw what had happened and avoided the orchard and two groups of four swooped in over the centre of the garden. With a tremendous

whooshing sound, the swans descended from the sky, led by Serena and Swinford. Their huge wide wings and swan-cries distracted and confused the magpies. They circled and turned to attack, beaks pointed and ready. The swans clashed with the magpies, causing great screeching and sending feathers flying. A few injured magpies fell to the ground, badly injured by nasty bites from the swans' sharp teeth. As they neared the ground, the cats leapt up to catch them. Again, the nasty birds turned to dust. Others reached the ground and then limped away to hide in the grass, only to be pounced on by the waiting foxes. They too turned to dust.

At the same time as all of this was happening, the nasty heron headed for the pond. Cyril didn't live in the garden at all, but he crashed in now and again, mainly to terrify the goldfish. His long skinny legs were great for wading in the shallower water as his beady eyes searched the pond for the quivering fish. His long neck and extremely long beak were also great for fishing. Knowing the cats hated water, he waded into the middle of the pond, well out of their reach.

The goldfish had retreated to their special hideouts, where they would remain until the danger had passed.

The ducks dived into the thickest reeds, and Ernie hid under a few well-positioned stones.

When he saw that wading would not work, Cyril changed his plan. Instead, he hovered low over the water trying to spy the goldfish over a wider and deeper area. He flew up and down, staying close to the surface, all the while trying to spy the hiding fish. While he was concentrating his gaze below the surface of the water, Timber suddenly leapt from the long grass at the edge of the pond and swiped at him with his big front paw.

THWACK!

The heron fell into the pond with a massive splash. Dougal bounded in and snatched the stunned bird out of the water. He shook the heron in his mouth and then dropped him on the ground. Cyril lay on the grass twitching and squirming, surrounded by the cats, dogs and foxes. He was well and truly caught. The Brigadier stepped forward and barked sharply at their prisoner.

'Tell us, who are you and why are you tormenting us? Why are you attacking our pond?' Cyril was crying with pain. He knew he was done for. His wing was broken, so he had no chance of escape. He would be in big trouble with Worfeus too, as he had failed in his task yet again. There was no way out. He was finished. He might as well tell the truth.

'I'm sorry,' he wailed. 'My name is Cyril. The warlock Worfeus took my mate, my lovely Harriet, when we were nesting near the edge of the forest. He said he would kill her if I didn't do what he told me to. He wanted me to keep everyone away from the pond, and especially away from that fountain. I tried to scare them off but they kept coming back to do their silly swimming race. Worfeus said that if I couldn't scare them away, I had to kill them. The magpies told him everything I did. He said that if I failed again, he would kill my Harriet. That's all I know. I'm sorry, I'm sorry,' he sobbed. 'Worfeus will kill Harriet now, so I might as well be dead too. I didn't want to do it. I was only trying to save her.'

'All you had to do was ask us for help, you know,' said the Brigadier, feeling a bit sorry for the heron. He was inclined to believe the bird's story.

'And what could you have done?' asked Cyril. 'Harriet is a prisoner in Worfeus' lair. How can anyone get her out without doing what he asks?'

The residents looked on, wondering what they

should do with Cyril.

'I have an idea,' said Eldric slyly. 'Cyril, very shortly you will die from that broken wing or from the nasty bites that we could give you. Unless, of course …' Eldric stopped and whispered to the others. They all nodded in agreement.

'Huh?' croaked Cyril. He hardly cared anymore and his eyes were half closed in pain.

'… Unless, you nasty heron, we heal your wing and in return you promise to help us defeat the warlock. This is the only way you will save Harriet, and yourself,' said Eldric sharply.

'Wait! How do we know he's telling the truth?' asked Teddy.

He was worried that perhaps they were too quick to believe the heron's story. After all, he could have made a different choice and asked them for help, just like the Brigadier had said.

'The butterflies,' said Sylvie. 'Let's ask the butterflies. They are never wrong. They can tell us if what Cyril said is true.'

Everyone looked at the butterflies. But unfortunately they couldn't speak unless they had a vision.

'Perhaps the butterflies could *indicate* if the story is true,' suggested Timber.

'Good idea!' said the Brigadier. He trotted over to the butterflies. They were perched nearby on a bunch of pink roses.

'Ladies, could you please land on my head if the heron's story is true. If it is false, please stay exactly where you are.'

Everyone held their breath, waiting for the response. The enchanted butterflies flitted gracefully over to the Brigadier and landed on his head. It was true, then.

'Thank you, ladies, thank you,' said the Brigadier. Everyone felt reassured.

'Now we can continue,' said Sylvie.

'Cyril, all the magpies are either dead or have already flown away,' said Eldric. 'There are none still in the garden to spy on you. If we agree that you can leave here healed, you must return to the forest and pretend to Worfeus that your wing was only bruised and you escaped us by hiding. You can tell him that from now on, instead of attacking the pond, you will perch on top of the statue, listening and watching. That way Worfeus won't be suspicious of you being here without attacking us all the time. When you return to the forest, keep your eyes and ears peeled for any information that might help us. You will be *our* spy from now on, not his.'

They waited for an answer from the exhausted heron. Timber nudged Cyril a few times with his big, strong, thwacking paw to remind him of what had just happened.

'Cyril, you won't get a better deal than this,' he said.

He hoped the heron would agree to their terms, otherwise they might have to kill him, and somehow that just didn't seem right. After all, the heron wasn't something created from dark and evil magic in a warlock's cauldron. He was a real bird, a bird that should be their friend.

Cyril weakly nodded his agreement. He had been caught, he was injured and he was probably dying. He had lost everything. It was a generous deal after all the trouble he had caused. How foolish he had been, how weak.

As they all waited for Ernie to arrive to heal the heron's broken wing, their thoughts turned to Harriet and to the wicked warlock, Worfeus. Was Harriet still alive? How would they free her from the warlock's lair? Were they crazy to take on this evil warlock at all?

Chapter Eleven

SO THE QUEST BEGINS

The residents stood in a circle to watch as Ernie hopped over to the injured heron. At Timber's woof and the Brigadier's nod, the frog kissed Cyril on his broken wing. It healed instantly.

'Oh my!' gasped Cyril. 'What can I do now?' he asked, still a bit nervous.

'Well,' said Timber, 'as we said, you can be our spy and let us know what Worfeus is up to. If you hear anything about a secret scroll that he is looking for, that might help us too.'

'I have heard of it, but I only know that he is terrified that someone will find it before he does. He doesn't know where it is, just that some boy hid it or something, but apparently that same boy is missing as well. It all sounded very complicated. Worfeus gets a bit crazy at any mention of the scroll.'

The sound of wheezing and rustling in the long grass grabbed everyone's attention.

'Help, someone, help!' squeaked Norville. 'Get this horrible thing off my back. Please, someone, help!'

The hedgehog struggled into the centre of the group. There was a magpie stuck on his back.

'This disgusting thing was stung by the bees and fell out of the sky. It has taken me all this time to get here, he is so terribly heavy.'

'Let me see, Norville,' said Eldric. 'I'd be happy to pull him off. I don't think he is quite dead yet or he would have turned to dust like the others. Hold on there.'

Eldric and Teddy clawed at the magpie to get him off Norville's back. When they did, the magpie turned to dust, just as expected.

'Oh, thank you, that was horrible,' said Norville, greatly relieved. He shook his spikes till they almost rattled.

'That's what happens to friends of Worfeus,' said Timber to the heron, pointing to the pile of dust that was once a magpie. 'Are you absolutely sure you are ready to join us now? There will be no mercy if you break our trust.' He spoke sternly, wanting to be certain that the heron was really on their side.

'I'm sure,' said Cyril humbly. 'I don't see any other way to save Harriet, or myself for that matter. And you're right. I made the wrong choice before, and the least I can do now, is to try to put things right somehow.'

Cyril was feeling deeply sorry, wishing he had never agreed to help Worfeus at all, even if it had been all for Harriet. He should have known better and instead have asked for help from the residents of the garden.

'Very well, then,' said Timber. The big dog stood up and threw back his head. He made the biggest, longest wolf howl he could muster. 'Aroo-woo-woo, Aroo-woo-wooooo.'

He was letting everyone in the neighbourhood know that Grindlewood and all its residents would defend their territory, no matter what Worfeus had planned.

'Well, Timber, that was a job well done, I think,' said

the Brigadier proudly, as they trotted back towards the kennel.

'It certainly was,' agreed Timber. 'And young Dougal did very well too.'

'He has really grown up these past few weeks. He is going to make an excellent dog, just like you and me, ha ha!' said the Brigadier. 'See you later.'

The Brigadier went for a snooze while Timber checked around the garden once more. The rain was falling quite heavily, washing away all traces of feathers and magpie dust that had been strewn around the garden. The wind had picked up too, so the rain would pass quickly enough. It would be nice to have some cheerful sunshine in the garden after such a frightful morning.

Later in the day, as the weather did indeed begin to improve, the residents all went about their usual routines. The Grindles came home from the market with some lovely cakes and pies, and the children ran out to play with their pets. Normality returned, at least for a while.

The residents knew that more trouble lay ahead, but now they felt they knew their purpose. They were determined to find and decipher the secret scroll, to defeat the evil warlock and to save Grindlewood. This had been Wanda's quest and now it was theirs. They knew they had to succeed before Worfeus found a way to get out of the forest. Although the good witch was gone, she had certainly enchanted some of the residents, and more importantly, she had cursed the warlock, keeping him locked in the forest. This meant the residents had a little head start, at least for now.

They all hoped, too, that they would find Luke, the missing boy. The quest had really begun for the residents and the clock was ticking. It was time to put their search plan into action.

Chapter Twelve

CYRIL VISITS THE WARLOCK

September arrived and the children were preparing for their new school. Their bags were packed and their new uniforms were hanging in their bedrooms ready for the first day. Greg and Gloria still had no grand plan for the wild and unruly garden. For the moment they were busy doing up the house. Outside, the residents were holding meetings on a regular basis to keep everyone up to date with any news about the wicked warlock Worfeus. The race was on to find the secret scroll, which they now assumed must be hidden somewhere in Grindlewood garden.

Without drawing too much attention, the residents carefully searched the garden again and again. They found nothing. There seemed to be no clues at all, and no one could think where a secret scroll might be hidden. They had to get some information from the only other person who knew enough about the scroll to want it so badly: Worfeus, himself.

A couple of days after the aerial attack, Cyril had to muster up the courage to report back to Worfeus and explain his failed attack on the pond. Worfeus would be expecting him, and as always he would be angry and impatient. The magpies had already informed the warlock of the heron's failings, but at least his nasty birds had stayed well clear of the garden since the last attack. To their surprise, nearly two-thirds of their group had been caught and killed. Despite feeling angry and wanting revenge, they had to wait for the warlock's instructions, and he was waiting for the heron.

Cyril ignored their cackles and taunts as he flew straight to Worfeus' lair. He landed gracefully on a dead tree stump and waited. He knew Worfeus would keep him waiting and that it would be a most unpleasant meeting. The poor heron was very nervous. When Worfeus eventually emerged, he was much more than irritated or angry. He was absolutely livid. He was also stuck in the form of a wolf, something that made him mad as hell.

'CYRIL! You stupid scrawny wretch! How many

times did I tell you that if you messed up again, I would kill your pathetic Harriet? Explain yourself and your repeated failure to do as I command!'

Worfeus was raging so much he was foaming at the mouth. He was a truly disgusting sight. But Cyril had to be brave. It was important that he remained calm and didn't mess up this moment.

'Worfeus, I'm very sorry it didn't go as planned, but the residents of the garden were very well prepared. They killed several of your magpies, as you know.' Cyril tried his best to sound upset.

'I know all that – the other magpies told me. You should have killed the goldfish while all that bedlam was going on. And where have you been hiding until now?'

'I was hit by one of the dogs and my wing was badly injured. I managed to hide in the bushes when the animals left, and then I stumbled away to recover. I returned here as soon as my bruised wing healed enough to fly again.'

Worfeus stared hard at him. His eyes were like tiny black slits, edged in red.

'You are nothing but a useless bunch of feathers. You can't even catch a few goldfish! You are pathetic, a complete waste of my time, you stupid bird!' The wolf roared right into Cyril's face, as the heron leaned back to avoid the stench of wolf breath. There was a slobber of oozing green froth on his muzzle, left over from the potion he had recently drunk.

'Worfeus, I think …' began Cyril.

'WHAT? YOU! THINK? WHAT DO YOU THINK?' Worfeus continued spitting and snarling into poor Cyril's face, his stinking breath almost causing the heron to gag.

'Perhaps I should just watch the pond.' Cyril forced the words out quickly, as the wolf at last calmed down a little. 'Perhaps I should watch the pond from *within* the garden. That way I could see what all the residents are up to. That's what you really want, isn't it?' asked Cyril gingerly. He desperately hoped the enraged warlock would agree.

'Hmm, I don't know if you can do anything right. What makes you think this plan will work?'

Worfeus was very frustrated, but he clearly wanted a new plan. The idea of one of his spies sitting in the garden all day was quite tempting.

'Why don't I give it a try? I'll let you know each day what I see and hear, and whether the goldfish, or the others, get up to any mischief. After all, I can get a clear view of them if I perch on the fountain. That should keep them under control, I em, think.'

Cyril was afraid that he had said too much, and began to feel sick in his tummy and wobbly on his legs. He hoped that Worfeus would agree quickly and not think about it too much. If he did, he might sense something was wrong. Taking the warlock for a fool was a very dangerous game. Worfeus eyed him suspiciously for a long time.

'All right, you idiot bird, I'll give you one last chance. It might be time for a subtle change of plan. But you had better make it worth my while, or you know what I will do, Cyril, you know what I will do …' Worfeus put his grizzly muzzle right into Cyril's face again, making his threats all the more real. The terrified heron took a quick gulp of air, straining once again to avoid the wolf's revolting muzzle.

'Yes, yes of course, Worfeus. I will find out everything I can.'

'Yes, you will, or it won't just be Harriet who ends up in my dinner, or in that cauldron,' the wolf snarled. 'AND, if you have any thoughts of double-crossing me, be warned Cyril. You will suffer more dreadfully than you ever thought possible in that little pea-brain of yours. I will certainly make those residents suffer. I know their game! How dare they think they can keep that scroll from me! I'll make them suffer, and you too, Cyril, if you mess up one more time!'

Worfeus was still snarling as he turned and walked away. Suddenly he turned back and swiped Cyril with his hind leg, sending him tumbling and sprawling towards the cackling magpies and snivelling vole, who had gathered to hear their master's rant. They pecked and poked at Cyril as he tried to right himself. Finally, bruised and battered, Cyril took to the air and headed back to Grindlewood. He was greatly relieved that he had managed, somehow, to pass a very difficult test.

Chapter Thirteen

SEARCHING

Cyril flew into the garden and landed on the fountain to 'stand guard over the pond' as he had agreed. The residents spotted him and were eager to know all that had happened, but that would have to wait until later. They knew the magpies would be watching the heron for a while, at least until they got bored. It also meant that their search plans would have to wait too, until the magpies left.

A few of the residents gathered in the kennel for a chat. The new dog kennel was proving very popular. Teddy decided to take up the storytelling before the Brigadier began to tell more tales of his hunting days. It was time for something new, and Teddy had just the thing. He decided to tell everyone about Timber's brave deeds during their time in Alaska.

Poor Timber was very embarrassed by all of Teddy's

praise, so after the storytelling, a few jokes and a bit of teasing, they all moved off to return to their search. The magpies seemed to have left for the day, but they still had to be careful.

The cats searched the area nearest the house in case they were seen by the Grindles. It wouldn't look too odd if they were searching around, as cats are always very curious. They rooted around absolutely everywhere: in the barns, in the bins, in the work shed, much to Greg's annoyance, as they nearly knocked over several work tools, paints and glues. Late at night the cats crept around the house, sticking their heads and paws into every cupboard, box and crate, searching for the scroll or something that would lead them to it.

The dogs searched further down the garden, sniffing and digging so many holes that it ended up looking like the rabbit field next door. For a couple of weeks it was the same routine.

'Greg, what on earth are the dogs up to? They are digging holes all over the garden,' said Gloria, very confused by their behaviour.

'Yes, I noticed that. Every morning there seem to be more holes. I guess their noses are overloaded with all the new scents and smells. They're probably trying to figure out what's what and who's who out there, you know, territorial stuff in the animal kingdom. I saw it on one of those nature programmes Jamie loves. I don't think the dogs have uncovered any bones out there, have they?' asked Greg.

'I haven't seen any, thank goodness. Maybe that's what they want. I'll ask the butcher in the village if he has some big bones for the dogs to chew on. I'm sure they'll love them, and hopefully it will put an end to all that hole-digging.'

'Good idea, Gloria, and there's no point in planting any new grass or flowerbeds while all that is going on. We should wait till this digging phase is over, I think.' Greg chuckled to himself. It appeared to him that the dogs were having a hole-digging competition!

The foxes and the hedgehog were in the third group, even though poor Norville couldn't always keep up. His legs were much shorter, so the foxes were able to sniff, dig, search and run on to the next patch much more quickly than he could. But this did give Norville the chance to take a little break now and again, when he was left on his own for a bit. He was glad of every opportunity to rest, as he wasn't great at physical activity. So every time the foxes came back to look for him, he tried to look busy again. But when he was tired he started to moan.

'More searching, more searching. Why can't we find this silly scroll?'

'Norville, this scroll isn't silly, it's terribly important. It contains the only spell that can destroy the evil warlock – who, if I have to remind you, is presently stuck in that nearby forest,' said Eldric impatiently. Everyone was getting cross.

'Yes, yes, I know, of course I know, but we haven't found anything yet. Where do we look next? We have searched everywhere,' said Norville, still whining.

Eventually, after another fruitless hunt for everybody, they gave up for the day and they all went about their own business.

Later, the dogs were resting after some lively tricks with the children. The cats were just waking and stretching from their afternoon nap, when all the pets noticed the butterflies were moving about the statue.

'Oh no, not again!' said Eldric as

he waited for the moment they would fly over to the Brigadier with their message.

'Oh dear, so soon?' said Norville nervously.

'Let's hope that it's good news this time,' said Serena, who had just flown in for a swim on the pond and a chat with the ducks. As the butterflies flew off towards the Brigadier, everyone waited to hear what they would tell him.

'Oh, good! Ooooh, how wonderful! Wait, wait, who is it? Wait!' He called after the butterflies but they had fluttered back to the flowers. Their enchanted speech was already gone.

'What is it, Brigadier? What did they say?' asked Timber.

'It's good news, everyone, good news! We are going to have a wedding!' cried the Brigadier with delight, followed by confusion. Everyone looked pleased, then surprised, then puzzled. Who could be getting married?

Teddy eyed Cindy. No one knew his little secret, not even Timber. So who could be getting married if it wasn't them, he wondered? Everyone was curious to know who it could be and the news travelled quickly around the garden.

'Well, Eldric is it you, at last?' asked Norville.

'Of course not, you silly hedgehog,' replied Eldric with a snort.

'Oh, I was just wondering,' chuckled his friend.

'What about you, Norville? Any thoughts of finding Mrs Hedgehog?' asked Eldric.

'Oh no, I have no plans like that. I like my own company best of all,' answered Norville.

Eldric stifled a few chuckles as he trotted off. The thought of Norville being bossed about by a Mrs Hedgehog made him laugh.

The wedding question developed into a frenzy of betting excitement. The rooster had worked out the odds, but had managed to confuse everybody. He had never really been any good at doing sums. Some thought it might be Oberon who was getting married. When he had decided to move into one of the barns in the yard, he found that a pretty barn owl had just moved in. Oberon very politely asked permission to move in too, and the barn owl had agreed. She was a quiet sort of bird who kept to herself and didn't bother Oberon, nor did he bother her. And she had very generously offered to help Oberon with the search of the lofts. But some of the residents thought that the two owls must be the happy couple.

'There's just one big problem with that,' said Eldric to the rooster. 'Oberon is a snowy owl, and the other one is a barn owl. They will never get married.'

Eldric rolled his eyes to the sky, thinking the others were being quite absurd about all this love business. The rooster got into a total flap. He had to re-do his betting odds, and this time he didn't have a firm favourite, so he was in a total mess.

'I'm afraid it's true, Roosevelt,' confirmed the owl. He had come out to hunt just as it was getting dark. 'I have no wedding plans with the barn owl, or with anyone else for that matter. You'll have to look elsewhere for your answer.'

The rooster was plucking at his brown and orange feathers so much, he almost had a bald patch. He had been so sure about Oberon. Now it was back to the drawing board. If he didn't have a clue about who was getting married, then neither did anybody else. They would just have to wait and see.

Chapter Fourteen

NEW FRIENDS

The children loved their new school and were making lots of friends, many of whom were invited to Jemima's eighth birthday party. Jemima had told all her friends about her wonderful garden, her pets and all the amazing wildlife that lived there, and they were really looking forward to seeing it all. It was a lovely bright day in early October, and Jemima was very excited. She danced around the garden all morning, hugging her pets and chasing any other residents she could find.

She was thrilled with her birthday present from her mum and dad. Greg had made a beautiful doll's house, and Gloria had made all the furnishings and decorations. Jamie gave his sister a very special book about magic that he and his mum had found in the village bookshop. He was looking forward to the party too, as some of his friends were also invited. He was getting ready to play cowboys and Indians with the boys, followed, of course, by some football.

There were shrieks and squeals of delight as the pets were presented to all the visitors. They were a huge hit, and Timber did his special howl for everyone, but not before Gloria warned the children and some nervous-looking parents that his howl was particularly loud!

One of Jemima's friends, Abigail Allnutt, arrived at the party looking a bit forlorn. Her mother had come with her, carrying a large carry-box with a huge fluffy rabbit inside. This was Abigail's present to Jemima. Abigail's mum had heard that the Grindles had a big garden and lots of animals, so she thought that their family pet, which had grown too big for their little garden, would be a great gift for Jemima. Abigail loved her rabbit, but had reluctantly agreed with her mum that her pet might be happier in a bigger space.

'What a beautiful big rabbit, Abigail! Thank you so much. She's gorgeous!' cried Jemima as she reached for the bewildered bunny.

'Her name is Ramona. She has lovely soft white fur. She is so big she can be a bit clumsy, mind you.

Her hind legs and feet are very big, but she is a sweet thing. We, um, Abigail thought you would love to have her. She'll be, ahem, so happy with all your other pets, I think,' said Abigail's mum, hoping the Grindles would accept yet another pet. Greg was a little surprised, but he replied politely.

'Well, the more, the merrier, I guess. What do you think, Gloria?' Jemima had taken the rabbit out of the carry-box and was cuddling her closely. Ramona had already spotted the big garden and was keen to hop around.

'Well, yes, why ever not?' replied Gloria. She noticed that Abigail looked a little sad.

'Don't you worry, Abigail,' Gloria whispered to her. 'We will take really good care of Ramona, and you can come and see her whenever you like. We have a very big garden here and Ramona will have lots of room to play.'

This cheered Abigail up and she ran off with Jemima to show the big rabbit to all their friends.

Ramona was indeed a lovely big rabbit. With her

extra-large hind legs, Ramona could get rid of most trouble coming her way by simply kicking it clear out of sight. As the children ran about the garden and the parents watched from indoors, the pets came over to sniff Ramona and offer their usual friendly welcome.

'Don't come too close, you guys,' said Ramona. 'See these hind legs? I could kick you clear over that hedge if you get frisky with me. Be warned!'

Timber was amused. He stepped forward, and smiled down at her.

'Are you sure, Miss Ramona? I am quite a heavy dog, you know.'

'Well, maybe not you, then. You do look a bit big, even for me, but those two, or the cats or foxes, they'd be no problem. I'm almost the same size as them,' said the rabbit, trying to appear tough. She didn't think she could kick Timber over any hedge, not in a million years. She looked more confidently at the others though, who were a bit surprised at her remarks. Poor Dougal was completely baffled.

'But why would you want to kick us over the hedge?' asked Dougal.

'Don't worry, Dougal,' said Timber. 'Ramona won't do that if you don't upset her. Right, Ramona?'

'You bet!' said Ramona firmly. 'The neighbours' dogs at my last house used to chase me around for fun, and I just got tired of it. So when I realised just how strong my legs were, I decided to use them for more than just hopping, if you know what I mean.'

'Yes, indeed we do,' said the Brigadier quickly. 'Welcome to Grindlewood, Ramona. You will have no trouble from us. We like to live in harmony and we look after one another. There will be no need to kick any of us anywhere.'

While the Brigadier was politely reassuring Ramona, Timber was thinking that those strong hind legs could come in useful some day. But there was time enough to tell Ramona about their recent troubles. It was best to let her settle in and perhaps meet some of the other rabbits, who were arriving in large numbers through the hedge, curious to meet yet another cousin.

'Enjoy the garden, Ramona. There are many residents who will be keen to meet you. Have fun!' said Timber, as he trotted off with the other dogs. Dougal was still trying to figure out why a rabbit would want to kick a dog over a hedge.

Some of the rabbits who peeped into the garden to see the new bunny had suddenly become target practice for the boys' game of bows and arrows. But they escaped unharmed as they hopped so fast they could bounce through the hedge before the boys reloaded with new arrows. Ramona then started playing with the boys' football, kicking it with her strong back legs. The boys thought this was hilarious. Over in the yard, the girls were excited to see all the clucking chickens and chased them around for a while. Everyone loved the pond, of course, and thankfully, no one fell in.

During the afternoon, the pets received most of the attention, and they were all petted and cuddled more times than they could count. Dougal was completely confused by all the tricks he was asked to do, despite having practised so hard. The Brigadier was exhausted. Sylvie too needed time out and escaped for her afternoon snooze. Teddy and Cindy lapped up all the attention and the tummy rubs, never having purred so much in their lives. Timber howled on demand, and it was a great fun day for everyone.

Abigail was the last to leave the party. Before she went home, she asked if she could play with her rabbit for a few minutes.

'Come on, Abigail,' said Jemima. 'Let's go and find her. I think she must be down at the end of the garden, where the boys were playing football.'

'She always loved kicking a ball, even in our little garden,' said Abigail.

The two best friends raced to the end of the garden, and looked around. They couldn't see her at first, but they could hear some shuffling in the long grass and overgrown bushes that hadn't been cut in years.

'I think I hear her over here,' said Jemima quietly, not wanting to startle the rabbit.

'Do you? I think I can hear her over here,' giggled Abigail.

The two girls went in different directions as the rabbit could have been hiding anywhere. Abigail suddenly tripped over a large brick, and tumbled into some bushes. As she turned to get up she glimpsed a low wall under all the nettles and brambles. She pushed herself up, and then cried out sharply. Jemima heard her and ran over.

'What happened?'

'Oh, I'm OK,' said Abigail. 'I tripped on that brick over there and fell over. I nearly hit a wall or something, there, underneath all that stuff.'

Jemima went to look, but the nettles and brambles kept her back.

'I think I can see something but I can't get in behind all that prickly mess. Are you sure you're all right?'

'Yes, thanks, I only grazed my knee. Oh, I cut my hand as well – ouch!'

'That looks sore. I think you have a splinter,' said Jemima.

Abigail managed to squeeze the little wooden splinter out of her hand.

'I leant on something as I got up from the fall. Look that's it, that stick did it,' said Abigail, pointing to a thin, slightly bent stick.

'Oh, that looks just like a wand!' said Jemima, laughing. 'How funny! Maybe the splinter will be lucky!'

'Wow, yes it does,' agreed Abigail, picking up the stick. The two girls looked carefully at it and practised waving it about.

'You keep it, Abigail. You found it,' said Jemima generously.

'Oh no, it's your birthday, you must have it. Go on,

take it,' said Abigail, handing over the wand.

'Thanks, Abigail, I know it's only a stick, but it does look a bit like the real thing. At least it looks just like the ones in my book of magic, doesn't it?'

'It sure does. Who knows, maybe?' said Abigail, winking and giggling at Jemima.

'Yeah, who knows? said Jemima. 'Come on, you need a plaster for that cut. And look, here comes Ramona!'

The two girls ran after Ramona as she emerged from the bushes, munching some dock leaves, and bounded back towards the house. After Abigail's hand was fixed up, it was time to go. Her mum was waiting for her.

'Have fun with your lucky wand, Jemima,' whispered Abigail, 'and don't forget to check out that corner of the garden as soon as you can. I think there's something hidden under all those brambles down there. Let me know what you find.'

'I sure will, Abi. See you soon,' Jemima called back cheerfully as she waved her friend off.

A few quiet days followed all the fun of the birthday party, and Ramona settled in well. Very soon she had her own big hutch, which sat proudly in the yard, and she found it very comfortable. It was quite close to the chickens, who thought Ramona was most amusing. They had never seen such a huge rabbit before, and certainly not one with so much attitude! But all was well.

One lovely autumn evening a few days later, just as dusk was falling, Waldorf Woodpigeon was sitting high up in a tree, coo-cooing the arrival of autumn. He was glad of the rest after more searching with the other Grindlewood birds. They had divided up into groups and searched every tree, and every nest in every tree. They even searched outside the garden and politely asked permission of all the neighbouring birds if they could also look in their trees and nests. Most of them said yes, but a few were understandably put out. In the end, though, the birds got the job done and returned to Grindlewood garden, tired after a long day. A few went out and about looking for food. The rest were happy to listen to Waldorf cooing softly in his tree, lulling them to sleep.

Then, out of the blue, he was surrounded by a group of magpies who had been hiding nearby. They flew directly at Waldorf, screeching wildly. He was in deep trouble. No one had been expecting this and he was quite alone. The magpies flew in very close, pecking and stabbing at him. He was startled and terrified. They landed on branches all around him, blocking his escape. Their sharp beaks prodded him harder and harder. Within a few seconds he was badly injured and it seemed that his life was in danger.

Eventually, the residents noticed Waldorf had stopped singing mid-song, which was most unusual. When they heard the magpies screeching they knew there was trouble in the trees.

From his new perch on the statue, Cyril was closest to the trouble. He flew quickly to the top of Waldorf's tree. With his long, dagger-like beak, he stabbed at one magpie from behind, but the other magpies turned and stabbed the heron even harder. Now the heron was in real danger. There were just too many magpies, all clustered in one part of the tree, surrounding the two resident birds. Cyril urgently needed help but most of the garden birds were not at home.

WHAM! Another big bird no one had seen before landed with a thump on top of one of the magpies, surprising him and knocking him clear out of the tree. Cyril and the new bird saw their chance and fought off the rest of the magpies as best they could. Poor Waldorf was pecked to bits and soon his helpers were also suffering.

'To-wit-to-woo, to-wit-to-woo!'

Oberon had been woken up by all the noise in the tree and he flew over to help Cyril and the newcomer to defend Waldorf. His sharp owl beak tore at one of the magpies. Luckily, he wasn't alone. The barn owl flew after him and followed his example. After much screeching, pecking, tearing and stabbing, several magpies fell to the ground. The dead birds turned to dust, just like the others had on the day of the last attack.

The rest of the magpies retreated and flew off

into the darkening sky, back to the forest. Waldorf managed to stutter down from the tree to recover. He was joined by some of the little birds who had just returned, having heard the fight.

'Quick, Dougal, run to the pond and get Ernie. Waldorf is badly injured,' said the Brigadier as he and the other dogs arrived at the foot of the tree. Dougal barked and ran off to get Ernie. Cyril also had nasty pecks on his face and neck, but the two owls were uninjured. The newcomer, another woodpigeon, was also in need of Ernie's help. She was bleeding in a few spots and quivering all over.

Ernie hopped around as quickly as he could and set about healing everyone's wounds.

'Well, that's a new tactic for the magpies, cornering only one of us like that,' said the Brigadier. 'Luckily we had help at hand. Well done, Cyril, Oberon, and brave new friends.' He nodded to the barn owl. She tooted and flew back to the barn.

'And many thanks to you too, Miss Woodpigeon,' said Timber.

Waldorf was gazing at his lovely new friend.

'My name is Waldorf. Thank you so much for coming to help me.'

'You're welcome, Waldorf,' she said, bowing her head shyly. 'My name is Wendy. I've been listening to your lovely singing. That's how I got here so quickly. I was just behind you in that chestnut tree. I was hoping to say hello, when those nasty birds attacked.'

'We have been having some trouble with magpies lately,' said Eldric, joining them. 'But you birds did a great job. Worfeus must have cooked up more nasty birds in his cauldron.'

'Yes, indeed,' said the Brigadier. 'Well done, everyone!'

Waldorf and Wendy chatted quietly together, reliving every peck and squawk of the moments before. Timber looked at Oberon and the two of them joined Cyril.

'Cyril, that was a very brave thing you did, helping Waldorf like that. I can see by your sad face that you realise what else you have done,' said Timber.

'Yes. The magpies will tell Worfeus that I am a traitor, and he will kill my Harriet, my lovely Harriet!' Cyril started to weep. It was obvious now that Harriet had no chance. Worfeus would kill her in revenge, if he hadn't already.

The other residents huddled around, trying to

comfort the poor heron. Delilah and Danville invited Cyril to stay with them and the rest of the ducks on the little island that night. Cyril needed some company. The three swam over to the nesting island as the other residents went home. Cyril could be heard sobbing through the night. He blamed himself for everything that had gone wrong.

The next morning, after the rooster's wake-up call, Waldorf and Wendy were heard singing softly together. They seemed to have forgotten the events of the night before, and the residents' conversations of that morning.

'These attacks are really hotting up. I'm telling you, we're in for a lot more trouble from Worfeus,' said Norville.

'We knew that the warlock would come up with more nasty plans, Norville. This is no surprise. He is an evil monster,' said Eldric.

'I expect Worfeus will make each attack more cunning and more violent than the one before. We need to prepare for just about anything,' said Timber.

'Yes, indeed we do,' agreed the Brigadier, wondering what on earth to expect next.

'Um, how do we do that?' asked Dougal. This was

a simple question but a difficult one to answer. No one said anything for a few moments.

Their silence was interrupted by Ramona, who came bounding into the group. She was full of energy and good humour. 'Hello there. What on earth was that rumpus last evening? I was busy meeting all those rabbits in the field last night. I couldn't believe just how many there are. Then those magpies made a lot of noise and –'

'Good morning, Ramona. I will explain,' said the Brigadier. He took Ramona aside and told her the whole story. Timber joined them when the Brigadier had finished. He was sure that Ramona's kicking talent could be useful in fighting off some of their enemies, if Ramona was willing.

'Well, sure, but you won't be able to get me up in the trees to kick those menacing magpies,' said Ramona, almost disappointed.

'No, but you could be very helpful on the ground, if there are problems here as well as in the trees,' said Timber. 'And perhaps you could teach some of the bigger rabbits to kick like you do. In fact, why don't you organise a whole team?'

'Sure, when can we start?' said Ramona, excited by the idea.

'How about today?' said Timber.

'Great idea, Timber,' said the Brigadier. 'It might be best to keep the lessons confined to the field next door, though, while they are, um, practising, ahem, yes.' The Brigadier expected complete mayhem from a bunch of over-excited, kick-boxing bunnies. They would also draw too much attention from the family if they were doing their lessons on the partially cut grass or amongst some newly tidied flower beds.

'Yes, most of the rabbits live there anyway,' replied Timber quickly. 'I'm sure they will all agree. Let's go and have a chat with some of them now, and you can get started.'

With the rabbits all organised, the dogs, cats and foxes had another chat in the kennel later that afternoon, while the children and their parents were out.

'We are going to need every possible advantage to defend the garden while we continue with Wanda's quest to find the scroll, cast the spell and destroy the warlock for ever. Worfeus is definitely going to send more nasty 'search parties' in here. I'm sure that the magpies aren't all he has up his sleeve, or paw, you know,' added the Brigadier. He was flustered again.

'If only we knew where this secret scroll was hidden, we could get to the bottom of all this much more quickly,' sighed Teddy.

'Worfeus must be getting desperate, too. He searched for years, then he got stuck in that forest, and he hasn't been able to come up with much while he has been moping about in there. The scroll simply must be here somewhere,' said Timber, gnawing at his paw. 'Where else could it be?'

Like the rest of the residents, he felt frustrated. They had so few clues, or so it seemed.

'So, where oh where would you hide a secret scroll?' asked Eldric, looking around as if someone actually knew the anwser. No one did.

'We will simply have to search every inch of the garden, all over again, and again and again until we find it,' said Sylvie wearily.

They were all a bit disappointed that they didn't have a better plan, but they left the kennel to spread the word. The search was on, yet again.

Chapter Fifteen

MORE SEARCHING

The residents spent many more days searching the garden for anything that looked like a secret scroll, or a clue to where it might be, or even a clue to finding a clue. But no one found anything.

'No wonder Worfeus is so frustrated. We can't even find it, and we live here!' said Norville, having spent a week searching the hedges with the foxes again. All four of them looked quite cross and untidy having rummaged around in the bushes and brambles for so long.

The latest round of searching had been very close to Norville's den and this was upsetting him too. He didn't want his home all messed up. Unfortunately, the dogs were digging an awful lot of holes, big holes.

'Just keep looking, Norville,' said Eldric. 'It's got to be here somewhere. And don't mind the dogs, they're doing a great job.'

'We're all doing a great job, but no one is digging up the kennel!' said Norville.

Timber noticed Norville was rubbing his nose in frustration again.

'Don't worry, Norville. We'll be digging in and around the kennel just as soon as we get a chance. And sorry about all these holes, but it really is the best way to find out if anything is buried here. We'll all work together to put it back as tidy as possible.'

'I just love this digging!' said Dougal, happily making the biggest mess of all.

'Yes, good work, Dougal! Keep it up. We only have another acre and a half to go I think,' said the Brigadier.

'I'm not sure we'll get away with that many holes, Brigadier,' said Timber, trying not to laugh. The Brigadier was so dedicated to his work, that he sometimes didn't spot the obvious. 'I think the Grindles are getting a bit tired of all these holes, and they're wondering what we have been burying, not knowing that we are actually looking for something,' said Timber. Then he just couldn't stop himself laughing. 'And anyway, I don't think we have made nearly as many holes as the rabbits, no matter what

Jamie and Jemima have been saying. The rabbits have totally destroyed the field next door with all their digging!'

Then all the animals started laughing, and the laughter made them all feel a bit better.

'Did the garden look very different five years ago?' asked Timber, changing the subject slightly, and trying to get back to the serious work of searching.

'Not really, Timber,' answered the Brigadier. 'It was a lot less overgrown of course, but I think it was more or less the same. When the master was here, we spent more time in the house with him, and we were out with the horses a lot. Luke used to come over sometimes and help the gardeners tidy the flower beds and that sort of thing. That's about all I remember.'

'Hmm, I think I might ask Oberon about that spell business again. There has to be a clue lying around here somewhere.'

Timber trotted off to talk to Oberon, talking to himself as he went. Eldric was impressed. He hadn't met such a clever animal before, other than foxes of course. The Brigadier was doing his best, but he was becoming more and more flustered and that wasn't helping. Timber on the other hand was staying calm and he never stopped trying to work things out. It was great to have both Timber and Teddy as part of their team.

Over on the pond, some of the ducks were still comforting Cyril and trying to persuade him to go for a little swim with them. Other ducks were searching around the edges of the pond, sticking their bills into the reeds and rushes in case the scroll was there. They looked quite amusing, so many ducks all in a row, looking like they were stuck upside down!

Serena had organised a similar search on Lindon Lake much to the surprise of the many visitors there. They couldn't understand the swans' unusual behaviour, rummaging around in the reeds, flapping about in what looked like a mad panic.

Serena left the search after a couple of hours and flew to Grindlewood to help comfort Cyril. She invited him to visit the swans on Lindon Lake. But all Cyril could think about was Harriet. He had to know what had happened to her.

After listening to his endless sobbing, little Pippa had an idea. She flew off to find the snowy owl. When she reached the barn, Oberon and Timber were going over the history of Grindlewood.

'Excuse me,' said Pippa as daintily as ever. 'I have an idea.'

'Great,' said Oberon. 'What is it, Pippa?'

'Cyril is very upset and I don't think he will fully recover until he knows what has happened to Harriet. I was wondering if tonight, when it's fully dark, you could carry me to the edge of the forest, and I could try to find out what has happened to her. After all, Cyril can't go in there any more, and I've gone into the forest a few times already.'

'Good heavens, Pippa, that's very risky! I have to admit, though, it would be a good way of finding out, not just about Harriet, but what else Worfeus might be up to,' said Oberon keenly.

'I agree,' said Timber. 'Are you sure, Pippa?'

'Oh, yes, I insist.'

Timber and Oberon looked at each other. They weren't sure Pippa understood how dangerous her mission might be.

'Oberon, would it be better if the barn owl went with Pippa? Your white feathers are quite noticeable, even in the dark. Her brown feathers are much harder to see,' suggested Timber.

'Did someone mention me?' tooted the barn owl.

She had been listening to the conversation from the comfort of her nest in a corner of the barn.

'Oh, hello there, um, Miss.' Oberon suddenly realised that he didn't know her name.

'My name is Bryony. Yes, Bryony – it's an unusual name, I know. I understand that you need some help. I'd be delighted to fly you to the forest, Pippa.'

'Thank you very much, Bryony.'

'Well, I guess that's settled then,' said Timber. 'Bryony, you saw what happened before. Please be very careful. We would like both of you to return safely. Oberon, can you hide nearby, say at the edge of the next field, just in case they need some extra help?' asked Timber.

'Of course I will. Pippa, no wandering off, getting lost or falling asleep, understand? You must fly in and out as quickly as possible. Return with Bryony safe and sound, even if you don't find out anything.'

'Yes, Oberon, I understand. You can count on me.' While Pippa sounded calm and confident, Timber and Oberon, and probably Bryony too, thought this visit to the forest might be very risky.

It was time to introduce the newcomers to the Rules of the Garden and for each animal or bird to publicly promise to obey them. The Brigadier and Sylvie had scratched the Rules onto a big granite stone, many years ago. They read:

To permanently live in Grindlewood Garden, all residents must obey these seven Rules of the Garden:

- *Do not kill, injure or steal*
- *Help each other out when there is any kind of trouble*
- *Be kind, pleasant and thoughtful to everyone*
- *Solve all disagreements quickly, quietly and fairly*
- *Put your talents and strengths to good use for everyone's benefit*
- *Follow your dreams and your heart's desires*
- *Always remain the best of friends*

There had been quite a number of new residents in the garden over the last few months. There was Cyril, who had once been their enemy, but was now their friend and ally. Then Oberon had rescued Pippa and told them about the quest. Ramona was a gift and now a family pet, and then Wendy had come to Waldorf's aid. Finally of course there were Timber and Teddy. They were the official pets of the household, just like the Brigadier and Sylvie had always been.

Word was sent out to everyone to attend a formal reading of the Rules. The ceremony would take place in a couple of days' time. Before then, they would be waiting anxiously for Pippa's safe journey to and from the forest. With a bit of luck, she would bring back some news, and some valuable new clues.

Chapter Sixteen

BAD NEWS AND VERY BAD NEWS

As soon as it was dark enough, Bryony set off towards the forest with Pippa tucked safely into her feathers. It wasn't a long journey for the bright young owl and they arrived in a few minutes. She landed at a suitably safe place.

'Remember, Pippa, don't stay too long. I'll be waiting here for you. If you hear me hoot, come back straight away, as it will mean trouble. Good luck!'

Pippa flew on and on, deeper and deeper into the forest. It was so dark in that dead place, that it was quite difficult to see. Her keen little ears quickly picked up some strange gurgling sounds. She followed the noise, past many dead and dreary trees, dead leaves, blackened twigs and branches strewn about everywhere. Then just ahead, as the gurgling got louder, there was a small chink of light. She had found the wolf's lair.

Pippa perched on a tiny branch, watching and listening, silent and invisible to the horrible creatures moving around the fire. Two ugly old hags with wild scraggy hair and bloodshot eyes were stirring a huge cauldron over a blazing fire. They were struggling to stir the big black pot, full to the brim with a thick and lumpy gloop. They cackled and screamed at each other, arguing over something. Nearby a few magpies were scrapping over the ragged remains of a dead mouse. Then the wolf emerged from his lair, barking and snapping at the hags. He wasn't happy.

'Keep stirring! Stir harder, faster, you ugly old hags,' roared Worfeus. 'I need more birds, bigger birds, meaner birds. Keep stirring or I'll put you two in the cauldron as well!'

The hags stirred harder and harder, so much harder that they looked like they might fall over. The wolf circled them again and again. He was impatient and snapped at their ankles.

'Do you really want to be thrown

into the pot as well? STIR, STIR, STIR! Those stupid magpies couldn't do what I told them. Perhaps I should cook the rest of them too! YES! I'll cook a few more!'

The wolf pounced on a couple of magpies who were cackling near by, and tossed them into the cauldron. It hissed and bubbled furiously before settling back down to a simmer.

'I need crows, big, strong, clever crows to do my work. No slacking, hags, KEEP STIRRING, OR YOU'RE NEXT!'

He paced up and down, then around and around the cauldron, watching the hags closely. The last few magpies shuffled about uneasily. They moved out of his way, as he continued to grumble.

'As for that snivelling scrawny heron, how dare he play games with me? As if I would ever have trusted him. AS IF! His skinny little Harriet never had a chance. I had no intention of keeping her alive. Throwing her into the cauldron only weakened those last magpies I made. She messed up the whole brew!'

Pippa was frozen to the spot with fright, but she heard every word. Harriet had been killed long ago, boiled in the cauldron. Worfeus had never intended to

return her to Cyril. All his suffering and hoping had been for nothing.

The noise from the cauldron grew louder again. Something in there was splashing about wildly. Worfeus lapped up some green slop from a dirty old bucket and slowly and painfully resumed his normal form. He strode over to the steaming pot and took up a strange position. With his eyes half closed, he raised his arms over the cauldron. He leaned back awkwardly and muttered a strange-sounding spell. He looked completely mad.

Then the bubbling increased and became louder, and splashing out of the boiling cauldron flew four carrion crows, squawking, flapping and stretching their wide black wings. They were very big birds, strong, jet-black and mad-eyed. They flew around above the cauldron before landing at the warlock's feet. They bowed to him and waited for instructions. Worfeus bent down low to them and whispered in an ancient tongue. The birds cackled and bowed again to the warlock.

Their beady eyes darted about in their heads, taking in everything around them. They rose up from the ground together, headed towards the tree tops and flew off.

Pippa was struggling to breathe. She was so frightened. Just when the residents had thought they had got rid of the magpies, more hags had been turned into even bigger, more aggressive birds. 'Oh dear,' she thought, 'and there are still two more hags to go.'

Pippa was distracted by her thoughts when she got another fright. She heard a little shuffling noise very close to her and she started to tremble. There he was, Valerius Vole, rummaging around for insects and grubs. She had to be very careful or she might become a tasty part of his supper.

She moved back slowly, closer to the tree trunk, hoping he would pass her by. She remained absolutely still for what seemed like a very long time, when finally the vole moved back towards the fire as Worfeus roared for attention. Pippa was feeling quite sick. Valerius could so easily have caught her. She crept around to the other side of the tree trunk, and then flew straight back to the waiting owl. Bryony was still in the same spot, almost invisible, tucked closely in to the knotted branches of a dead tree. Pippa was exhausted after such a fright.

'All right, Pippa?' whispered Bryony.

'I'm not sure,' replied the ladybird.

'OK, hop on and I'll get you home. Hold on tight, here we go.'

Bryony took off smoothly and headed back to Grindlewood. Oberon saw them coming and gave out a gentle toot-toot to reassure them he was there too. They flew back to the garden side by side, to be greeted by the residents who were waiting anxiously for their return.

Waldorf and Wendy were busy setting up their new home in the finest chestnut tree in the garden. Everyone was looking forward to their wedding, which was planned for later that morning. The Brigadier was to be in charge of the ceremony. It was market day again so the Grindles would be out selling their ripe apples from the orchard, and shopping for treats. The garden residents could attend the ceremony without any interruption. Pippa's news from the forest had been troubling, but that morning everyone put their worries aside to celebrate with the woodpigeons.

The reading of the Rules was long overdue and had only been delayed because of the search for the scroll and the attacks on the garden. Otherwise it would have taken place much sooner. But it didn't take long for all the newcomers to make their solemn promise to obey the Rules, and everyone was keen to get to the wedding ceremony.

It was a lovely calm November morning. The sun was shining and there was only the slightest breeze. All the residents gathered in and around the lower branches of one of the chestnut trees to wish Waldorf and Wendy a long and happy life together. Ernie hopped out of the pond and sat on top of the Rules of the Garden stone to get a good view. The goldfish stood on their tails for as long as they could to catch a glimpse of the newlyweds. The Brigadier made a lovely speech, and Mr

and Mrs Woodpigeon sang a few of their favourite songs at the end of the ceremony. Everyone was happy, and delighted to be part of such a lovely celebration. Then Norville spotted the butterflies.

'Uh oh! Here we go again!' he muttered.

All the residents turned to look at the statue, where the butterflies had perched to watch the wedding. They had fallen asleep and woken up with another vision. The light-hearted mood of the wedding turned quickly into one of worry and unease. Timber, Teddy, Sylvie and the Brigadier walked over to the butterflies to hear the news. They didn't want everyone to hear it straight away, especially if it was bad news.

And it was bad news. It was very bad news indeed.

'More bird attacks. They are big birds, really big birds,' said Belinda Butterfly, almost fainting at the mention of them.

'And big ugly scurrying things with tails, everywhere, lots of them,' added Bethany, in a total tizzy.

'Oh dear, that doesn't sound good,' said a worried Brigadier.

'It sounds frightful,' agreed Sylvie.

'Ladies, can you tell us what the scurrying things are?' asked Timber.

The three butterflies were still hovering in the air as if there was another part of the message to come. Was there really more bad news? The cats and dogs waited. Eldric and Dougal joined them, and the other animals and birds edged closer too. Most were afraid of what they might hear. This message was taking longer than usual.

'Sparrows, sparrows,' repeated Beatrice Butterfly over and over again, as if she were in another dream. Then all three of them spoke together.

'Find the spitfire sparrows! They were Wanda's friends!'

Then off they flew, silent again. As the rest of the residents joined the group, they all wondered the same thing. Who were the spitfire sparrows?

Chapter Seventeen

THE SPITFIRE SPARROWS

Everyone's attention had quickly moved from the newlyweds to the butterflies, and many residents were apologising to the woodpigeons. But Waldorf and Wendy didn't mind in the least.

'Don't worry, everyone, we have had a lovely morning. Now we have to work out what the butterflies' message means,' said gentle Waldorf.

'I think I may be able to help with that,' said Oberon.

Everyone turned towards the wise snowy owl.

'Some more history, Oberon?' asked Eldric, suspecting, as Timber did, that there might be more to Grindlewood's history than they had already heard.

'Well just a little bit, Eldric,' replied Oberon.

Everyone gathered closely around Oberon to hear another piece of the puzzle.

'When the good witch Wanda lived in these parts, she had many friends in the forest. The spitfire sparrows were a group of about a dozen or so common-or-garden sparrows who befriended her. She was always kind to them, and they lived in and around her little treehouse in the forest, singing and flitting about. When Worfeus followed her to the forest, it was the sparrows who warned her. Wanda then moved to the garden, where the warlock eventually caught up with her.'

'Most of the time, the little birds kept her informed of his whereabouts and what he was up to. To thank them for their loyalty, Wanda enchanted their beaks with a stunning spell, and I think she may have given them extra-long life as well.'

'So many spells, so much magic,' muttered Dougal. He loved hearing about magic.

'Little birds with stunning beaks. That's amazing!' said Cindy.

'Who or what will be next?' said Norville, still irritated.

'And just how do we find these enchanted sparrows, Oberon? I don't see any of them around here any more,' asked the fox.

'You're right, Eldric. They left this place when Wanda died.'

'Right, let's figure this out quickly! Where could they be?' said Eldric.

The three clever foxes huddled together for a think-in.

'Hmmm.' Fern was thinking hard. 'Where did the sparrows come from?'

Everyone looked at Oberon.

'I believe some were local, and others, well, they came here from all around.'

'And where do sparrows normally live?' asked Freya.

'Usually near towns or villages or in the countryside, like us,' said Reggie Robin.

'Oh dear, that sounds like everywhere,' said Norville. 'This could take ages.'

'It could,' said Eldric, impatiently. 'Then perhaps all of you birds should fly around all the nearby towns, villages and countryside to see if you can find them.'

'It would make more sense if you split up into small groups,' said Timber sensibly.

'And if we're lucky, some of the local birds might know or remember them,' added Teddy. 'Not many birds have enchanted beaks. Someone is bound to know something.'

'Yes, but be careful,' warned Timber. 'The magpies will be watching and they may follow some of you. We must keep this a secret. We don't want Worfeus' spies upsetting our plans.'

'It's hard to imagine that little birds like sparrows could be helpful at all,' grumbled Norville. 'First the magpies, then the heron and now these crows, all causing us trouble.'

'Yes, but like the stinging bees, Norville, the spitfire sparrows might be very useful to us, if we can find them of course, and then persuade them to come back here and help us. Oh dear, it does sound like a lot to ask,' said the Brigadier, worrying again.

'That is all very well,' said Teddy. 'I think the other part of the message could be even worse. What are the big, ugly, scurrying things? They sound more dangerous than all the big birds put together.'

'They do, and I think they will attack on the ground,' said Timber. 'Ramona, we may need your kicking talent quite soon,' he said, glancing down at her big feet. 'You have arrived at just the right time.'

'Yes, she is indeed a whopper of a bunny!' whispered Eldric to Norville, who nearly choked trying not to laugh.

'Steady on there,' whispered Sylvie. 'You don't want that whopper practising her kicks on you two, do you?'

Eldric and Norville nodded to apologise. They most certainly did not want to get a thundering kick from Ramona's big feet. At least Eldric's little joke helped Norville to relax a little. He had been getting very cranky.

The group quickly settled down to organise which birds would fly where the very next morning. Luckily, garden birds are seen almost everywhere, so it wouldn't look too strange if they were seen flying out and about in the neighbourhood. If they spotted the magpies, they would just have to make their fly-abouts look normal.

The next part of the puzzle was to work out what the big scurrying things would be, and how to deal with them. Those difficult questions kept the meeting going well into the night.

Only Roosevelt's loud call was heard the next day. All the other birds had flown off to find the sparrows.

It was generally agreed that the next attack was likely to be a lot worse than the last one, so Timber and the Brigadier decided to chat with Ramona again about her kick-boxing team. It was very important that they were ready to defend the garden alongside the other animals.

'Eh, how are things going with the kick practice, Ramona?' asked the Brigadier.

'Oh, great, just great,' said Ramona cheerfully.

'That sounds good,' said Timber. 'Do you think you are ready for some real action?'

'Oh, yes, we are,' said Ramona confidently. 'I have two dozen rabbits all practising hard as we speak. You can have a look if you like. They are in the field next door.'

'That's OK, I'm sure they are fine,' said the Brigadier.

'I might take a look,' said Timber. He wanted to be sure that the rabbits were practising and not just playing around.

The two dogs stuck their heads into the hedge as far as they could to watch the bunnies kick and jump. They were pleasantly surprised.

'Ramona, you have done a fantastic job. Well done!' said the Brigadier.

'They look great, Ramona. Well done to all of you. Do the rabbits know what their kicking might be used for and that it might be dangerous?' asked Timber.

'Oh yes, I explained everything, and they are all set. I only asked the bigger rabbits as you can see, but they were all very keen to be involved. I must say, they learned how to kick like me very quickly,' said Ramona, proudly.

'Great, let's hope we don't need them to do too much. See you later, and keep up the good work,' said Timber, as he trotted off with the Brigadier.

'You bet!' cried Ramona, as she bounded through the hedge.

Worfeus, meanwhile, was rubbing his hands with glee. His own preparations were coming along nicely. The cauldron was bubbling and curdling magnificently, sending up piles of thick smoke that could be seen above the trees for miles around. The stench from the evil brew was worsening too. It was further proof that the next thing the big black pot would spit out would be foul, ugly, and very, very dangerous.

The birds were exhausted. They had flown from village to village, town to town, and in between, unable to get any useful information about the sparrows. They were almost about to give up, when the robins decided to stop for an early lunch. They were starving. They dropped into a lovely garden where there were bunches of juicy berries growing on a creeper along a wall. They were having a nice little nibble when all of a sudden, several little birds landed around them.

'Oops! So sorry, are these your berries?' asked a slightly nervous Reggie.

'Why, yes they are,' said one of them cheekily.

The robins eyed each other and then Ruby spoke. 'We're very sorry. We were so tired and hungry that we had to stop for a snack. You see, we're looking for a group of sparrows, and …'

Reggie gave Ruby a sharp nudge in the wing, just as she realised that she was actually talking to some sparrows.

'Do you know a witch, I mean, someone called Wanda, by any chance?' Ruby asked the question in

~ 187 ~

a whisper. She was so afraid of being overheard and then getting into all sorts of trouble. And the two robins were clearly outnumbered.

'Who's asking?' asked one bright little sparrow.

Reggie decided he might as well talk too.

'We're from Grindlewood and we're looking for Wanda's sparrow friends. Do you know them or where we can find them? It's a very urgent matter.'

The sparrows were quite impressed with this outspoken little pair.

'We might be those sparrows,' said one of them. 'What seems to be the trouble?' The mention of Grindlewood had got the sparrows' attention.

Reggie was too tired to think any more, so he blurted it all out. The sparrows stared back at the robins in a long, thoughtful silence. They had flown away from Grindlewood thinking that the happy days were over for ever. They had no idea it was still a lovely place, and that so far, Worfeus had been kept out. They were shocked to hear that the Grindlewood residents had taken up Wanda's quest, and how recent events had become so threatening.

'Yes, we are those sparrows. Welcome to our

humble new home. We loved Grindlewood and didn't like leaving, but after Wanda was killed by that evil warlock, we didn't have the heart to stay,' replied one of them.

'Is it true that you have enchanted beaks?' asked Ruby.

'Yes, we do, and we use them to get out of trouble,' replied another one.

'We liked Wanda. We were always happy to help her, and she helped us by giving us these enchanted beaks,' replied the cheeky one.

'Well, we need you to help us now. Wanda wanted to protect the garden, and to keep the scroll out of Worfeus' hands. He is planning more attacks, because he believes that the scroll is hidden in the garden. If he succeeds in finding it before we do, no one will be able to stop him. We need you to help us. Please, come with us now, before it is too late, for us and for Grindlewood.'

The sparrows eyed each other. They didn't need to think too long about it.

'Of course we will!' they cried. 'Let's all go to Grindlewood!'

The sparrows cheered and tweeted, and flew

around the garden in fantastic diving motions. No wonder they were called the spitfire sparrows!

On the way back, they spotted the blackbirds and the woodpigeons flying home as well. They were greatly relieved to see the sparrows had been found. The sparrows were another part of the puzzle, and one of the many enchantments Wanda had left behind her. But would these little birds really be able to make a difference?

Chapter Eighteen

THE FIRST INVASION

The garden was buzzing with excitement when the sparrows arrived. After all, they were Wanda's friends, and they were enchanted! The residents agreed to hold a meeting after dark. With the children due out in the garden for some play time before supper, it would be impossible to hold the meeting without interruption before then. All the birds gathered immediately in the trees to chatter.

'Mum, there are lots of extra birds in the garden today. I think they're building nests in our trees,' cried Jemima. She had been trying to count the sparrows, but they kept flying about from tree to tree, making it an impossible task.

'Why yes. I wonder where they came from all of a sudden?' said Gloria, peering out the window. There certainly seemed to be a lot of extra activity in the trees.

Over in the yard, the chickens' dancing rehearsals had been replaced by pecking practice. The rooster had been trying to prepare the chickens for the next fight, telling them how to pick and peck at any would-be attackers. It was unlikely that the chickens would be able to defend themselves very well, but they were at least going to give it a try. They had been so impressed by what the elder bees had done, they wanted to do their bit too.

So the pecking classes had begun, and the inevitable squawking that came with it puzzled the Grindles. They assumed that the chickens were making a commotion because the coop was too old and too small. They decided to make plans to build a bigger one.

When darkness fell, the residents gathered at the end of the garden to listen to the sparrows' story. Spindle Sparrow usually spoke for the little flock, and he stepped forward to address the group. He told again how Wanda had rewarded their friendship and loyalty with the enchantment of their beaks. Spindle said they knew of the evil Worfeus and his obsession with finding the secret scroll. He explained that Worfeus had always cooked up nasty things in his cauldron.

'It takes one hag and a particularly nasty spell to cook up either two crows or six magpies in the cauldron,' he said.

That explained why Worfeus probably tried using the magpies first. But the magpies had not done the job properly, so he had switched to creating the crows. With only two hags left, he needed to make something particularly evil this time.

'Yes, the scurrying things. What do you think they are?' asked Timber.

'No idea, I'm afraid,' replied Spindle.

Everyone groaned. They wanted to know what they would be fighting. 'Depending on how many of them there are, we may need even more help to deal with them. We should always expect the very worst from Worfeus,' Spindle added. 'You already know that magpies have beaks like swords, but the crows have beaks like spears. They are very dangerous. I hate to think what the scurrying things might be.'

The residents were very worried. Each attack was more terrifying than the last.

'What should we do? Is there anyone else we should ask for help? We really don't want anyone to get hurt, or worse,' said Teddy.

Spindle thought for a moment. 'While we were living away from here, we became friends with a huge flock of starlings. They helped us before, when some local crows tried to scare us off. There were so many starlings – hundreds, maybe even thousands – all spinning and swirling in the sky. In fact, whenever they do their sky dance, most other birds stay well out of the way.'

Some of the residents thought this sounded interesting.

'They might be useful in distracting some of these attackers, whatever they are, even if they are on the ground,' said Timber.

He was beginning to hatch a plan. The sparrows were too.

'Yes, I see what you mean,' muttered the Brigadier.

'The sooner we find the starlings the better. In fact, we should go tonight,' said Spindle. 'Perhaps we could hitch a ride with one of the owls? You can see so much better in the dark than we can and your bigger wings carry you much faster. Would that be OK? It would mean that with a bit of luck we could be back here by morning.' Spindle looked hopefully at Oberon.

'Ready when you are,' said Oberon confidently.

'Great. My friend Sparky will tell you the rest of our story, folks. Oberon, I think we should get going.'

The owl, Spindle and a couple of other sparrows flew off.

Very early the next morning, even before the rooster had crowed, trouble was starting. The magpies and crows had gathered in the trees around the garden, and there seemed to be more crows than Pippa had reported.

'Hmmm, Worfeus must have sacrificed another hag to create more crows. He can't have too many hags left now,' said Sparky. 'We must be prepared. They're definitely up to something, sitting up there at the top of those trees, cackling like that. I do wish Spindle would hurry.'

Then it began. There were at least twenty attacking birds. One crow took the lead in each attack, flying at the head of two or three magpies, squawking and zooming in for the kill. The blackbirds and woodpigeons tried to lure the magpies and crows closer to the ground where the cats and dogs planned to leap out from the bushes. This time, though, Worfeus' wicked birds weren't falling for any tricks. They had a clever plan of their own.

The blackbirds ended up stuck in the middle of two attacking teams. No amount of clever ducking and diving was going to get them all out safely. Bertram got badly stabbed by a crow, and Binky was hit by two magpies. They were lucky not to have been killed, and they had to stagger into the hedge for shelter. Barty and Billy had to dive for cover into a prickly bush and got dreadfully scratched by the thorns. The woodpigeons were too heavy and slow and soon became exhausted. They hid in a laurel bush to try to work out what they should do. The lead crow and his team screeched in delight and flew on to their next target.

At the very same time, two other attacks were happening. Another crow and two magpies headed for the chickens. They attacked the lock on the chicken coop door to try to get in. The poor chickens were terrified. It looked like the nasty birds might actually get into the coop. Finally, after hammering away at the lock, the biggest of the crows managed to break it. Then he and the magpies stabbed their way in and set about smashing the eggs.

Roosevelt rushed out of the barn and thundered

over to the coop. Bryony flew down from the loft and followed him. The rooster roared at the chickens to peck, peck and peck! At first, they were all too frightened to do anything, but once Bryony arrived and ripped into one of the magpies, and the rooster called out some further instructions, the chickens found their courage.

'Go for the eyes, go for the eyes!' roared Roosevelt from outside – he was too big to squash his way into the coop. The chickens finally heard the rooster's call and aimed their little beaks at their attackers' eyes. The magpie and the second crow were trapped in the coop and they couldn't avoid the chickens' frantic pecking. As the chickens' little beaks pierced into the beady eyes of their attackers, the crow and the magpies screeched in pain. They turned around and tried to leave the coop, only to meet Bryony at the doorway. She ripped angrily at one magpie with her sharp talons, and then finished him off with her hooked beak.

The foxes had heard the commotion and raced to help. As the crow tried to escape through the flock of flustered chickens, he backed straight into the waiting animals. The crow was quickly ripped to shreds and dissolved into dust. The chicken coop was saved, but not before a few chickens had been injured and most of the eggs smashed.

Next, the pond burst into a frenzy of splashing and screeching. Another crow and three magpies had zoomed over to the ducks.

The ducks and ducklings were quite defenceless. Cyril was having a very hard time trying to fend off all four attackers on the pond. He did his best with his long pointy beak, but his huge wingspan meant it was difficult to dodge the attacking birds. The ducks could do little but quack furiously. But once again, the majestic swans landed on the pond, ready to snap and bite at anything in their way. They swooshed around, some protecting the ducks, and others defending the injured heron.

But this crow and these magpies were not bothered by the swans. They were soon joined by another crow and two more magpies – the same trio who had driven off the blackbirds and woodpigeons.

The cats and dogs were leaping as high as they could, but the attacking birds had learned to stay out of reach. The pets kept trying to swipe or grab the nasty birds with their paws and claws but they had little success.

The heron and the ducks were still in mortal danger as the crows and magpies swerved around the swans, avoiding their huge wings and nasty bites. The swans really tried their best, but some ducklings were stabbed and poor Danville had been wounded on his belly. Delilah was hysterical and this wasn't helping at all. The garden birds were in grave danger.

High in the sky, something peculiar was happening. A sinister, dark cloud was moving towards the garden with extraordinary speed. It didn't move like an ordinary cloud, but swirled and shifted from side to side, sweeping up and down. It twisted back and forth in the sky against a backdrop of orange and gold as the sun slowly rose.

'It's Spindle! Look, it's Spindle!' cried Sparky from the chestnut tree. 'He's back and he's got the starlings!'

Oberon and Spindle were flying towards the garden at the head of all the starlings. The cloud was not a cloud at all, but a huge flock of birds, whirling through the air, heading for Grindlewood. The rest of the sparrows had been waiting in the garden for their leader. They never did anything without Spindle, so they flew up quickly to join him. They headed directly for the attacking crows and magpies and took aim, before stunning their targets with their enchanted beaks.

But Worfeus' nasty birds flew in a range of swoops and dives of their own, managing to avoid many of the sparrows. This wasn't going to be as easy as the spitfire sparrows had hoped. Some of the sparrows got stabbed first and fell injured into the pond. Cyril tried to save them from drowning, but got stabbed again by one of the crows.

Finally the huge flock of starlings whizzed down over the pond like a tornado. There were so many of them that they blinded and confused the attacking birds, herding them closer to the ground and making it easier for the animals to catch them.

For a few minutes, there was complete and utter mayhem. The entire garden was a swirling dark mass of feathers and beaks. The little sparrows remembered this from their past adventures and they darted in and out amongst the cloud of starlings, stabbing the crows and magpies side-on, stunning them completely. The dogs jumped into the pond and snatched the fallen birds out of the water. The cats and foxes waited on the grass and finished off the magpies and crows that fell near them. They watched them turn to dust, just like the other cursed birds.

When it all calmed down, the sparrows and starlings gathered in the trees, congratulating each other on a job well done. Almost all the crows and magpies had been destroyed. If one or two had managed to escape, it didn't matter. Grindlewood had definitely won this battle. Despite several injuries, everyone felt it could have been a lot worse. Ernie hopped out of the pond and worked his way around the wounded, kissing them better, putting his wonderful healing powers to good use. What on earth would they do without him?

And what would the Grindles have thought if they had seen such a sight?

Jamie and Jemima had woken quite early and they were in Jemima's room in the front of the house while all this was going on. They were reading her book about the history of Grindlewood.

'Jamie, it says here that many creatures who lived

in the forests were enchanted. They're talking about the animals and birds, Jamie. Do you think that any of our animals and birds could be enchanted, as well as the frog, I mean?' asked Jemima.

'I don't know. Why would they be? And what could they do if they were magical or enchanted?' said Jamie, hesitating. He wasn't quite ready to believe in quite as much magic as Jemima.

'Oh, I don't know, but some of the animals and birds in our garden really belong in a forest, and I'm sure they go in and out of the forest up on the hill. I think it's at least possible, don't you?' said Jemima, trying to encourage him to believe.

''Well, I'd need to see them do something, even something small. Then maybe, I suppose,' he muttered. He didn't want to look foolish either way.

'Well, I like to think that it's true. What about Ernie? We saw what he can do, didn't we?' asked Jemima.

'I suppose, but he might be the only one, and maybe there's a scientific reason for the frog, you know, something in his mouth. I've seen stuff like that on nature programmes. Oh, I don't know, Jem. I need more proof, I guess'.

They thought they heard some noise outside, and

both of them jumped.

'What was that?' asked Jamie, sitting up straight.

'Let's go see,' whispered Jemima.

The two children ran into Jamie's bedroom in the back of the house and looked outside.

Chapter Nineteen

THE SECOND INVASION

Mum and Dad Grindle had also woken early with all the commotion and went out into the garden, while the children were still struggling to get dressed and join them. The dogs ran over to greet them, wagging their tails as if everything was normal.

'Is there trouble in the garden, Timber?' Greg asked his big malamute, petting him on the head and looking closely at all three of the dogs. He noticed they were wet, and the cats were up and about early, too.

'Hello, my lovelies, are you all right? We heard a lot of noise out here. Did you have some unwelcome visitors this morning, eh?'

The pets just looked at him. The dogs mooched forward for more ear rubs. Gloria went over to the cats.

'Greg, I think there was something in the garden all right. The cats look a little unsettled. Maybe there was an intruder, or a row of some sort.'

Cindy and Teddy came closer to Gloria and rubbed against her ankles. Sylvie was sitting quietly close by, trying to look cool and calm.

'Hmm, maybe not,' said Gloria. 'Could it have been the foxes, I wonder? I heard the chickens squawking, too. I'll just go and check on them.'

'Yes, good idea,' said Greg. The two of them walked over to the yard.

'Oh, my, just look at the coop! All those feathers! And so many eggs are broken. Whatever could have gotten in to the coop?'

'I guess the dogs must have chased them off,' said Greg. 'The lock on the coop is broken, though. I wonder how that happened.'

'Well, we had better tell the children that their pets are OK, and it'll be an early breakfast this morning. We can tidy up later.'

'Yes, you go ahead, Gloria. If the children come down, try to keep them inside for the moment. I want to take another look around,' said Greg, still a little concerned about what had happened.

Gloria went inside, and Greg walked around the garden with the dogs beside him. He noticed an unusually large number of birds in the trees, but thought it might have something to do with winter migration habits or that sort of thing. He remembered seeing another one of Jamie's favourite nature programmes on television, which had described the amazing flight patterns of starlings at certain times of the year. 'Hmmm,' he thought, 'perhaps that's it, something in nature.' Satisfied for the time being, Greg headed back inside.

The next attack came just a few minutes later. The residents had just about recovered after the first round of action, when they heard a horrible, scary sound. At first it was quite faint, and then it got louder and closer.

'What on earth is that?' asked Timber, looking at the other pets. The sound grew louder still. It seemed to be coming from the direction of the forest. Suddenly, all the birds flew up from the trees into the sky, shrieking and hovering high above. They wanted to stay well away from whatever was coming. The residents on the ground all looked at each other. What was it? Then Waldorf shouted down the warning they had all been dreading.

'Look out, it's rats, dozens of them, and they're huge. There are dozens and dozens of giant rats!'

'Oh goodness me!' cried the Brigadier. 'Take care everyone!'

In a flash, the rats descended on the garden. They stormed in through the hedges and bushes that separated the garden from the neighbouring fields. They had run all the way from the forest, still steaming, having come straight out of the cauldron. They were big ugly nasty rodents, with huge buck teeth sticking out from their mouths. They were breathing hard, their nostrils stretched wide, and their mouths were dripping with white fizzing froth. The animals had faced rats before, but these ones were truly enormous. They were like rats from hell.

The residents quickly got into position and attacked as fiercely as the rats. There was a huge clamour of barking, snarling, meowing, scratching, biting, and skin and fur flying as the rats charged about the garden, attacking everything. Every resident animal was using

their teeth, claws, spikes, beaks – whatever they could.

Then the rats divided into groups and tore off in different directions. They ran towards the chicken coop, the pond, the orchard, the hedge, the lawn, and even up towards the house. This was very daring and clever. The warlock's plan was to attack them from all directions.

The residents were having a terrible time. They simply couldn't protect every part of the garden all at once, no matter how organised they were, and the rats seemed to be all over the place.

The chicken coop was under attack again. The chickens were clucking frantically, even though the two owls were bravely trying to defend them. Some rats had entered the pond and were swimming quickly towards the ducks, while others had dived under the water to find the frog and the goldfish. The rest of the rats were keeping the dogs, cats, foxes and hedgehog very busy.

The sparrows and starlings were preparing to attack again from the air, but it was taking some time to get so many birds organised. The swans' beaks were not very successful at biting through the rats' tough flesh, and the smaller birds weren't able to do much at all.

They were having a really tough time.

The pets and foxes were doing their best but it was extremely difficult with so many attackers coming at them from all sides.

Suddenly, out of the hedges, Ramona and her kick-boxing team jumped into action. They surprised the rats by bounding into the fight and thumping the rats into the air. The startled rodents landed in the jaws and claws of the angry cats, dogs and foxes, or straight onto Norville's piercing spikes.

'GOAL!' shouted Ramona, every time she clobbered another rat, sending him soaring into the air. 'GOAL!' she roared, again and again, kicking the rats like a football. The other rabbits followed her lead, thumping the rats from all directions. WHACK! WHACK! WHACK! Ramona was almost having fun with these horrible monsters. The rats were bewildered. They didn't expect to get such a thrashing, and certainly not from an army of fluffy rabbits!

The noise brought all the Grindles out to the back garden again.

'Oh no! Greg, rats! Look, they're huuuuge!' screamed Gloria.

'Children, go back inside, quickly,' Greg shouted to the children over all the barking and screeching, but they either couldn't hear their father or they ignored him. 'Gloria, get the hose. I'll get … a weapon.'

Greg looked around and grabbed his pitch fork. He charged at some of the rats, but they were too quick for him. Gloria looked for the garden hose, but Jamie had got to it first and turned it on at full power. He tried his best to blast the rats with the powerful jet of water, but it was hard to see them under all the spray, and they moved about so quickly.

'Jamie, what are you doing? Go inside!' Greg shouted over the din.

'It's OK Dad, I can do it. Look!' cried Jamie, as he forced a rat to slide back on the puddles of water, straight into the waiting jaws of the three cats. 'I got him!' cried Jamie. He was very pleased with himself. He ignored his father's shouts and went after another one.

Jemima had run inside and grabbed the broom from the kitchen and raced back to the action. She wasn't sure she could kill a rat with it, but she felt better with something big in her hands.

There was an awful lot of noise as Greg and Gloria

kept ordering the children to go inside. But Jamie and
Jemima were busy shouting instructions to each other
and the dogs. The animals were creating their own
racket too, so no one could really hear anyone else
clearly. Every so often, Jamie managed to blast another
rat with water, causing it to change course and run
directly into one of the animals. He was starting to
enjoy the fight.

Jemima took a few swipes at a passing
rat or two, managing to swoosh them
away from her and towards one of the
pets. Luckily, she didn't get into any real
trouble either. She even jumped in front of
her mother, swishing the broom around, whenever a
rat came too close.

'Don't worry, Mum, I'll clobber this one!' said
Jemima bravely, as she whacked another huge rodent
with the broom.

'Oh well done, Jemima, well done,' said Gloria,
startled by her daughter's courage.

Finally, the flocks of birds got themselves organised,
and together the sparrows and starlings swirled into
proper action. While the starlings swooped down to
confuse and distract the rats, the sparrows zoomed

out from the centre of the thick swirl and stabbed and stunned the rats with their enchanted beaks. But to their horror, the stuns didn't have quite the same effect that they had had on the crows and magpies. The rats seemed almost invincible, and they defended themselves with terrible bites. Clearly this was Worfeus' dark magic at work – magic more powerful than before.

But the plan was slowly starting to work. After a few more minutes, the rats saw that they weren't going to win this fight, and the last few were spotted heading back through the hedges, across the fields and into the forest, back to Worfeus' lair. The injured and stunned rats were killed off by the animals and, as expected, turned to dust.

The residents were shattered. Everyone except the Grindles was wounded. Greg stayed outside to check on the pets, while Gloria absolutely insisted that the children go inside with her and dry off. Everyone had been soaked from head to toe by Jamie's hosing and they needed to put on dry clothes. Gloria was just about to head back outside to Greg again, when the doorbell rang. It was Farmer Finlay.

'Hello there. I was out for my walk extra early

this morning, when I heard a lot of commotion. Is everything OK here?'

'Oh, Arthur, do come in. I'm afraid we were invaded by giant rats this morning. It was just awful. We have just come in but Greg is still outside. Ugh, I'm still recovering, myself. The rats were huge! Huuuge!' Gloria was still very flustered, rushing her words to get the story out quickly.

'Don't worry, Gloria, I'll go and join Greg. You three stay in here for a minute or two.'

Arthur went out to the garden.

'Greg, I hear you've had a bit of bother this morning.'

'Hello, Arthur, good to see you. Yes, we have had a rather nasty surprise. We had rats in the garden. They were truly enormous, lots of them. I've never seen anything like it before,' replied Greg.

'Oh, how dreadful! They must have come from that nasty forest. I'm not surprised that rats grow extra large in there. Are the cats and dogs all right?'

He looked carefully at the pets. They were licking their wounds nearby, waiting for Ernie to come and heal them. The other residents were nursing their injuries in the bushes and under the hedges, while most of the birds had returned to the tree tops.

'I think they're all fine, though I might call the vet to take a look at some of them,' replied Greg.

The two men continued chatting for a while. Meanwhile, Ernie was anxious to get out of the pond and start healing the wounded. He came out of his underwater hideout and was hopping over the lily pads towards the edge of the pond when there was a great big splash, followed by horrible high-pitched squeaking noises. The dogs started barking and the cats were hissing. Everyone ran to the pond.

'Oh no,' cried Greg. 'I think there are a couple of rats still in the pond!'

'Give me that pitch fork, Greg. I'll spear those nasty rodents!' roared Arthur.

Greg tossed him the pitch fork and Arthur waded into the water. Poor Ernie was still trying to hop out of the pond to help his friends, but now he didn't know where to go. He was in grave danger himself. Timber ran further down the side of the pond and barked over to him.

'Ernie, forget about us. Get away from those rats!'

Ernie heard him and his eyes bulged even bigger

with fright. He looked around. One rat had seen him and was heading his way. Arthur was getting into quite deep water and had to tread slowly. The rat was closing in on Ernie. Timber jumped into the pond to help, but Greg immediately called him back.

'No, Timber, no! Come out of the water. Stay! Sit!' he ordered his dog.

Timber reluctantly obeyed. Greg didn't know that Timber wanted to save the frog, or just how important their little green friend was. But Ernie was a terrific little acrobat and he bounced and hopped his way across the pond. While keeping a safe distance, he bravely lured the rat towards Arthur, who was taking aim with the pitch fork. As Ernie hopped from one lily pad to another, he finally landed on a rock at the edge of the pond. Then the rat came close enough for Arthur to strike.

The children had actually snuck back out to the garden when Gloria had been talking to Arthur. Jamie had grabbed his bow and arrows and ran straight to the pond. He was quite a good shot and now he quickly took aim. As Arthur got ready to throw the pitchfork straight at the rat, Jamie let go his arrow. The arrow and the pitchfork both struck their target and killed the rat immediately. To their great surprise, the rat turned into a dirty mound of dust that fell through the prongs of the pitchfork. The arrow floated away on the surface of the pond.

'Well I never!' cried Arthur, amazed.

'Wow, Dad, what happened? I know I hit him, so did Mr Finlay. Where's the rat?' cried Jamie.

Jemima pulled Jamie by the sleeve. 'It must be magic, Jamie, dark magic'. She looked very seriously at her brother. Jamie looked directly back at her, but he didn't know what to say.

'But the rat must be dead, and he must be somewhere,' said Jamie.

'That's very odd,' said Greg, relieved the rat was dead, but confused by the dust.

Once again, they were startled by more splashing in the pond. Cyril was diving in and out of the water, stabbing at something.

'I think there's another one,' cried Greg.

'Let me get him, Dad,' said Jamie.

'Whatever you do, don't miss, Jamie, if this is dark magic, it could be very bad if you miss,' whispered Jemima urgently.

Jamie glared at her, and then he turned to aim carefully at the rat.

Ernie had hopped out of the pond and was starting his healing duties. No one noticed the little miracles going on behind them while they were busy watching the last rat in the pond. Timber, Dougal and the Brigadier were straining to go after the rat, wanting to help Cyril.

This rat was very determined. He dived down into the pond and swam around and around the fountain. There were lots of little nooks and crannies where the goldfish could hide at the base of it, and the rat had realised this.

Cyril kept diving too, trying to distract the rat and lure him to the surface. The terrified goldfish were trembling in their hideouts. The rat had found them and was scratching at the base of the fountain, trying to force the goldfish out.

Finally, the rat had to come up for air, and Cyril knew that this was the only chance he might get. He charged with all his remaining strength, stabbing the rat deep in the neck. Cyril screamed in pain as his beak broke, but he had done enough. The rat was mortally wounded. Arthur scooped the rat out of the pond with the pitch fork, and the cats jumped on him to finish him off before anyone could stop them. Before their very eyes, the giant rat turned to dust. Everyone sighed with relief. The double-trouble was over.

Chapter Twenty

AFTERMATH

Greg, Arthur and the children walked back to the house. Greg was very concerned. So was Arthur. A rat problem would be dreadful. The children were feeling quite elated. Jamie was very proud of his archery skills, while Jemima was more interested in the possibility of more magic at work in the garden. The children decided to talk about the magic stuff later.

'I think we should put down some rat poison, Greg. We should put it here and also in and around my fields next door,' said Arthur quietly.

'Yes, I think so,' agreed Greg. But something else was on his mind. After a few seconds he turned to face Arthur and blurted it out.

'Arthur, have you ever seen anything like that before? The dust, I mean.'

'No, I haven't, but some people think that all sorts

of nasty creatures live in that forest. Those people would tell you that those rats are cursed or something. My son used to talk about wizards and witches living in these parts centuries ago, and all sorts of other fantastical stuff. Apparently they all killed each other off, or so the story goes.' He laughed a forced kind of laugh, but there was nothing funny about what they had just seen.

'But if there is some strange stuff going on, or some nutter hiding in there, I'll be after him and his rats all right, dust or no dust.' He thrust the pitchfork in the air. 'He won't get away from this,' said Arthur, no doubt still thinking of his son Luke, and the rumours that he may have been 'taken' by the forest.

'They won't escape my bow and arrow either,' said a defiant Jamie.

'Aye, you're a good shot, Jamie,' said Arthur, smiling at him.

'You sure are, Jamie,' said his dad. 'I didn't know you had practised and improved so much. Well done today.'

Jamie was thrilled. Jemima was still in a world of her own, trying to understand the magic side of things.

When they were all inside, the children were

worried that they could still hear Timber howling around the garden, on patrol with Dougal and the Brigadier.

'Don't worry, kids, the pets are all fine – just a couple of scratches, really,' said Greg.

'I want to check on them again, Dad,' said Jemima.

'Come on, Dad, we just want to make sure they're OK. We were out there helping to fight the rats already,' said Jamie. 'We're not afraid to go out there again.'

They both looked imploringly at their father.

'Well, all right, we'll go back out into the garden together. And why don't we give the pets a few treats for their breakfast? I think they've earned it.'

They went back out and Greg called to the pets. They quickly scampered over, glad of their morning feed.

'Just look at that!' cried Greg. 'Not a single mark on them! Well, well, well!'

The adults checked the animals carefully and found no trace of wounds or scratches anywhere. The dogs gave a few extra shakes to remove the water from their coats. Otherwise they looked perfect.

'Well I never!' exclaimed Arthur.

'Goodness gracious!' said Gloria.

'Hooray, hooray!' cried Jamie.

'It's more magic!' cried Jemima.

Greg, Gloria and Arthur exchanged glances, but none of them said another word. It was a very strange start to the day.

The three adults went to look at the chicken coop. It was very badly damaged and the chickens were in an awful state. Roosevelt looked a total mess, sitting in the middle of the yard, utterly exhausted. Several of his feathers were scattered around him.

'Just look at the poor rooster,' said Gloria.

'Yes, and I think you'll need a bigger, stronger coop for this lot,' suggested Arthur, pointing to all the bedraggled chickens.

'We certainly will,' replied Greg. 'How are you fixed later today Arthur?' asked Greg, hoping his friend would help him out again.

'No problem at all. I'll let you get started with the tidying up while I head down to the village to get that rat poison and a few supplies. I'll pop back here after that.'

'That would be great, Arthur. Thank you. We must warn the villagers about the rats too, just in case there are more around the place. Would you mention it when you're down there?' Greg wondered just how big a problem it would turn out to be.

'Will do,' called Arthur as he headed around to the side gate.

When the garden was at last cleared of children and adults, several of the residents gathered to talk about what had happened.

'Well, well, that was quite a battle. Those rats were monstrous!' said the Brigadier, still feeling a bit wobbly after all the fighting.

'It most certainly was,' said a relieved Sylvie. 'Poor little Cindy is still shaking. Some of the rats were bigger than her.'

Teddy went over to Cindy and gave her a few little licks on her ears.

'Are you all right, Cindy? You were very brave,' said Teddy gently.

'Yes, I'm fine, thanks, but I'm not sure I want to see another rat ever again.'

Sylvie trotted past and purred in agreement.

'Yes, yes, everyone was so brave,' said the Brigadier.

'Whatever would we do without Ernie?' asked

Dougal, still feeling jittery.

This was so true. Ernie had been very busy healing the wounded, but even the frog couldn't bring anyone back from the dead.

'It looks like Worfeus knows about Ernie's talents,' said Timber.

'Yes, those two rats in the pond were definitely after Ernie, and the goldfish too for some reason. I just don't understand why they would be interested in the goldfish. What sort of threat are they?' said Teddy.

'The attacks started in and around the pond, isn't that right Brigadier?' asked Timber.

'Yes, that's true, but we have never understood why,' replied the old dog.

Timber was puzzled. Ernie's healing powers were so important, but what was it about the goldfish?

'Oberon, do you know what the rats were after?'

'No, I don't. It is very strange,' replied the owl.

'Well, at least we got three of the four crows, and all but two of the magpies, by my count,' said Norville, trying to be cheerful.

'Yes, we did,' snarled Eldric. 'But one or two rats

got away. Who knows where they are now.'

'Yes, I'm worried about that too,' muttered Timber.

'Worfeus really planned this attack very carefully, didn't he? There was one group attacking the chicken coop, another at the pond, on the ground and in the air. They behaved like a small army would,' said the Brigadier, getting carried away with ideas of armies and battles again.

'So what will happen next?' asked Freya.

All the residents were silent. They really didn't know what to expect next.

'Worfeus is increasing his attacks in both strength and frequency. He must be very certain that the scroll is here in the garden,' said Eldric. 'So, my friends, where is this wretched scroll?'

It was time for the visiting starlings to depart. They were thanked warmly by everyone, and then they said their goodbyes and flew off.

Three of the spitfire sparrows had been lost in the battle and the remaining birds were very sad. They had all been happy to help save the garden and protect the scroll, but their help had come at a terrible price.

Still, the survivors decided to stay. They did not want their friends to have died for nothing, and they were determined to help the residents to complete the quest. They knew it was what Wanda would have wished.

The ducks were not at all happy. Danville and Delilah were sitting with Serena and some of her swan friends at the edge of the pond. Danville was still sobbing.

'Delilah and I lost three of our brood this morning. This is so awful. It cannot happen again.' He took a deep gulp of air and went on. 'With a new bunch of ducklings arriving next spring, we have decided to move to Lindon Lake immediately.'

The residents were shocked.

'You mean you're leaving?' cried Dougal.

Danville said nothing more. Then Delilah burst into tears. Serena waddled slowly forward.

'Unfortunately, they simply must. It would be unwise to hatch a new brood of ducklings on the pond, when we don't really know what is going to happen next. Swinford and I have also decided to postpone our move here until the spring, when we see how things are.'

More residents gasped. The swans had been expected to move in before winter, and then to stay permanently.

'We have obviously let you down very badly,' said the Brigadier.

'No, no, not at all,' replied Serena. 'All of you were incredibly brave. If anyone let the ducks down, it was perhaps us swans. We did so well when the magpies and crows attacked, we thought we could handle anything. But the giant rats, well, they were much more difficult, and we all suffered many more injuries, serious injuries. One of the Lindon Lake swans nearly died of rat bites before Ernie reached her.'

Serena stopped talking and no one else spoke. They had all hoped to have swans on the pond for the first time ever, and the ducks had been there for years. Everyone was very sad to hear they were leaving. There would be no birds on Grindlewood pond for the first time in decades, maybe even a hundred years.

'We will be very sorry to see you go, but promise us that as soon as this nasty business with Worfeus is over, you will return to this wonderful garden,' said the Brigadier. 'And it still is a wonderful garden, isn't it?'

His voice trailed to a whisper. All the residents nodded and waited, hoping the ducks and swans would agree.

'Of course we will, and of course it is,' they replied in unison.

And so it was time for farewells and goodbyes. The swans and ducks prepared to leave Grindlewood for the time being. The remaining garden birds promised to visit them on Lindon Lake and to let them know if they were needed.

The residents' thoughts turned again to Worfeus.

'Oh, I am so very worried,' moaned the Brigadier after the pond birds had left. 'We really never had troubles as worrying as this, before.'

'Never mind, Brigadier, we'll manage,' said Timber. 'Eldric, Norville, are you going anywhere this winter?'

'No, Timber,' replied Eldric. 'We foxes thought you might be glad to have us around!'

'Yes, we certainly would,' said Timber.

'No, we don't actually hibernate. Once we have enough to eat, we can stay out in the cold. Any chance you could get some extra rations for us?' the fox asked cheekily.

'I'll see what I can do,' replied the good-natured malamute. 'What about you, Norville? Will you stay out and about too?'

'Well, like Eldric, I will need extra food. I have made my den quite cosy, but if it gets really cold, I might need to move in with the foxes for extra warmth. You don't mind a few spikes, do you Eldric?' Norville sniggered.

'No problem to me, Norville, but perhaps you would like to check with Freya and Fern too, hmm?'

For a moment Norville had forgotten that there were already three foxes in the den. But that would just make it even warmer, once his spikes didn't bother anyone. Eldric thought it might be quite amusing sharing the den with his friend Norville. Really, they enjoyed each other's company – they just pretended to find each other difficult. He wondered if the two lady foxes would be troubled by Norville's spikes – hopefully not.

With all that more or less settled, Timber had one more question. He wandered over to the butterflies who were perched nearby. They were shivering. It was time for them to find somewhere cosy for the winter too, and this would probably mean that they wouldn't be around until the spring, if they returned at all. Butterflies didn't usually survive through the winter months. What would that mean for these enchanted butterflies? No one knew, but either way, there wouldn't be any more visions until they returned.

'Belinda, could you and your sisters do us one last favour before you retire for the winter?' Timber asked politely. The butterflies fluttered off their perch, twirled around and landed again. They waited for the request. 'Would you mind having one last nap on the statue, just in case you might have another important message for us before you go?' The butterflies nodded, and they flew over to the statue. They landed on the statue's wings and, in the soft winter sunshine, they soon fell asleep. The residents would have to wait until they woke up later in the day to hear their news, if indeed there was any.

And so the residents moved off to their usual late morning spots for snoozing, hunting, wandering, or just plain sitting. Most of them were still feeling the effects of the early morning attack and were happy to take it easy. Lots of drilling and hammering had begun in the yard, where Greg had started on the new chicken coop. How the chickens would get out of this one to do their dance rehearsals or pecking practice, no one could even imagine. But that wasn't really important any more. Worfeus' attacks had become more threatening and more merciless. The residents would have to be prepared for just about anything. As the day wore on, many of them kept one eye on the statue. It was increasingly hard to relax, wondering what on earth could be next, and what the butterflies might say.

Chapter Twenty-one

THE FAIRY HOUSE AND THE WELL

The chickens were almost too scared to come out of the barn where they had been living for a couple of days. But their new coop was ready and it was time to move in. With a little encouragement and a few handfuls of grain, they clucked and squawked their way out into the yard to view their new home. They were pleasantly surprised. Greg and Arthur had done a fine job, and the new coop looked splendid. It was at least twice the size of the old one and was much more comfortable too. They all hopped in and settled down to some cheerful clucking and egg-laying.

Next the Grindles decided to clear some of the garden, at last. Overall, the weather had been very changeable so gardening work had been put off for a while. They hoped now that removing some of the thick undergrowth might keep the rats away. At least it would mean that there would be fewer places for them to hide or breed. Luckily, Arthur managed to find a few gardeners from the village for the coming weekend and everyone was looking forward to it.

'Jamie, I think we should have a look around that corner of the garden, before the gardeners come and chop it all away. Abigail and I were sure we found something there. It was just too hard to get at it,' said Jemima eagerly.

'Sure, but we better wait until Mum and Dad are busy, because it's really messy down there, and they're already complaining about how dirty I am from climbing the trees and looking for the footballs. Ramona keeps kicking them into the dirtiest and messiest parts of the garden,' replied Jamie.

'Yes, I know, that's how we found this wand,' said Jemima.

'That looks like a slightly bent stick to me, Jem,' said Jamie.

'I know, but I like to think it's a wand. Anyway, I told you that Abigail and I thought there was a wall or something behind all that bushy stuff, or at least a lot of bricks. They must have been there for a reason, part of something. Let's check it out as soon as we can. I promised her I'd let her know what we found.'

When work on the garden got started, the cats wandered off, disliking the noise, while the dogs watched from the kennel, barking at the strangers and the noisy chainsaws. The children were warned to stay out of the way too, but they crept closer and closer, all the time watching the gardeners. They hadn't had a chance to look for the low wall that Abigail had spotted, as the weather had been so wet and windy beforehand, they hadn't been out in the garden. Luckily it had dried up just when the gardeners were due to start.

The men were working hard at the far corner of the garden, cutting and chopping, when suddenly, CLANK! CLANK! WHIRR, SPLUTTER, CHUG, CLUNK! The hedge cutter broke down. The blade had snapped. One of the men had hit something very hard, but he couldn't quite see what it was.

'Over here, look! There's something over here!' he cried.

'Let us in there. Move aside now,' said Greg, as he and Arthur pushed past the workers and pulled back some heavy foliage. The children pushed in beside their dad.

'Well, just look at that!' cried Greg. 'I think we found ourselves a little well!'

He looked around at the others.

'Oh my!' said Gloria, appearing behind him. 'How nice, and it looks so old, so small. We weren't told it was here. Did you know it was here, Arthur?'

'Not a clue,' he replied, scratching his head.

'It looks like a magic well,' sighed Jemima, secretly delighted.

'How come?' asked Jamie, nudging her. He needed more proof of magic.

'Everything about it looks magical,' said Jemima quietly to Jamie. 'It's so small and dainty, and why is it here at the end of the garden, and so far from the house?'

'That doesn't prove it's magical,' Jamie whispered back. 'Is this what Abigail found?'

'I don't think so, which means there must be something else in there,' said Jemima quietly.

'OK, let's see what else is under all this thick, prickly stuff,' said Greg. 'Take a break lads, and I'll sort out some stronger cutting tools.'

The gardeners went off for a tea break, and Greg and Arthur looked around the barn for some stronger cutting tools. The children got their chance, at last, to explore a bit for themselves.

'Come on Jamie, let's see if we can crawl under some of this stuff, it might be easier now,' urged Jemima.

Jamie liked a challenge and ran ahead of her to the spot nearby where Abigail had fallen. The gardeners had cleared some of the overgrown nettles and brambles in that area too.

'I think we could sneak under here. Come on, hurry,' he said quietly.

The two children crawled under some cut and half-cut foliage, often getting snagged by thorns and prickles as they went. Their clothes were quickly ruined, but in the excitement, they didn't seem to notice or care. Jamie stopped abruptly when he got a bump on the head.

'Ouch, that hurt,' he said.

'It must be the wall – I told you, Jamie. This is definitely the spot where Abigail fell. Quick, pull this stuff out of the way,'

'I'm OK thanks,' said Jamie, as Jemima was distracted by what they might find next, rather than whether Jamie was hurt or not. They pulled and tugged at some thick old ivy that was clinging tightly to something hard.

'It must be the wall, Jamie. Come on, pull harder,' said Jemima, getting more and more excited.

'I'm trying, I'm trying. Help me with this bit here, will you, it's really stuck.'

They both pulled with all their might, and at last the ivy came away. Both of them fell backwards with the force of all the tugging. And there it was – part of a little low wall.

'Wow, is that part of a house?' asked Jamie.

'I'm not sure. It could be. We'll have to get help to clear more of this away. We'll never do it all by ourselves. Let's go back and tell Dad. He'll ask the gardeners to do it for us. Come on, let's go,' said Jemima, already heading back. Jamie was still rubbing the bump on his head, but he ran quickly after her.

'Dad, Dad, we think we found something. Jamie bumped his head off a wall,' said Jemima, out of breath after racing back to the yard.

'Dad, there's something there, something hard, it could be a wall, or even a house, I think,' said Jamie, also panting.

'More discoveries! Oh dear, just look at your

clothes! Come on then, let's go and see what you've found,' said Greg.

Greg and Arthur followed the children back to the spot, and this time the men were carrying much heavier chainsaws. They cut back a wide area of undergrowth and all sorts of wild plants and weeds. There it was – a low wall, a buckled little door, and two little gaps that might once have been windows.

'Oh this is great, it's a fairy house!' shrieked Jemima.

'This is so cool,' said Jamie. 'I wonder what it used to be. But it's ours now, OK, Dad?'

'Well, sure, but we need to uncover it completely, Jamie, and then it might need to be supported. That little roof, or what I can see of it back there, that will need repairing before it is safe, and I'd also like to strengthen the walls, hmm …' Greg continued looking and muttering. The children were very excited but they weren't allowed go one step further in case the little house fell down. It really was quite a shambles. Greg and Arthur peered into the remains of the small dwelling, carefully looking above and below in case any more of the old roof or floor collapsed.

'Did you know anything about *this*, Arthur?' asked Greg.

'I certainly didn't,' replied Arthur, looking around in amazement. 'I never really ventured this far down the garden after the place had been searched several times for Luke. There was no mention of this little building.'

'It is so very, very dainty. Who could have lived in this?' muttered Gloria, having arrived at the fairy house. She had noticed the children suddenly charge down the garden a few moments earlier, and thought something must be up. Jemima told her mother it was a fairy house as soon as she arrived to take a peek. They all looked around, wondering who or what could have lived there. And someone might have lived there – there were little pots and jars and crockery, mostly broken and scattered about. There was a little table of sorts, a rickety chair, scattered old logs, and what probably had been a little bed of dried ferns.

'Wow, Mum, Dad, I bet it was a real fairy house! It must have been,' cried Jemima, straining to see more. The dogs had trotted down to take a look too.

'Do not come in here until we are sure it won't fall down,' repeated Greg. 'The whole place could collapse quite easily.'

Gloria took the children and the dogs back to the

house, at Greg's insistence. The men worked hard all day, cutting, chopping and clearing that peculiar little corner of the garden. No one knew anything about the mysterious little fairy house or the tiny dried-up well. The children chatted excitedly all evening about the amazing find. It was too dark to go back out in the evening, so they would have to wait until the next day to see it again.

The dogs were allowed back into the garden, as Greg and Arthur had quickly fenced off the well and the fairy house. The residents were all intrigued and the garden was buzzing with questions again.

'This is amazing! How could we all live here and not know about this little house and the well?' asked the Brigadier.

'Indeed,' said Eldric. It seemed that nothing about their quest was straightforward.

'Does anyone know anything about this?' asked Sylvie, as the cats joined the group.

'Perhaps we can help,' chirped Spindle. 'The little house belonged to Wanda.'

The residents looked around at each other wide-eyed. Then all heads turned back towards the sparrows.

'But how did no one find it before?' asked the Brigadier.

'Another spell, by any chance?' suggested Timber.

'Quite right,' replied Spindle. 'There used to be some sort of stone shed or playhouse in that corner, but Wanda turned it into a little garden cottage, when she was on the run from the warlock. The old man in the big house never came down to this overgrown end of the garden. He always stayed in or near his house,' he explained. 'Wanda wanted to protect the residents from any trouble, so she enchanted her little cottage to make it invisible. She called it a cloaking spell. Wanda didn't tell the local boy, Luke, about this little house because she didn't want to endanger him in any way. She preferred to meet him in the forest, where she would go to pick mushrooms, though sometimes he would come into the garden to see the pets or tidy up the pond. We thought the house would have completely fallen down by now.'

'Slowly the pieces are falling into place,' muttered Oberon.

'What do you mean? We still don't know where this secret scroll is. Do any of you know anything else about Wanda?' Norville asked the sparrows crossly.

'Hmmm, no, I can't say we do.'

Spindle was a little disappointed that he didn't know where the scroll was. He had been a very good friend of Wanda's but she hadn't told him where she had hidden it.

'She did mention one other thing, though,' chirped up Sparky.

All eyes and ears turned towards the other little sparrow.

'Well?' said Eldric impatiently.

'Wanda often said that you should keep important things under lock and key.'

Eldric rolled his eyes on hearing what seemed so obvious.

'Under lock and key,' repeated Timber. 'Then perhaps we have to find a lock or a key, or both. I think we will have to search the garden again,' he said, amid groans and moans from everyone. 'And perhaps, as soon as we can get in, we should search Wanda's house too. We just might find something in there.'

'If the gardeners don't find it first or throw it away,' said Norville. He was fed up with all this searching. Nothing had turned up so far, why ever would it turn up now?

'Don't worry, Norville. We'll keep a close eye on what they are doing, and make sure we don't miss anything. The birds are in the best position to keep a look out from the top of the trees. We can keep a look out on the ground.'

While discussing the fairy house and the secret scroll, everyone had forgotten about the butterflies. They had been sleeping on the statue all this time.

'Look, they're awake! They're moving!' cried Dougal.

'Why are they flying towards the house? Quick, follow them!' cried Sylvie.

The pets scampered after the butterflies, who were totally entranced as they headed straight for the house. They fluttered near the kitchen window, which was slightly open. The pets watched as the butterflies flew inside and landed on Jemima's hair. This was so different from the butterflies' usual routine. The animals didn't know what to make of it.

'Oh, something must be wrong,' said Eldric, standing a little further back, 'or else the butterflies have finally gone gaga!'

'Might they have a message for Jemima?' muttered Timber to himself.

They all watched and waited. The pets inched closer to the kitchen window, while the other residents stayed further off, out of sight. They heard Gloria come into the kitchen to start fixing the supper.

'Mum, do you have a special key?' asked Jemima, looking rather quizzical.

'What key, dear, a key to what?' she asked her daughter.

'I don't know, just a key, a special key. The butterflies just told me that I have to find it. It's really important.'

Jemima looked very seriously at her mother. Gloria assumed that Jemima had been reading fairy tales again, but she reassured her daughter that if she found a key she would let her know. Then she spotted the butterflies.

'Oh, Jemima, those are lovely butterfly slides in your hair. Where did you … Oh, my goodness, they are real! Stay still now.'

Gloria gently lifted the butterflies, who were about to get tangled in Jemima's lovely curls, and released them out the window. The pets were waiting under the window sill and gently woofed and meowed, hoping for some information. But it was too late, and the butterflies flitted off into the twilight air without a word. As it was getting rather cold now it was unlikely that they would be seen again for months. The residents were very disappointed. They felt helpless. Suddenly the winter looked like it would be a very long and dark one indeed.

Chapter Twenty-two

THE CRYSTAL KEY

The next day, Greg, Arthur and the volunteers started work early. They took down some of the shakier parts of the little house, and put a sturdy wooden cover over the well to make it safe. They continued to cut and chop away at all the overgrown bushes and brambles in that corner to clear it out once and for all. The children were allowed to play in the garden with the pets as long as they stayed well clear of the work. They had discovered the big stone with the Rules of the Garden scratched on it, but they had no idea what all the scratches and scrawls meant. The cats and dogs looked on amused as the children tried to work it out.

Jamie ran off to get some rope to make a second swing on the oak tree, and Jemima went to watch the goldfish.

Unknown to anyone, one of the giant rats was still

in the garden. He was hiding in the rushes near the pond, nursing his wounds. As Jemima approached the pond, the rat rushed out, heading straight for her. She screamed loudly when she saw it. Terrified, she hopped up onto the granite stone to try to avoid the ugly rat, whose buck teeth were bared as it snarled and charged at her.

Greg, Arthur and the volunteers didn't hear her screams at first over the noise of the equipment. But Timber heard them. He jumped up, barking loudly, and charged over to Jemima. The barking woke Teddy from his morning snooze with a fright, and he jumped straight up in the air, his fur on end. He quickly followed Timber and rushed towards Jemima.

She was standing on the stone, waving a small branch she had pulled from a tree to try to shoo the rat away. Finally, her father heard her screams. He raced towards her, followed quickly by Arthur, only to see the giant rat leap up at Jemima.

'NOOOOOOOOOO!' yelled Greg.

Timber was there in a flash. With a menacing growl, he leapt up and grabbed the giant rat by the neck, wrestling him to the ground. Teddy arrived and jumped in too, ripping at the rat with his sharp claws. The three fought furiously on the ground for a few seconds, rolling and snarling. Timber refused to let go his grip on the rat's throat. The other dogs and cats rushed over, barking and hissing.

Greg reached them with the chainsaw, shouting at Timber and Teddy to get out of the way. Just as Greg lunged forward with the hefty saw, Timber gave one last crunching bite and snapped the rat's neck. The nasty creature turned to a dirty mound of dust.

Gloria and Jamie had run across from the yard. They hurried over to Jemima. Gloria hugged her daughter and checked to make sure she was unharmed. They all looked at the mound of dust.

'I want to know what that is. I want to know,' Greg demanded. 'You saw the rat, I saw the rat, in fact we all saw the rat. So what is that, that mound of dirt – again?' Greg was shaking, pointing to the place where the dust lay.

'Very strange, very, very strange,' muttered Arthur. 'I don't know what to say, Greg, I'm sorry.'

Jemima was about to say something, probably about magic, but stopped as Jamie stared hard at her and shook his head from side to side.

Timber was the hero again, and he patrolled the garden, howling to ward off any further threats. It was a noisy afternoon with all the barking and sawing, and with Jamie shouting out 'Timber the Super-mal' and 'Teddy the Super-cat' again and again, eventually driving everyone mad. Later,  when the garden was clear, the pets joined the residents who were waiting patiently for them.

'Wow, that was impressive, Timber and Teddy,' said Dougal.

'Wow,' purred Cindy. Teddy was chuffed.

'Well done!' said the Brigadier.

'You were fantastic,' twittered all the birds who were near.

'Poor Jemima,' said Sylvie. 'Just think what could have happened if the two of you hadn't got there in time.'

'Best not to think of that,' said Timber. 'Jemima's fine, but I'm surprised we hadn't smelled that ugly wretch before now.'

'I'm not,' said Spindle, dropping down from an apple tree. 'Remember, that giant rat isn't really a rat. It's a horrible hag and cooked in a cauldron with other evil ingredients. It's all dark magic, you see, the rats have no scent.'

'That explains it, I suppose. But it makes it more difficult for us,' said Timber.

'Yes, Worfeus is wickedly clever,' said Spindle.

Gloria decided to take the children out for lunch in the village. The pets stayed in the garden, repeatedly checking that everything was OK. Despite the earlier fright with the rat, the children ran straight outside again once they returned home. They simply had to explore around the newly discovered fairy house, even if it still wasn't safe to go inside.

'Hey, Jamie, look what I found!' cried Jemima.

In amongst the debris around the little fairy house, she had spotted the broken old well bucket, and stuck in the splintered bottom of the bucket was a strange looking object.

'Oh, it's an old key, I think,' said Jamie, looking closely at the find. 'I wonder what that belonged to.'

'It must be the key the butterflies told me about. It's so small, and look, it has a little bit of squiggly writing on it.' She rubbed it with her sleeve. 'I think it's made of glass.'

'Hmm,' said Jamie, wondering about it. 'Let's wash it and see if it fits something in the house.'

The children took the key inside to clean it up, passing the gardeners as they returned to work.

After long hours of clearing away the debris and rubble, as well as all the overgrown bushes, the work at the end of the garden was done. The fairy house looked quite pretty, even though it was well and truly tumbled down, and the little well and broken bucket looked sweet.

The children decided to keep the key a secret for the moment, while they tried to find out what it was for.

'Jamie, let's check all the cupboards in the house, just to be sure. And we should check the attic and the cellar in case there is anything there that the key might fit.'

'Good idea,' agreed Jamie, 'but let's try not to disturb anything or Mum and Dad might take the key.'

'So you think it really might be important then?' asked Jemima, glad that Jamie seemed to be coming around to her way of thinking.

'Well, we don't know yet, do we? But it does look rather special. Let's hope it is,' said Jamie, a little embarrassed that he was almost admitting his interest. It was usually Jemima who believed in the strange stuff.

The children's thoughts and conversations were interrupted by supper, so they didn't talk about the key again until bedtime, when they went into Jemima's room to discusss it again. Jemima was very certain of her facts.

'Jamie, the butterflies told me that we have to find a key,' said Jemima, 'and I think this must be it. What other key could it be? And, my *History of Grindlewood* book says that butterflies were always revered – that means that people thought they were very special. So if our butterflies are special, and they told me to find a key, and we found *this* key, then maybe the key will lead to something really important.'

'Huh? Hmmm, maybe,' said Jamie. 'What do you think it might open?'

'I don't know, Jamie. I was hoping if we found the key it might be obvious what it opened, but I guess it's not that obvious after all.'

The two children continued to talk about the key

for ages, imagining all sorts of exciting things it might unlock. Eventually it was time for sleep.

The cats had been curled up on the duvet and heard the conversation about the key. They hurried outside to tell the others.

'Where is it?'

'What does it look like?'

'What does it open?'

'WHAT?'

Everyone had questions, but as usual there were no quick or easy answers.

'If the butterflies said it's important, then it has to be the key we are looking for. Now, where is the lock? Anyone?' asked Eldric, but no one answered.

So, while Eldric tried to tackle this second, more difficult, question, the others worked out a plan. They decided that the dogs would distract the children with some game or other in the garden, allowing the cats to take the key. They would then borrow it for a short while until they could figure out where it belonged.

Finding the crystal key was certainly a piece of

good fortune. It could have lain in the dirt or sunk in the mud for another five years, or even five hundred years, without ever having been found. But what exactly had the key got to do with the scroll? Where was the lock for the key? So far, this hadn't been an easy quest, and it wasn't about to get any easier.

Chapter Twenty-three

INSCRIPTION RIDDLE

Jamie and Jemima ran around the house trying the crystal key in every possible lock. They grew rather tired of this after having no success, and they had other important things to think about. Christmas was just a couple of weeks away and there were so many distractions. They had to decorate and light up the house, bake the Christmas cake and pudding with their mother, do lots and lots of shopping for presents, and of course, decorate the enormous Christmas tree. In the end, they decided that the crystal key would make a lovely Christmas decoration. They put it on the tree, where it hung low and sparkled beautifully. The pets couldn't believe their luck.

The cats unhooked the key from its branch late one night, and brought it outside to the waiting residents. They all took a look, but Oberon looked particularly closely. He was very interested in the tiny inscription running down one side of the key.

'Can you read it, Oberon?' asked Timber, as everyone waited eagerly.

'I'm afraid not. But I do recognise some of it. It belongs to an ancient witch language, a language as old as the hills. I suspect Wanda was an expert in ancient magic and scripts. There are very few experts still alive who might be able to translate this. Hmmm, yes, very unusual indeed.'

'Great, just great!' moaned Norville. 'Just when we make some progress, along comes another riddle.'

'Oh, do be quiet, Norville,' barked Eldric. 'Give Oberon a chance.'

'Oberon, keep at it, will you? You might come up with something,' said Timber.

But after a few minutes and a lot of muttering and sighing, Oberon gave up.

'I'm afraid I can't do it,' he said. 'My expertise is in the history rather than the magic. But I think I know someone who can translate it.'

Oberon paused. He looked very serious. Was it another case of good news followed by bad?

'Well, tell us, Oberon, who is it?' asked the Brigadier eagerly.

'There is a golden eagle named Gildevard who lives alone high up in the mountains. He is extremely clever and knows a lot about such things. I think he would know this ancient language,' the owl explained.

'That's great. Where are these mountains, then?' asked Dougal.

'Ah, yes, well, quite far away, I'm afraid. At least three or four days' flying to get there and back, and that's if the weather is good,' replied Oberon.

'Would you be able to do that, Oberon?' asked Timber, knowing it was a lot to ask in the winter weather.

'Yes, yes, I could, but it really will take that long, no less. And that's if I find the eagle straight away. He sometimes goes off studying and researching ancient magic. So he could be away for days or even weeks. I will also need to rest for a day or two when I get there. And I will have to take the key with me. Gildevard must see it to decipher it.'

Oberon bent low over the key again, examining

every little detail. There were groans of disappointment from the residents. It could easily be about a week before Oberon returned. Oberon looked around the worried group of animals and birds.

'Don't worry. I'll be back as quickly as I can. I'm sure the key will be back on the tree for Christmas,' he said, trying to lift the mood. Secretly, he wasn't sure it would be that easy at all.

They wished him well as he prepared to go. He tucked the key tightly inside his great talons. He took off with a flourish and a few toots, heading for the mountains, off to find the golden eagle, the great and glorious Gildevard.

The snowy owl had been to the mountains once before. Then he had been a young owl and rather afraid of meeting such an important and learned bird of prey. Gildevard was well known to be a grumpy and short-tempered fellow, but he was very clever and knew all sorts of strange and wonderful things. Oberon hoped he would feel more confident meeting him this time.

The owl was in luck – the golden eagle was at

home. To show his respect, Oberon perched on a ledge just beneath the eagle's large, untidy nest, which sat close to the cliff top. He bowed politely, asking permission to join the eagle for a moment.

'Come,' said the eagle. 'What is it you want, Oberon?'

'Thank you, Gildevard. I am pleased that you remember me,' replied Oberon politely.

'I always remember the clever ones. You, Oberon, are one of the clever ones. Tell me, why do you seek my help?'

Oberon explained the situation, and placed the crystal key in front of the proud and clever eagle. Gildevard's eyes opened wide with interest and he studied it very carefully, almost greedily.

'Ah yes, I recognise this script. This is the most ancient tongue of the Wandelei people. It is very complex. This key holds ancient magic, Oberon, ancient and somewhat dark. It is not to be meddled with. It is most certainly not for the foolish or the weak. The inscription is quite simple. It says only that this key will unlock the plinth.'

Oberon looked perplexed. 'Is that all it says?' He paused, waiting for Gildevard to say something else, but the eagle did not speak again. The owl felt it was time to leave. 'Thank you, Gildevard, and good day.'

The owl bowed low once more and secured the key tightly in his talons. He flew off to get some food and then to rest before starting out on the long journey home.

Gildevard watched him go out of the corner of his eagle eyes. He frowned. The key was indeed a very interesting item. Perhaps he had dismissed Oberon too quickly. Then his frown changed to a smile, a knowing smile. He need not worry. There was no doubt at all that he would see both the owl and the key again soon – very soon.

Chapter Twenty-four

A MAGICAL CHRISTMAS

The excitement of Christmas had taken over at Grindlewood. Everyone was in great form and the children were very excited about Santa Claus' first visit to their new home. Even the pets were caught up in all the excitement. The dogs were barking and wagging their tails a lot, following the energetic children around. Cindy and Teddy were fascinated by all the sparkling, twinkling baubles on the tree and once or twice they nearly toppled it over! Sylvie watched from a distance, hoping no one would notice that the crystal key was missing. The children had more or less forgotten about it with all the other distractions.

A few days before Christmas, just as it was starting to snow, Oberon finally appeared in the night sky. He looked like a strange white blob, barely visible, flying through millions of falling snowflakes.

'To-wit-to-woo, to-wit-to-woo!' he called out, to let the residents know he was coming. One by one, all those not in hibernation came out of their cosy homes to brave the cold and hear the news. They huddled together in the little fairy house, which was now quite safe to enter. It provided just enough shelter from the weather despite its tumble-down state.

'Welcome back, Oberon. You must be exhausted!' said the Brigadier.

'Well, how did it go? What did Gildevard say?' asked Timber quickly.

Oberon placed the crystal key down carefully.

'Luckily, Gildevard was at home and he translated the inscription. All it says is, "The key will unlock the plinth." That is all, my friends.'

The residents looked at each other.

'Great! Uh, what's a plinth?' asked Dougal.

Most of the other residents didn't know what a plinth was either. Timber walked slowly out of the fairy house and looked over towards the pond.

'It's the fountain,' he said, turning around to face the residents who were watching him. 'It's the fountain. The plinth is the base of the fountain.' The other residents gathered around him, staring at the fountain through the falling snow.

'Well at least we know what a plinth is and where it is. Now how do we get at it?' asked Teddy.

They all stood staring out of the fairy house. The pond was frozen and the plinth was under the ice.

'There's nothing we can do for the moment,' sighed Timber. 'We must hide the key safely until the ice melts. When the goldfish and Ernie leave their winter tank in Jamie's bedroom, they will be able to swim down there and take a look.'

It was a lot to ask of pond life, though. Then Timber had another idea.

'Cyril, would you be able to dive to the bottom of the plinth when the ice melts?'

'I could give it a try, but the goldfish would be able to have a better look as they don't need to come up for air like I do,' said Cyril.

Unfortunately, it was probably going to be a job for Ernie and the goldfish, once Cyril had taken a couple of dives to check it out. Frequent diving into the pond would probably draw too much unwanted attention anyway. Whatever they decided, nothing was going to happen until the thaw came.

'So where is the safest place for the key while we wait?' asked Eldric.

'Why don't we put it back on the tree?' suggested Cindy. 'It was safe there in the house before now.'

'That's a good idea, Cindy. Well done!' said the Brigadier.

It was decided that Sylvie would return the key to the Christmas tree. In the New Year, she would borrow it once again when they were ready to use it. Hopefully the frozen pond would have thawed at that point. If not, they would have to find another safe hiding place before the tree came down and the children thought about the key again. Sylvie carefully picked up the key and trotted silently back inside. The rest of the residents dispersed.

Everything was ready. All the preparations for a wonderful Christmas were complete. The house looked beautiful, all the decorations sparkled and lots of presents were sitting under the tree, all brightly wrapped. On Christmas Eve, the pets gathered around the fire with the family. The children were terribly excited about Santa Claus. Just like last year, it was difficult to persuade them to go to bed.

As usual, around midnight, Jemima crept downstairs

again and snuck into the sitting room. She wanted to see Santa Claus so badly and ask him all about the magic of Christmas. Every year she had missed him, but this year she was determined to stay awake. She sat close to the Christmas tree, watching the crystal key sparkle in the light of the dying embers of the fire. She was getting sleepy, and it was getting cold. Timber mooched over and lay down close to her to keep her warm. She cuddled in beside the dog, and soon fell asleep.

Greg and Gloria had expected Jemima to try to stay awake that night, but they knew that she would fall asleep, just like every Christmas. They tip-toed downstairs and Gloria lifted her up to bed. Greg patted Timber on the head for being such a good dog, then let him back outside.

Timber woofed gently around the garden as he did his final patrol of the day, said goodnight to his friends, and then trotted back towards his kennel. The snow was falling heavily, making the garden look more enchanted than ever. Most of the residents peeped out to see the magical Christmas snow scene.

Shortly after Jemima was put back in bed, Jamie crept into her room and woke her.

'Jem, Jem, wake up! There's something I have to tell you – and show you.'

Jemima was very sleepy but she woke up with a few more shakes from Jamie.

'What is it, Jamie? What's up?' said the sleepyhead.

'You have to see this. Quick, come to the window in my room.'

Jemima was suddenly wide awake and she ran to the window in Jamie's room. The two of them looked out, but Jemima was looking up.

'Not up there, silly, down there, in the garden,' said Jamie.

'What? Oh, Timber is outside again, and, oh, foxes, and a hedgehog, and is that a snowy owl? Wow!' said Jemima.

'That's not all Jemima. I've seen them do this before, lots of times, all together, and they seem to be, well, talking to each other. Jem, it's really weird. I didn't tell you before now because I wasn't sure, but I've been watching them a lot lately. It seems to happen at night-time. Look, here come the cats. Watch, they're moving really close, like they're all talking about something. Look!'

Jamie was right, the animals were all huddled together in such a way that it looked like they were having a meeting. And of course they were, but the children hadn't figured this out before now.

'It sounds kind of crazy to say that they're talking to each other, doesn't it?' Jamie asked the question but somehow he knew that it wasn't so crazy at all.

'I don't think it's crazy, Jamie. After all, the butterflies were happy to tell us things as soon as they met us. I'm not surprised the other animals talk to each other, but why don't our pets talk to us? And what are they talking about? That's what I want to know.'

'I don't know,' muttered Jamie.

They watched the residents hold a quick meeting near the kennel, and decided to find out some more.

'Jem, let's go out and ask them. Timber will tell us something – I know he will – if he can.'

'That's a good idea, but we mustn't get caught. It is Christmas Eve you know and …'

'Yes, I know, Santa Claus is coming. But right now,

I really have to know if Timber can really talk, and maybe all our other pets too!' said Jamie, very excited by the idea.

'Come on then, let's go down,' said Jemima.

The two children dressed in a hurry and tiptoed downstairs. They crept outside to the kennel as quietly as possible. Some of the animals heard them coming and ran off, but the cats purred and the dogs wagged their tails as the two excited children approached them.

'Hello, Timber, come here and tell us what's going on,' whispered Jamie.

Timber trotted closer.

'We do know there's something going on. We can tell. You're all talking together, aren't you?' asked Jemima.

Timber was closest to the children, and the other five pets were just behind him. What should they do? Would the children understand them?

Timber turned his head around and growled softly to the other dogs and cats waiting behind him.

'I think we could do with their help. They would believe all of this, you know – the quest, the spell, everything. I'm sure of it,' he said to the others.

'Yes, but how do we do that?' asked the Brigadier in his own low growl.

Timber turned towards the children again and growled and woofed softly. He nudged them affectionately with his wet nose.

'He is definitely trying to tell us something,' said Jamie eagerly. The idea that his dog could sort of talk was thrilling.

'I think so too, Jamie. They seem to understand us so well, but how do we understand what they are saying?'

Timber continued to woo-woo softly, shake his head, wag his tail, and lick the children's hands.

'Timber, do you really understand us, all the time?' asked Jamie gently. He really wanted to know the answer, and he badly wanted the answer to be yes.

'Woo-woo, woo-woo,' said Timber.

'That's a yes, it has to be,' said Jamie excitedly.

'I believe you, Jamie, but how can we be sure?' Now Jemima had a small doubt. This was quite fantastic, even for her.

All the pets approached now. It was an extraordinary scene: the two children standing in their snow-covered garden in the middle of the night on Christmas Eve, with all their pets – three cats and three dogs – purring, softly growling and nuzzling them. The animals were clearly trying to communicate in a very special way.

Jamie and Jemima just looked at them, then at each other, then back at the pets again.

'OK, I think they do want to tell us something, Jamie. I can feel it. They want to tell us something about the garden and magic and, and … I don't know what else, but there must be more and it must be important, because this has never happened before …' Jemima's voice trailed off as she thought of what the pets might know.

'Wow, Jem, this is amazing. What do we do now? How do we know what all their barks and meows mean?'

'I don't know Jamie,' whispered Jemima, wondering how they could work this out. 'Oh, I don't know how we can do it, do you?'

'Yes, yes, I do!' said Jamie, suddenly. 'Look, they're all clever animals, right? They seem to understand us all right, so we just have to learn how to understand what *they* are saying. We'll teach them how to talk to us with tricks and signs! Easy!' said Jamie, rather loudly.

'Shh, you'll wake Mum and Dad. They'll think we've gone crazy. We must keep this quiet. Come on, it's really cold out here. Let's talk about it inside,' said Jemima. 'And let's look at my book of magic and the *History of Grindlewood* book as well, just in case there's anything in there about talking animals.'

'Oh, OK, I think we could just teach them, you know, we don't need spells and stuff,' said Jamie. He was buzzing with his own practical ideas.

'This is so exciting, Jamie!' squealed Jemima as quietly as she could. And the two went inside and back to bed. They poured over the books, and whispered for hours about what their pets and all the Grindlewood wildlife might be up to.

Outside, the pets trotted down to the end of the garden to tell some of the other residents the latest news.

'I really think we could do with their help,' said Timber, 'but we mustn't put the children in harm's way.'

'That could be tricky,' said Eldric. 'They might not realise just how dangerous it would be to join us on this quest.'

'You're right, but I agree with Timber,' said Teddy.

'There are so many ways that they might be able to help.'

'Yes, it was the children after all who found the key, and Jemima is already convinced that there is magic about the garden,' said Oberon.

'They both might be surprised to learn that we are on a quest, a real quest,' said Timber.

'And Jamie is going to try to help us learn words to communicate with us,' said Dougal. 'That should be fun!'

'Perhaps, Dougal,' said Sylvie, 'but I don't think it will be quite as easy as it sounds.'

'Well, it is quite a discovery for the children to make. Now they know we can all talk to each other,' said the Brigadier.

'Well, let's see how it goes,' said Timber. 'Their safety comes first. Then, if we can talk to them and get them to help us, it could be just the sort of help we need to get this quest moving. There's nothing more we can do tonight. Goodnight, everyone. Keep warm and merry Christmas!'

Christmas morning was full of good cheer. The

children couldn't wait to open their presents.

'A super train set, and Lego, and lots and lots of chocolate! Great!' Jamie was thrilled and started putting his new train set together straight away. Jemima shrieked with delight when she opened her presents.

'Oh, look! More magic books, and a magic set, just what I was hoping for. And lots and lots of chocolate!'

But the biggest surprise of all was out in the yard.

Greg had got up before everyone else and pulled the snow sledge carefully out of his workshop. It was painted red and gold, just like the one that Santa Claus had. Timber was thrilled to be harnassed to a sledge again, and he pulled it proudly through the snow over to the Finlays' farm and back again. Afterwards the children spent some time with their pets, playing snowballs and making snow angels in the thick snow that blanketed the garden. It would be impossible to start the pets' talking lessons in front of their parents, but no doubt there would be time enough over the Christmas holidays.

After a sumptuous Christmas dinner, the pets were allowed in to snooze by the fire. Teddy and Cindy purred to each other, drowsy and content after so many treats, in the comfort and warmth of the house.

Sylvie watched them through sleepy eyes, purring contentedly too. The Brigadier and Dougal were sound asleep in front of the fire, stuffed with treats and exhausted from all the snowballing.

Timber was still wide awake, though. He had really enjoyed pulling the sledge and having fun in the garden, but at the back of his mind was the residents' quest. They still had to find the scroll, defeat the warlock and save Grindlewood. He was eager to get to the plinth under the fountain and find out if the scroll was really there. It was very hard not to think about it all. Then he heard a noise outside in the distance, and he wanted to go and check it out.

'Want to see some more snow, Timber?' asked Greg.

Timber gave a little woof and was let out. He trotted around the garden, making a low, rolling growl as he went. He felt responsible for everyone at Grindlewood, not just the Grindles but all the residents of the garden whom he had come to know and love over the previous six months.

As Timber patrolled the garden, Worfeus, back in his wolf form, climbed to the highest point of the forest. He gazed down on Grindlewood. As the moon rose and the snow fell, he let out his most haunting

howl. It was a very scary sound in the stillness of that beautiful night. But Timber wasn't going to let him get away with that. This was his territory now. He threw back his head and let out his loudest and longest howl ever.

'AROO-WOO-WOOOOO, AROO-WOO-WOOOOO!AROO-WOO-WOOOOO, AROO-WOO-WOOOOO!'

It was a powerful howl and a fitting warning to Worfeus. It was clear, even on that lovely Christmas night, that the wolf and the malamute were preparing for a terrible showdown.

Coming soon

Grindlewood Book 2: The Secret Scroll follows the animals of Grindlewood garden as they continue the quest to save their enchanted home. The odds are stacked against them as they struggle to understand the ancient language of Wanda's secret scroll and use its magic to defeat the evil Worfeus. Slowly Jamie and Jemima learn that their pets are caught up in something both sinister and special and that somehow they must find a way to help. All the while, the wicked warlock is growing more powerful and threatening. The race is on to unlock the secrets of the scroll before Worfeus frees himself from the forest and enters the garden himself, intent on revenge and the destruction of Grindlewood.

Grindlewood Book 2: The Secret Scroll
will be available in spring 2014.

Acknowledgements

This book would not have been possible without the advice, help, support and encouragement of so many wonderful people, all of whom deserve a special mention.

Heartfelt thanks to: my marvellous editor, Robert Doran; my illustrator, Fintan Taite, for all his wonderful artwork; to Chenile Keogh, Vanessa O'Loughlin, Sheila O'Flanagan, PJ Cunningham, Rosemary O'Grady, Paul McNeive and Una Armstrong for all their advice and encouragement; to my extended family and friends for believing in me and for not being at all surprised at my wish to become a writer! A special thank you also to my enthusiastic young readers who 'road tested' my book and gave me some very insightful advice.

I would also like to give a special mention to the inspirational Peri Burnside, who introduced me to her wonderful Alaskan malamutes. To me they are the most beautiful dogs in the world.

Lastly, and above all, I owe so much to my wonderful husband, Angelo, without whom these stories would probably never have been told. I will be forever grateful for his unconditional love, encouragement and support, and also for his extraordinary expertise and sound advice.